The Clinician's Thesaurus 3

The Guidebook for Wording Psychological Reports and Other Evaluations

Third Edition, Revised

Edward L. Zuckerman, Ph.D.

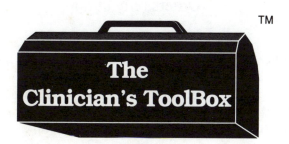

TM

The Clinician's ToolBox

Dedication

To my beloved daughter Molly.
This is what I was doing all those nights I was not with you.

ISBN 0-9622281-4-1   OCLC # 20591234

Copies of this book are available from the distributor you purchased from:

If you are unable to purchase from the above source the publisher will gladly supply copies for $29.95 (plus $3.55 postage and handling) until at least the end of 1996. Bookstores pay shipping but receive a discount of 25% from the list price. Discounts for quantities above ten are available; please call or write for details.

This book is available at significant discounts for bulk purchases for educational uses, business gifts, and premiums. Specialized editions can also be created to meet specific needs; please contact the publisher.

The Clinician's ToolBox™ Series, including *The Paper Office 1* and *The Clinician's Thesaurus: Electronic Edition*

is published by

The Clinician's ToolBox™
Post Office Box 81033, Pittsburgh, PA 15217
412/ 521-1057 - Voice and Answering Machine
412/ 521-8187 - Attended Fax
Orders only at 800/

1. Introduction

If you create psychological documents such as Psychological or Psychiatric Evaluations, Progress Reports, Treatment Summaries, Testing-based Reports, Assessments, Intakes, Psychosocial Narratives, Staffing Reports, summaries of Interviews, or similar studies, *The Clinician's Thesaurus 3/* can make your work easier at the same time as it makes your reports better.

This *Thesaurus* is designed to assist you in writing inventive, tailored, fresh reports. The use of even five percent of the words and phrases collected here for any aspect of your observations will enhance the clarity, precision and vividness of your reports. And it can assist you in other ways as well:
- It is organized so that you can do a Mental Status Examination using its sequence and sampling from the questions offered.
- It can serve as a guide to organizing your thoughts when writing or dictating reports to ensure that you have addressed all the topics of relevance.
- It can suggest behavioral observations to individualize and personalize a report or description.
- It can stimulate your recall of client characteristics (We all can recall more with the prompting of our memories).
- It can help to replace the drudgery of creating a narrative with playfulness, spontaneity, and serendipity.

For more detail on the use of this book, please see Chapter 4, "How You Might Use this Book."

Because of its behavioral and observational bent and its gathering of clinically descriptive terms *The Clinician's Thesaurus 3* is suitable for any clinical orientation or evaluation purpose.

To use *The Clinician's Thesaurus* most efficiently, please understand that it is organized into <u>six</u> <u>parts</u> corresponding to the ***sequence of constructing a report.***

1. The first part contains two collections of questions that can be used to structure the interview with the patient. The first collection is the traditional **Mental Status Questions** (and variations on them) for eliciting aspects of mental, cognitive, and emotional functioning of concern to the clinician. Then, if the clinician wishes to follow up on areas of clinical concern, the second collection contains questions designed to elicit information about specific **Symptomatic Behaviors**.

The rest of *The Clinician's Thesaurus* consists of five more parts designed to serve as a guide to writing or dictating the actual report.

2. Second is the required contents of the **Introduction** to any report, the **Background** and History of the patient, and **Reasons for the Referral**.

3. Next is for the body of the report: **Behavioral Observations** of the patient, his or her **Presentation of Self** and **Behaviors** noted during the interview, including characteristics of Speech and **Affects**.

4. The fourth part is for ending the report: **Diagnoses, Summary, Prognosis, Recommendations, and the Closing.**

5. The fifth part's Sections provide standard statements for other aspects of the patient's functioning: **Activities of Daily Living**, **Social and Community** functioning, the qualities of client's **Relationships, Vocational** performance, **Recreational** pursuits, and other dimensions' clinicians are often asked to evaluate.

6. The last Section offers **Resources**: a list of **Medications**, cues for **Psychiatric Masquerade** of medical conditions, useful **Abbreviations, Normal Curve Conversions**, and Citations and **References**.

The Clinician's Thesaurus is, very simply, a tool to assist the clinically competent professional in carrying out his or her report-writing tasks. It is not a textbook or a treatise on "How to Write a Psychological Report" nor on clinical interviewing. Nor is it a set of psychological tests' interpretation statements; I have assumed that the reader is already well-versed in these sophisticated clinical skills.

I must clearly acknowledge my debt to my colleagues from whose clearest thinking and best writing I have borrowed liberally to fill these pages. There are more than two hundred of you who have furnished the more than ten-thousand reports from which I have culled the 19,000 or so unduplicated wordings incorporated here. Although you are too numerous to credit please accept my gratitude and appreciation. While I have borrowed many of the words and phrases, I alone must assume responsibility for the content and organization of *The Clinician's Thesaurus,* whatever its merits or limitations.

The formatting of this material as a book is ideal for those clinicians who dictate/handwrite/typewrite their reports but for those who must write a lot of reports or are computerizing their offices, there is now a **computerized version of this book**. Please see the last pages of this book for more information and to send for a free demonstration disk.

In this, the third edition of *The Clinician's Thesaurus,* there is sixty percent more content than in the second edition which, in turn, expanded the first edition's content by about twenty-five percent. Each edition has added several tools useful to the report writer. I intend to keep this book in print and would greatly value your ideas about how to make it even more useful to us clinicians. If you have suggestions or make additions to your copy, please send me a photocopy of those pages. When your suggestions are adopted into the next edition I will send you both a free copy and my sincerest thanks.

Edward L. Zuckerman
August 10, 1993
Pittsburgh, Pennsylvania

2. Table of Contents

3. Acknowledgments

With appreciation for both their expertise and generosity, I am happy to publicly acknowledge my debt
to the following professionals for their contributions to this revised edition:

Robert W. Moffie, Ph.D., of Children's Hospital, Los Angeles, CA

Joseph Regan, Ph.D., of Toronto, Ontario

Dorothy H. Knight, of Passavant Area Hospital, Jacksonville, IL

Fay Murakawa, Ph.D., of Los Angeles, CA

Susan G. Mikesell, Ph.D., of Washington, DC

Richard L. Bruner, Psy.D., of Hightstown, NJ

Jeffry Burkard of Colvis, CA

Nora F. Young, of Cedro Wolley, WA

Leslie J. Wrixon, Psy.D., of Cambridge, MA

Dolores Arnold of Lawton, OK

Marcia L. Whisman, of ACSW, St. Louis, MO

Patricia Hurzeler, M. S., R. N., C. S., of Bloomfield, CT

Henry T. Stein, Ph. D., of the Alfred Adler Institute of San Francisco, CA

An Invitation to Contribute

What is missing from this book?

What would you have put in or taken out?

What have I gotten wrong?

Tell me and three good things will happen:
> 1. You will get **a free copy of the next edition.**
> 2. Your contribution will be fully acknowledged here.
> 3. You will receive my (and our fellow clinicians') sincere appreciation for adding to our
>   knowledge, and for making our work easier.

4. How You Might Use This Book

4.1 What is *The Clinician's Thesaurus 3*?

It is a giant, 19,000 item, externalized checklist. It probably closely approximates the internal checklist you have developed already and from which you construct your reports. It is easier to work from an external checklist: it converts a free recall task into a much simpler recognition task. Also we all do a more thorough job when using a checklist.

It is a tool and a coach:
- to learn or teach report writing/construction and then occasionally refer to
- to structure an interview or assessment to assure that you cover everything of relevance
- to structure a report to make certain you haven't missed anything of importance
- when you are stuck for a word/turn of phrase, use it to reference and re-access your knowledge base.
- to rewrite/tighten up an already written report
- to browse and enjoy the precision language offers and the serendipity of variety

4.2 When you interview:

You can use the two sections at the beginning, Mental Status Questions and Symptom Questions, to guide your interview. You might simply read the questions to the patient or you might copy out a few to ask, or you might use them to refresh your memory of the questions appropriate to the referral concern(s).

4.3 When you dictate a report:

This book is organized in the same sequence as the "classic" psychological report and so by paging through it you could dictate about all the appropriate sections. Alternately, you can turn to some sections to focus on particular topics and select the best wordings. If you need to do a very comprehensive evaluation you can use all the (numbered) headings as a checklist to make certain you haven't overlooked any important point.

As you use *The Clinician's Thesaurus 3* you may find it valuable to highlight in color, underline (I have always liked pencil as degrees of emphasis can be indicated by the darkness of the underline), or box some words or phrases that best suit your style of writing or dictation and those most relevant to your own practice and setting. You may find it practical to use paper clips or to sticky tabs to more quickly find sections of the book. Space is purposely left blank so that you can add notes, comments and, especially, suggestions.

4.4 When you teach:

You can offer only a small fraction of the variety of behaviors a clinician must understand. When you focus on a few diagnoses or processes students may miss the breath they will need. If you discuss theory your students may miss the concrete; if you offer cases they may learn only a few example and not the big picture. As a teacher, I have struggled with these choices. This book provides another option: all the aspects of each syndrome and pattern are in this one book. The whole language of the mental health field are in here.

When they need to interview all the questions are here to follow up any referral question. When they sit down to write up their findings all the choices are here. They and you can concentrate on the higher level functions, weighing, winnowing and choosing, not on re-inventing the right language.

Students love this book because it reduces their anxiety as well as making them more competent. When they see that everything they will need is in this one book they breathe a sigh of relief. They may even realize that they will only use 5% of it for any report. They'll still have to learn what the words mean and when to use them but at least the task no longer seems endless. The book does not replace their clinical education; it simplifies the process. It is equivalent to giving a calculator to a math student; they can concentrate on the problems, not the details of computation.

4.5 When you supervise:

Lower-skilled professionals or students may sometimes fail to think deeply or may write a superficial report. The usual supervisor response to this situation is to interview the student trying to pull out of them observations or understandings of the patient which they probably never made and did not record because they lacked the terms for categorizing the phenomena of concern. Even Socrates couldn't ask the right questions and so this approach is frustrating and unproductive (except of bad feelings between you).

Try this instead. Refer the students to the appropriate sections of *The Clinician's Thesaurus 3* and ask them to find, say, three more words to describe, say, cognitive aspects of the patient's depression. Not only does this make the problem into a game instead of a contest of who is smarter, it puts the burden of discrimination on the student where it belongs. Moreover, the process of weighing the alternatives which is required by this assignment trains a kind of "clinical judgement" which is otherwise almost impossible to teach.

It is not a "cheat book." It does not write reports for you. It is not canned. Students still have to know the meanings and tailor them to the client.

A Cautionary Note

The entries of this book are presented simply as what has been used in the field and their presence here does not imply any endorsement by the author or publisher. These wordings are offered without any warrantee, implied or explicit, that they are the only or best way to practice as a professional or clinician.

When you use any of the words, phrases, descriptors, sentences, or procedures described in this book you must assume the full responsibility for all the consequences: clinical, legal, ethical and financial. The author and publisher cannot, do not, and will not assume any responsibility for their use or implementation in your practice or with any patient, client or student and shall not be liable in the event of incidental or consequential damages in connection with or arising out of any use by a purchaser or user of the materials in this book.

If more than the material presented here is needed to manage a case in any regard, the reader is directed to engage the services of a competent professional consultant.

5. General Notes about this *Thesaurus*

5.1 Descriptors:

The terms or descriptors offered in *The Clinician's Thesaurus* are arranged as either:
> A. **Columns** of quite similar but not identical terms which provide a cluster from which to select shadings of meaning. Columns are arranged across the page, where marked by this sign (<->), in order of increasing intensity of the trait. Where a word is the standard term used by clinicians for that cluster it is **Capitalized**:

QUALITIES OF CLOTHING: (<->)

filthy	seedy	needing repair	plain	neat	stylish
grimy	disheveled	threadbare	out of date	careful	immaculate
dirty	neglected	rumpled	old-fashioned	dresser	meticulous

> or B. a **Paragraph** of words and phrases having no ordering principle but simply often used together:

Presentable, acceptable, suitable, appearance and dress appropriate for age and occupation, business-like, professional appearance, nothing was attention-drawing, modestly attired

> or C. a **Spectrum** of words indicated by this sign (**<->**) organized by increasing (or rarely, decreasing) intensity of the trait or behavior described:

(<->) Institutional, odd, unusual, eccentric, peculiar, unique combinations, carefully disordered, dressed to offend, un/conventional, attention seeking/drawing, outlandish, garish, bizarre

Where multiple phrasings are offered they are separated by a **slash mark (/)**.

Words in **quotation marks (" ")** are slang or inappropriate in a professional report but are self-descriptors frequently offered by persons being evaluated and are placed under appropriate headings to assist the clinician unfamiliar with such phrasings in understanding their meanings.

Comments by the author, Ed Zuckerman, are put in **square brackets [ ]**.

Most wordings apply to both adults and children. However, words used in the evaluations of children, but not adults, are listed at the end of each area where they apply and are indicated by **For a Child.** Similarly, uses are indicated, such as **For a Disability Examination**.

Commonly used **acronyms** are indicated by underlining the initial letters of the longer wording. For example, Activities of Daily Living are often referred to as "ADLs."

The phrasings offered in this book are standard American English usage and the conventional language of the mental health field. The terms offered are only rarely defined here. You may find useful a specialized psych. dictionary such as Hinsie and Campbell's (1970) or *Steadman's Medical Dictionary* (latest edition) or Steadman's *Psychiatric Words*.

5.2 Forms of Language:

For compactness and simplicity, adjectives, adverbs and nouns are sometimes mixed in a list.

The **pronoun forms** used here are intended to lessen the sexist associations and implications whose harmful effects are well documented in this field. An attempt has been made to simply alternate male and female pronouns or to use combinations such as her/him and s/he to not further gender associations. When pronouns of a single gender are employed that phrasing should not be taken to imply any association of gender with behavior or disorder.

5.3 Attributions:

The psychologist, psychiatrist, social worker, nurse, therapist, counselor, clinician, behavior specialist, educator, teacher, advisor, interviewer, examiner, writer, author, undersigned, reporter, respondent ...

can be said to report, offer, observe, document, note, relate, record, state, summarize ...

about the patient, client, claimant, resident, student, subject, individual, person, citizen, man, woman, child, adult.
N.B.: Use of a first or given name is acceptable only for children. Use Mr./Ms./Mrs./Dr./Esq. and other titles only where necessary to prevent misunderstanding and it is relevant to the intention of the report.

He or she can be said to report, allege, submit, describe, claim, concede, indicate, maintain, attest to, mention, tell me, reveal, disclose, contend, aver, certify, state, offer, evidence, exhibit, present, view, register, speak of, deny, disavow, disclaim, etc. Also acceptable is "was found to ...", and "appeared to be ...."

5.4 White Spaces under the text and in the margins:

Blank space is provided so you may customize the entries with your favorite phrases and statements.

I would be grateful for and attentive to your suggestions and improvements and will send you a free copy of the next revision of *The Clinician's Thesaurus*. Please see the Chapter 3 Acknowledgments.

5.5 The Formatting used in this book is:

1.   Chapter   18 Point Times Bold

1.1. Section	14 Point Times Roman
HEADING	12 POINT, SMALL CAPITALS
Sub-heading	*12 Point Times Italic*
Sub-sub-heading	**12 Point Bold**
Text	12 Point Roman
Topic ideas or **names** in the text	**12 Point Bold**

5.6 Beginning the Interview

There are dozens of specialized interview methods (See Hersen and Turner, 1985, for guidance to many) and structured interviews which should be used to increase reliability and validity over open-ended approaches.
The format below addresses some points crucial to all interviews.

SELF-INTRODUCTION:

"Hello, I'm (Title) (Name) _____ . And you are _____ ?"

With each client be alert to the client's possible **limitations** of hearing and vision and inquire if you have any reason to suspect a handicap. Ask about any need for glasses/contact lenses or hearing aids if not worn and comment in your report on the effect on the client's performance. Ask the client for suggestions to improve conditions, such as minimizing the background noise, or changing the lighting. Don't cover your mouth and speak clearly. Take into account the cognitive variations of many of the hearing impaired or users of <u>A</u>merican <u>S</u>ign <u>L</u>anguage.

BACKGROUND:

Ask: Ask early and if the subject seems unforthcoming.

"What have you been told about this interview/our meeting?"
"What do you expect to happen here?"
"What did you think and feel before you came in here/met me?"

"Because I have spoken with _____ /read reports from _____ /know you from _____
I already know some things about you/why you have come here/we are talking."

"However I'd like to hear from you why you have come to see me/come here."

"I'd like to talk with you for a few minutes in order to _____ ."

CONSENT: See section 8.7 for Consent statements

Obtain fully informed and voluntary consent to the interview or evaluation.

Explain the purposes of the interview: Attend to the client's and examiner's perceived expectations of referring agent, what information is to be gathered, by what means, what is then to be done, and if a report is written or made, who will see it.

"Would that be all right with you?"

OTHER ASPECTS TO BE CONSIDERED AT THE BEGINNING OF THE INTERVIEW:

Current medication prescribed/taken: Name(s), dosage(s), frequency

Consider client's use of alcohol and other drugs.

Handedness/preference/dominance: comment here or under section 11.4 Beh. Observations, Praxis

5 • General Notes

Understanding and use of English or in what language the interview was conducted, American Sign Language, etc.

Use of or need for an interpreter and consequences such as ambiguity, distortions, psychological naivete or sophistication of interpreter, interpreter's opinions of client's language and thoughts, etc.

BECAUSE OF MY SETTING **I should remember to <u>always</u>:**

Do the following:

Say:

Warn about ...

Explain:

Remind the client of:

ELICITING THE CHIEF CONCERN/COMPLAINT: See section 8.6 for descriptors of Chief Concern

"Would you please tell me why you are here/we are meeting/you are being evaluated?"
"What brings you to the hospital/clinic/my office?"
"What concerns you most?"
"What has been going on?"
"Why have you come to see me?"
"What do you hope to have happen because we have met?"

DIMENSIONALIZING THE CONCERN/PROBLEM(S):

"For how long has this been happening?"	(Duration)
"How often does this happen?"	(Frequency)
"Think back to the last time this happened and tell me:	
"What led up to its happening?"	(Antecedents, Cues, Controlling Stimuli, Latency, Sequences, Progression, Chains)
"What were you thinking and feeling?"	(Expectations, Beliefs, Meanings, Affects)
"Who else was around and what did they think and feel?"	(Both of above)
"What happened next/afterward?"	(Sequences, Reinforcers, Payoffs)
"How typical was this occasion?"	
"Was the first time it happened different?"	
"What could have made a difference in this incident?"	(Expectations of outcome, changeability, treatment, treaters, understandings of causation)

6. Mental Status Test Questions/Tasks

These questions are about COGNITIVE FUNCTIONS.
Questions about SYMPTOMS and ABNORMAL BEHAVIORS are in the NEXT chapter.

6.1 Introduction to the Mental Status Questions:

Over the years clinician's have found questions which seemed face-valid, heuristic, or revelatory and passed them down to their students. With current standards, most of these are found to lack reliability, validity or both and the whole area of interpreting of the patient's response is unstandardized. For reliability there are available a number of standardized brief mental status tests[1] (i.e. Mini-Mental State, Blessed Information-Memory-Concentration test, the Short Portable Mental Status Questionnaire) and short batteries (Washington University SDAT Screening Battery, Iowa Screening Battery for Mental Decline). Even with these tests norming and validity are still less than ideal. It is suggested that the following questions are appropriately used only as screening devices, that unusual responses be investigated further with standardized tests, and that patterns of unusual responses be investigated with neuropsychological, neurological or other appropriate scientific methods.

You can, of course, use the questions from the age-appropriate Sections of the Binet or the Wechsler subtests of Information, Arithmetic, Comprehension, Similarities or Digit Span for the advantage of precise scoring of the responses. However, some of the questions offered below may be suitable

---

[1] For citiations of some of these measures see the annotations to the list of citations in Chapter 38.

alternatives for subjects who have recently been formally tested on these instruments or for other reasons.

No assertion or implication of any kind of validity is made nor should be inferred about the use of these questions. As far as I know, there has been no research conducted on them and there are no published norms available to guide the clinician in interpreting the responses obtained to the questions asked. The internal "norms" of the experienced and well-trained clinician are the only basis for evaluating such responses.

These areas of mental/cognitive functioning/tasks are LISTED IN ROUGH ORDER OF INCREASING COMPLEXITY and demand on the client because you would probably ask them in this order.

Sensorium:

Sense organs: vision, taste, hearing, skin sensation, kinesthesia, balance, touch, smell, etc.
   Intact, defects in _____,
Often included under sensorium are: orientation, memory, calculation, general knowledge, and abstract thinking
Glasgow Coma Scale: Teasdale and Jenvet, (1974) can be used for more precise numerical rating.

6.2 Rancho Los Amigos Cognitive Scale: can be used to assess the level of function in carrying out purposeful behavior.

Level I   No response to pain, touch, sound or sight.

Level II   Generalized reflex response to pain.

Level III   Localized response. Blinks to strong light, turns toward/away from sound. Responds to physical discomfort. Inconsistent response to commands.

Level IV   Confused - Agitated. Alert, very active, aggressive or bizarre behaviors. Performs motor activities but behavior is non-purposeful. Extremely short attention span.

Level V   Confused - Non-agitated. Gross attention to environment. Highly distractible; requires continual redirection. Difficulty learning new tasks. Agitated by too much stimulation. May engage in social conversation but with inappropriate verbalizations.

Level VI   Confused - Appropriate. Inconsistent orientation to time and place. Retention span/recent memory impaired. Begins to recall past. Consistently follows simple directions. Goal-directed behavior with assistance.

Level VII   Automatic - Appropriate. Performs daily routine in highly familiar environment in a non-confused but automatic, robot-like manner. Skills noticeably deteriorate in unfamiliar environment. Lacks realistic planning for own future.

Level VIII Purposeful - Appropriate.

6.3 Background Information Related to Mental Status: See also Chapter 9 Background Information

"How far did you go in school/how many grades did you finish in school/did you finish High School?"

"In school were you ever left behind a grade/not promoted to the next grade/ have to take a grade over again?"

"Were you ever in any kind of special classes/special education/classes for the learning disabled/slow learners/retarded/socially and emotionally disturbed or disabled?"

6.4 Orientation: See section 15.3 Orientation for descriptors

To assess the period of disorientation and confusion after traumatic brain Injury you can use the GOAT: Galveston Orientation and Amnesia Test (Levin, *et al.*, 1979)

To PERSON: Ask:

"Who are you?"
"What is your name?" (Pay attention to nicknames, childhood versions of name, hesitations, aliases)
"Are you married?"
"What kind of work you do/did you do?"

For a child: What school do you go to? What grade are you in now?

To PLACE: Ask:

"Where are we/you?" (Setting, address/building, city, state/province)
"Where do you live?" (Setting, address/building, city, state/province)

To TIME: Ask: (If he/she indicates not knowing ask for a guess or an approximation)

"How old are you?", "When is your birthday?"
"What day is today? Which day of the week is today?, What months is it now? What is today's date?"
"What time is it? Is it day or night?"
"What season is it? What year is it?"
Ask for the dates/duration of hospitalization(s): "When did you first come here?"

To SITUATION: Ask:

"Who am I?"
"What am I doing here?"
"What is the purpose of our talking?"
"Why are you here?"

To Familiar Objects:

> Hold up your hand and ask: "Is this my right or left hand?"
> "Please name the fingers of my hand."
> Hold up/point to a pencil, a watch, eyeglasses and ask the S to name the object, its uses, and parts.

To Others: Ask:

> "What is your mother's/father's/spouse's name?"
> "What are your children's name(s)?"
> "What is my name?"
> "What is my title/job?"
> "What are the names of some staff members?" Ask about their titles, functions, etc.
> "What are the names of some other patients?"

6.5 Attention:

Active information processing about a single or particular stimulus with filtering out of irrelevant stimuli. See section 15.4 Attention for descriptors.
For Attention Span questions see sections 6.6 Concentration and 6.9 Immediate memory.

Tests: (<->) Ask the client to:

> "Please say the alphabet as fast as possible." (Note the time taken; normal is 3-10 seconds)
> "Spell 'World'/ 'House' And now, please spell it backward."
> "Repeat your Social Security number backwards, please." You may need to clarify the sequence by adding "One number at a time, from the end."
> *Digit span* forward and reverse. See section 6.9 Immediate Memory.
> Name three objects and have S repeat them or repeat them to the S until all are learned - count the trials until the subject is able to repeat accurately.
> "Count and then tell me the number of taps I have made." Tap the underside of the table or in some other manner make several trials of 3-15 sounds out of the subject's sight.

6.6 Concentration: See section 15.5 Concentration for descriptors

The maintenance of/holding attention by excluding irrelevant stimuli, or the performance of linked mental acts.

Tests: (<->) Ask the subject to:

> "Name the days of the week backwards starting with Sunday."
> "Please name the months of the year." "Now please say them backwards."
> "Say the alphabet *backwards* as fast as possible."
> Ask the S to write a fairly long and complex sentence from your dictation.
> Ask the Subject to tell you when a minute has passed while you talk or don't talk to him/her and record the time taken. Repeat 3 times.
> Ask the S to point to/underline each 'A' in a written list presented on a full page of letters: e.g. B, F, H, K, A, X, E, P, A, etc.
> Mental arithmetic problems: See 6.15 for examples including the famous "Serial Sevens."

6.7 Comprehension of Language:

RECEPTIVE: Response to a series of commands such as:

"Close you eyes, open them, raise an arm, raise your left arm."
"Show me how you brush your teeth/comb your hair."
"Put your right hand on your left knee three times and then touch you left ear with your right hand."
"If today is Tuesday raise one arm, otherwise raise both."

Follows a three stage command: "Pick up that paper, fold it in half, and put it on the floor."

"Please, read and obey this sentence." (Presented on a card): 'Close your eyes.'

FLUENCY:

"Please tell me as many words as you can think of which begin with the letter F. Don't give me names/proper nouns or repeat yourself and keep going until I stop you." Stop the subject after 60 seconds and repeat with the letters 'A', 'P', or 'S.' Score is the total number of words meeting the criteria on each trial.

EXPRESSIVE:

"Repeat after me" (one at a time): "One, top, pipe, basket, cabinet, affection, stentorian, pleurisy, Methodist Episcopal; No ifs, ands or buts; liquid linoleum; Third Royal Riding Artillery Brigade."

Ask him/her to read and explain some sentences from a magazine or newspaper.
Show him/her a photograph (e.g. in a magazine) and ask for the name(s) of what is depicted.
Ask him/her to describe a picture portraying several actions.

6.8 Eye/hand Coordination/Perceptual-Motor Integration/Dyspraxia/Constructional Ability:

TESTS: Ask the Client to:

Pick up a coin with each hand.
Spin a paper clip on the tabletop using each hand.
Touch each thumb to each finger as you name them (not in order)
Copy a design of two overlapping pentagons from an illustration on a card.
Draw a house, a tree, a person, a person of the other sex, themselves.
Ask the client to draw, from your dictation:
    a Diamond   the outlines of a Cross
    a Smoking pipe   the edges of a transparent Cube
    a Clock face and then indicate the present time as he/she estimates it to be or "twenty after six."

6.9 Memory: See section 15.7 Memory for descriptors
TYPES:
Clinical: Recognition ("identify, select, pick, or find"), Reproduction ("say, repeat, or copy"), Recall (remember without cueing)
Theoretical or Processes: Registration, Retention, Decay, Reproduction

Kinds: Verbal: words, phrases, stories, associated word pairs
Visual: colors, designs, pictures
Spatial: positions of objects
Episodic: contexts, situations, components, details, sequences, themes
Practical: can demonstrate/pantomime how to open a can, brush one's teeth, butter bread

TESTS OF MEMORY:

It is probably best, if it is available, to use the Wechsler *Memory Scale - Revised* or a similar validated test for precise evaluation.

Introductory questions:

"Has your memory been good?"
"Have you had any difficulty concentrating or remembering what you read/watch on television/ recipes/telephone numbers/appointment times?"
"Have you recently gotten lost/forgotten an important event/something you were cooking/left some appliance on too long?"
"Have you had any difficulty recalling people's names or where you know them from?"
"Have other people suggested to you that your memory is not as good as it was?"

Immediate memory or memory span (about 10-30 seconds when in the experimental laboratory; what was just said, done or learned during the evaluation when in the clinic):

Digit Span: forward and reverse.
"I would like to test your ability to concentrate. I am going to say some numbers one at a time. When I finish please repeat them back to me. Ready?"
Start with two digits (single digits, not 17, 36, etc.) and when repeated correctly on a first or second attempt (with different digits) increase the length of the list by one digit until the Subject fails both trials/number sequences offered. Write the numbers down as you say them, speak at a consistent rate of one digit per second, do not emphasize ending numbers with changes in your voice, and avoid consecutive numbers and easily recognizable dates or familiar sequences. Or use you own Social security number or telephone number.
Then say "Now I am going to say some more numbers but this time I want you to repeat them backward. For example, if I said 6-2, what would you say?"
The score is the maximum number of correctly recalled digits in correct order on either trial. 'Five forward with one mistake' is four forward.
Normal is about 5-8 forward and 4-6 backward. A difference of 3 or more in maximum Forward minus maximum Backward suggests concentration deficits. Five or more forward is considered unimpaired in younger or middle-aged adults.

Ask the subject to "Tap a pencil on the table each and every time I say the letter 'C'". Present a series of random letters at the rate of about 3 each 4 seconds with the letter 'C' randomly distributed but occurring about every 6-8 letters. Normal is making about 1-2 errors (not noticing a 'C') in 30 seconds/45 letters.

Delayed recall: after interference: (variously defined as recall after any intervening activity, a few minutes time delay, recent daily events or intra-interview events):

Name (for auditory retention) or point to (for visual retention) three items (E.g. Broadway-New York city-taxi; book-pen-tablet; scissors-stapler-pad, apple-peach-pear), tell the subject that you will ask him/her about them later, and then ask for recall after 5 minutes of interspersed activities.

Offer 4 items from four categories (E.g. "House, table, pencil, dictionary") and record the number
    of trials taken to learn the list. Ask for recall in 5 or 10 minutes. If not recalled prompt with
    category descriptions (E.g. "A building, a piece of furniture, a writing tool, a kind of book"). If
    still not recalled ask the subject to select the words from a list of four similar items (E.g. for pencil:
    pen, crayon, pencil, paintbrush).
Give the subject three colors or shapes to remember and ask him/her to recall them in 5 minutes.
Tell the subject your name and ask him/her to remember it because you will ask for it later. Ask in 5-10
    minutes and if not correctly recalled re-inform and teach, then re-ask every 5 or 10 minutes more
    and note the number of trials to mastery or failure to learn.

Short-Term Retention: Short-term retention is a few minutes up to 1-2 hours.

   Ask the subject read a narrative paragraph from a magazine or newspaper and produce the gist of
       the story upon completion without being able to refer to it.
   Ask about the events at the beginning of the interview (i.e. Any others present?, What was asked
   first and next? Which history items were sought).

Recent memory: A few hours up to 1-4 days, today's events.

   Ask about yesterday's meals/television programs/activities/companions (Ask only if these can be
       verified). Or ask the route taken/distance to this office, the examiner's name (if not over-used in
       the interview), events in the recent news.

Recent past memory: The last few weeks and months: (Ask only if these can be verified)

   "What did you do last weekend?"
   "Where did you take your last vacation?"
   "What presents did you get on your last birthday/Christmas?"
   "What were you doing on the most recent holidays (July 4th, Labor Day, Christmas)?"
   "Name any other doctors you have seen, any hospitalizations, tests received, when the present
       illness began/first felt troubled/ill, etc."

Remote memory: From approximately 6 months up to all of lifetime or premorbid/symptom onset:

   Client's home address, and phone number.
   "Where were you born?"
   "What is your birth date, your mother's first/maiden name, your first memory?"
   "What was the name of your High School?"
   Ask about
       Childhood events, in correct sequence, places lived, schools attended, names of friends.
       Life history: parents full names, sibling's names and birth order, family deaths, first job, date(s) of
           marriage, birth dates/ages/names and ages of children.
       More difficult alternatives are sib's birthdays, dates of hospitalizations, names of doctors, school
           teacher's names.
   Activities on holidays about a year ago or which stand out.
   Local historical events
   Historical events (which you can verify): Sputnik (1957), Watergate (1971), Men landing on the moon
       (Summer, 1969), name of the President who resigned (Nixon, Aug. 9, 1974), The fall of Saigon
       (Apr. 29, 1975), Presidents during wars (WW II - Roosevelt, Korean War - Truman, Eisenhower,
       Viet Nam - Johnson, Nixon), Challenger Disaster (Jan. 28, 1986), etc.

6.10 Fund of Information: See sectio 15.8 Information for descriptors

BASIC ORIENTATIONS:

"What is your

Birth date?	Social Security number?	Area code?	Phone number?	
Address?	Zip code?			
Height?	Weight?	Shoe size?	Dress size?	Waist size?

"Tell me the time." "What time will it be in an hour and a quarter?"
"How long will it be until Christmas?"
"How many days are there in a month/year?"
"Name the days of the week/months of the year."

"Where are we?" (state, county, city, hospital/building, floor, office)
"Name the local sports teams."
"What is the capitol of this state?"
"Which states border this one?"
"Name five large American cities."
"How far is it from here to _____ ?" (one of the large cities named above).
"How far is it from New York City to San Francisco?"
"In which country is Rome/Paris/London/Moscow?"
"Name three countries in the Middle East/Europe/South America."
"What is the current population of this city/state/the United States (258 million in 1993), the world (5.6 billion in 1993)?"

INFORMATION ABOUT PEOPLE:

"Who is the current President? and before him?, and before him? Name the presidents backward starting with the current one." [Presidents of the U.S. since 1900 in reverse order: Clinton, Bush, Reagan, Carter, Ford, Nixon, Johnson, Kennedy, Eisenhower, Truman, Roosevelt, Hoover, Coolidge, Harding, Wilson, Taft, Roosevelt. Note: The failure to recall these is not pathonomic.]
"Where does the President live?" (in the White House, Washington, D.C.)
"Who was the first President of the United States?"
"Who is the Governor of this state/Mayor of this city?"
"Who is Dr. J., Prince, Michael Jackson, Jesse Jackson, Jackie Robinson, Martin Luther King Jr., Thurgood Marshall, Barbara Jordan, Clarence Thomas, Hammer?"
"What was George Washington/Thomas Edison/Jonas Salk/Albert Einstein famous for?"
"Who invented the airplane?"
"What does a pharmacist do?"
"Who was JFK/Gorbachev?"

For a Child:

"Who is Arnold Swartzenegger/Mr. Rogers/Big Bird/Ronald McDonald/your teachers' names?"

INFORMATION ABOUT THINGS:

"Name five foods."
"Name five animals."
Ask about local geography: rivers, mountains, streets, downtown, parks, highways, stores, schools
"How many sides does a pentagon have?" [5]
"Name three animals beginning with C."
"Name three cities beginning with D."

"How many ounces in a pound?" [16]
"What are houses made of?"
"Which is the longest river in the United States?" [Mississippi]
"In what direction does the sun rise?" [East]
"Please identify these." (Show some coins and bills of common US currency)
"Who/whose face is on a penny/nickel/dime/dollar bill/five dollar bill?" [Lincoln/Jefferson/
     Roosevelt/Washington/Lincoln]
"At what temperature does water freeze?"
"From what do we get gasoline?"

INFORMATION ABOUT **EVENTS**:

"What do we celebrate on the 4th of July/Christmas/Thanksgiving Day/Labor Day/Memorial
          Day/Easter/Passover/Ramadan/Kwansa?"
"Who won the last Superbowl/World Series?"
"Please name some events/big stories that are current/recently in the news/that you have read about
     in the papers or seen on the TV news."
"What has happened recently in (specify a place)?"
"What did (person's name) do recently? What happened to (person's name) recently?"
"Name some recent wars the US has been involved in and their dates [World War I (1914-1918)
     World War II (1939-1945), Korean War/Police action 1950-1953, Viet Nam/Indochina War
     1965-1975, Lebanon, Granada, Panama, the Persian Gulf, Somalia,], and the issues involved."

For those over 50 years of age:
"What was the date of the attack on Pearl Harbor?" [Dec. 7, 1941]

For those over 40 years of age:
"What was the date President John F. Kennedy was assassinated?" [Nov. 22, 1963]

6.11 Opposites:

"Please tell me the opposite of each of these words;"

Hard	fast	large	out	high	child

6.12 Differences:

Use the format   "What is the difference between _____ and _____?" or
                  "In what ways are a _____ and a _____ the different or not the same?"

lie - mistake	duck - robin	midget - child	orange - baseball
kite - airplane	water - land		

"Which of these is the different one?"
   Desk, apple, chair, lamp. "Why?" [apple is not artificial, not furniture, is edible]
   Pottery, statue, painting, poem. "Why?" [Poem is not tactile, Statue does not begin with a 'P']

6.13 Similarities:

Use the format "In what ways are a/an _____ and a/an _____ the same or similar?" Question any vague responses until you obtain a clear estimate of the level of comprehension and abstraction involved. For example *train/bus - bicycle* can be interpreted on a spectrum (<->) from "Has wheels/people ride on them/means of transportation/technological artifacts".

Ask "Please tell me more about that" and, if necessary, ask "What type/class of things do they belong to?"

EASY:

truck/car - bus	duck - chicken	dollar - dime	shoes - pants
scissors - saw	book - newspaper	bucket - mug	violin - piano
apple - orange	bottle - can	work - play	happy - sad
car - airplane	ship - airplane	elbow - knee	candle - lamp
stone - egg	wheel - ball	mountain - lake	joy - anger

MODERATELY DIFFICULT:

door - window	moose - whale	tree - branch	sun - moon
fox - dog	ladder - steps	wings - legs	barn - house
cat - lion	bread - milk	tree - forest	prison - zoo

DIFFICULT:

paper - coal	telephone - radio	theater - church	lamp - fan

6.14 Absurdities:

You can, of course, use Absurdities from the Stanford-Binet, Form LM or you might select from your experience examples which are tailored for the particular person being examined. The following are similar to those of the Stanford-Binet, 1980 Revision.

Ask "What is wrong with/foolish/doesn't make sense about this?"

"The doctor rushed into the Emergency Room, got out the bandages, and after eating a sandwich, bandaged the bleeding man."
"Bill's ears were so big he had to pull his sweaters on over his feet."
"An airplane pilot ran out of gas halfway across the ocean so he turned around and flew back to land from where he took off."
"A man was in two auto accidents. The first accident killed him but the second time he got well very quickly."

Only if you believe it useful, ask about absurdities/contradictions/paradoxes in everyday life:
The government pays farmers to grow tobacco and also pays for programs to reduce tobacco consumption.
A lemonade mix contains no real lemon but only artificial flavoring and a "lemon" detergent contains real lemon juice.
Please give me an example of "Catch-22"

6.15 Tests of Calculation Abilities: See section 15.11 Arithmetic for descriptors

These require attention, concentration, memory and education. On all math problems make note of the answers given, the effort required/offered, speed and accuracy, changed performance when given a prompt of the next correct answer in a sequence, and/or when given paper and pencil to perform the calculations. Also note self-corrected errors, later self-corrections, use of fingers to count upon, requests for paper and pencil, complaints, excuses, etc.

EXAMPLES: (<->)

"How much is 2+2? And 4+4? and 8+8=?" Continue in this sequence and note the limits of skill. More difficult versions are 3+3's and 7+7's.
One-step: 3 + 4 = ?, 6 X 4 = ?,
Two-step: 7 + 5 - 3 = ?, 8 X 4 + 9 = ?, 4 X 6 ÷ 3 = ?
"Which is larger: one third or one half?"

VERBALLY PRESENTED ARITHMETIC PROBLEMS: (<->)

"How many quarters are in $1.75?" [7]
"If oranges are priced at 2 for 18¢, how much would half a dozen cost?" [54¢]
"How much is left when you subtract $5.50 from $14.00?" [$8.50]
"How many nickels are there in one dollar?" [20]
"How many nickels are there in $1.95?" [39]

SERIAL SUBTRACTIONS/"SERIAL SEVENS" :

"Starting with 100 subtract 7 and then subtract 7 from that and continue subtracting 7."
Normal is 1 minute or less in subtracting to 2 with 2 or fewer errors (not including spontaneous self-corrections.)
In reporting responses to this, it is clearer to the reader if you underline the erroneous responses, such as on serial sevens: 93, 84, 77, 70, 62.

SIMPLER ALTERNATIVES:

Count to 20, count from 1 to 40 by threes, serial 3's subtracted from 31, serial 5's subtracted from 100, serial 4's subtracted from 100

6.16 Abstract Reasoning/Proverbs: See section 15.10 Reasoning for descriptors

The selection of which proverbs to offer depends on your initial assessment of the client's deficits and diagnosis because some are more difficult to interpret satisfactorily while others reveal coping strategies, the intensity of the cognitive dysfunction, or personalization.

Say: "What do people mean when they say...?"

PROVERBS WITH THEMES:

> All that glitters is not gold; You can't judge a book by its cover (appearances can be deceiving).
> Make hay while the sun shines; Strike while the iron is hot (using an opportunity, taking initiative).
> Don't cry over spilled/spilt milk (mature resignation and priorities).
> Every cloud has a silver lining; The grass is always greener on the other side; (depression, pessimism, optimism, envy, regret, dissatisfaction).
> Rome wasn't built in a day; Great oaks from little acorns grow (patience, frustration tolerance, deferral/delay of gratification).
> People who live in glass houses shouldn't throw stones (arrogance, tolerance, humility, guilt, impulse control).
> Birds of a feather flock together; Like father like son; The apple doesn't fall far from the tree (the effects of history, genetics or learning).
> Don't count your chickens before they are hatched; A bird in the hand is worth two in the bush (caution, realistic hopes/plans).
> The squeaking wheel gets the grease (modesty, attention-seeking behavior, self assertion).
> A rolling stone gathers no moss (positive and negative interpretations of stones/moss/rolling).
> When the cat's away the mice will play (control and rebellion).

Note: It is often advisable to ask if the client has heard these proverbs before.

6.17 Paired Proverbs:

These can be used to more carefully evaluate the client's ability, to make subtle distinctions and to hold simultaneously opposing views in mind by presenting them in sequence and without explanation. It parallels 'testing the limits' in intelligence testing.

PROVERBS:

Don't change horses in midstream	and	If at first you don't succeed, try, try again.
A bird in the hand is worth two in the bush	and	Nothing ventured, nothing gained.
Look before you leap	and	He who hesitates is lost.
Out of sight, out of mind	and	Distance makes the heart grow fonder.
A stitch in time saves nine	and	Don't cross a bridge until you come to it .
Haste make waste	and	Strike while the iron is hot
		Make hay while the sun shines.

6.18 Practical Reasoning:

QUESTIONS:

> "Why do we refrigerate many foods?"
> "Why do we have newspapers?"
> "Why do people buy life/fire insurance?"
> "Why should people make a Will?"

HAZARD RECOGNITION: (<->)

"What should you do before crossing the street?"

"Why shouldn't people play with matches?"
"Why shouldn't people smoke in bed?"
"What should you do when paper in a wastebasket catches fire?"
"What should you do if grease catches on fire when you are cooking?"

"What should you do when you cut your finger?"

6.19 Social Judgement: See also sections 6.18 Practical Reasoning and 15.14, .15 and .16

QUESTIONS: (<->)

"Why should you go to school?"
"What should you do if you lose/find a library book?"
"What should you do if you find a purse or wallet in the street?"
"What should you do if you are stopped by the police?"
"What should you do if you smell gas in your house?"

"Why do we have to put stamps on letters we mail?"
"Why do people have to have license plates on their cars?"

"Please tell me of a situation or incident in which you made a foolish or mistaken choice."
"Have you ever been taken advantage of/been a victim?"
"Have you ever made any bad loans?"

"How do you get along with others/people at work?"
"What should you do if someone is very critical of a job you have done?"
"What would you do if someone threatened/tried to hurt you?"
"Please tell me the name of a close friend of yours/someone you would confide in/talk with if you
        had a personal problem/talk over a serious problem."

"How would you spend $10,000 if it were given to you/you won the lottery?"

"Who is or was the most important person in the world/history? Why?"

"Why do people on an elevator always face the door?"
"What is the role of a free press in a democracy?"
"Why do people feel so strongly about the subject of abortion?"

For a Child:

"If you could have anything you wish for what three things would you wish for?"
"If you could live anywhere in the world, where would you want to live?"
"If you could change anything about yourself what would you change?"
"If you could be any animal, which would you choose and why?"

6.20 Decision Making:

"Are you satisfied with the decisions you make?"
"Do you have a hard time coming to some decisions? Which are hardest? Why?"

6.21 Self-image:

QUESTIONS:

"Please describe your personality."
"How would you describe yourself?"
"Which three words best describe you?"

"What was the most important thing that ever happened in your life?"
"Would/could/can you identify some turning points in your life?"
"What would be written on your tombstone/in your obituary if you were to die today?"
"Has life been fair to you?"

6.22 Insight: For descriptors of responses see section 15.17 Insight

GENERAL:

"Why are you here?"   "What causes you to be here?"
"What kind of place is this? What goes on here?"
"Why are you seeing me?"
"What do you think has caused your troubles/being disabled/being hospitalized?"
"What changes would help you most?"

INTO ILLNESS:

"Do you think there is something wrong with you? What? Do you think you are ill?"
"What is your diagnosis?"   "What does that mean?"
"Did you ever have a nervous breakdown/bad nerves/something wrong with your mind?"
"Do you think you need treatment?"
"Why did/do you need to take medicines?"
"Did you come here voluntarily?"
"What are your suggestions for your treatment?"

7. Inquiries for Signs, Symptoms and Syndromes of Disorders and Other Behavior Patterns

Questions here do NOT address the COGNITIVE FUNCTIONING or MENTAL STATUS; those are covered in Chapter 6. Mental Status Examination Questions.

Topics here are in simple alphabetical order so you can easily find the areas to explore based on the referral or intake reasons.

Abuse, Alcohol/Drug: See Sections 7.25 and 7.26 Substance abuse

7.1 Abuse/Neglect of Spouse/Elder (for a child, see 7.2 below) in the Physical/Emotional/ Psychological/Financial areas: See also sections 7.15 Impulse control and 16.1 for descriptors

Inquire of all patients about physical and sexual abuse, threats, fights, arguments

"How are things at home?"
"Are you alone at home a lot?"
"Are you afraid of anyone at home?"
N. B.: Neglect/abuse may show as weight loss, dehydration, withdrawal

BATTERING BY PARTNER: From NiCarthy, and Davidson, (1989)

"Has your partner ever[1] hit, punched, slapped, kicked or bitten you or your children?"
"Have you had bruises from being hit, held or squeezed?"
"Have you ever had to stay in bed or been too weak to work after being hit?"
"Have you ever seen a doctor as a result of injuries from your partner?"

EMOTIONAL ABUSE:

"Has your partner:
    "tracked" all of your time?"
    controlled all the money in the household and forced you to account for what you spent?"
    repeatedly accused you of being unfaithful?"
    bragged to you about his/her affairs with other women/men?"

    discouraged your relationships with family and friends?"
    prevented you from working or attending school?"
    humiliated you, called you names, or made painful fun of you in from of others?"

    gotten very angry or frightening when drinking or using drugs?"
    threatened to hurt you or the children?"
    threatened to use a weapon against you or the children?"
    regularly threatened to leave you?"
    punished the children or pets when s/he was angry at you?"
    destroyed personal property or sentimental items?"
    forced you to have sex against your will?"

A useful resource on diagnosis and treatment of the varieties of victimization's consequences in women is Coffman and Fallon (1990).
The National Coalition Against Domestic Violence is at 303-839-1852 for local referral.

---

[1] You can add "ever" for emphasis or to reduce denial.

7.2 Abused/Neglected Child: See also 7.1, above and 7.2 below

OPENING QUESTIONS:

"Are you afraid of anyone at home?"
"How do you get along with your father/mother?"[1]
"Are your parents strict?"
"What happens when you get into trouble?"
"Are you a happy kid?"

"Do you have problems with your teacher?"

PHYSICAL ABUSE: Note: Obtain experienced medical consultation if you have suspicions about injuries.

Look for evidence of injuries and inquire how they occurred and what was done about them.
Attend to:
> Explanations of the cause of the injury and especially any reluctance to explain, or different explanations by different care-givers
> Whether treatment was sought in a timely and effective fashion
> Previous similar or suspicious injuries
> Cooperation with previous treatments prescribed
> Risk factors: unwanted birth, prematurity, poverty, developmental delay, "difficult baby", colicky baby, inappropriate expectations, ignorance of development, poor baby/parent match or misfit, many small children at home, few supports, previous involvement with the authorities, drug or alcohol abuse, etc.
> Psychological patterns in the child such as depression, anxiety, avoidance, preference for isolation, acting out, etc.

If the injury was the result of disciplining the child inquire about when they discipline and how and what so annoyed the care-giver as to result in the injury, rationale for the punishment, current evaluation of the undesired behaviors/punishment, etc.

7.3 Sexual Abuse: Child and Adult: See also sections 7.1 and 7.2 above.
Note: This is a speciality area; if you are not experienced and trained get consultation or refer before going very far into the topic for fear of contaminating the truth.

INITIAL INQUIRY:

"What do you call your private parts? What do you call the other sex's private parts?"

Sometimes, in the right context, a gentle inquiry like "What has happened to you?" will open the door to these issues. This is preferable to 'What is your problem?' as it may not be seen as a 'problem.'[2]

---

[1] This stepwise approach and wording is from Nora F. Young, of Cedro Wolley, WA..

[2] This sensitive approach is from Nora F. Young, of Cedro Wolley, WA..

FOR A CHILD:

"Who has touched your private parts?" (Note: Do not add "when you didn't want them to" as
    that may not have been true or is yet unrecognized.)
"Who, when, where, why?"
"Whom did you tell? What did they do about it?"

FOR AN ADULT: From Root and Fallon, (1988).

"Have you ever been hit, slapped, shoved or spanked by a parent or a partner?"
"Have you ever been forced into sexual acts as a child or adult?"
"Has your husband ever insisted on sex when you didn't want to?"
"Was your first experience with sexual intercourse by choice or were you forced?"

SEXUAL VICTIMIZATION:

"Did anyone ever touch you sexually when you didn't want them to?"
"Who, if anyone, have you had a sexual experience with who was also a relative of yours?
"Have you ever been forced to have any kind of sex with anyone?"
    "What happened?   "With whom?
    "Where?   "When?
    "How many times did it happen?   "Whom did you tell or why not?
    "What did you do about this?   "How did this affect you, etc.?"

Evaluate the interventions needed:

SEXUAL OFFENSES:

"Have you ever forced anyone to have any kind of sex with you?"
"What happened, with whom, where, whom did you tell or why not, what did you do about this,
    how did this affect you, etc.?"

Estimate the risk to the community and self:

7.4 Affect/Mood: See also sections 14.3 Anxiety and 14.5 Depression

"How would you describe your mood today?"
"Are you happy, sad or what right now?"
"Using a scale where plus 10 is as happy as you have ever been, 1 is not depressed at all and minus
    10 is as depressed as you have ever been, please rate your mood today." (Less educated
    persons may need a scale from 0 to 10.)

"What is your usual mood like?"
    If negative ask "When was it last good?"
"When are/were you happiest?"

"In the last month, how many times have you cried/yelled/been afraid?"
"How long does it take you to get over a bad mood/upset?"

"What was your mood like during your childhood/adolescence/earlier life?"
"Were there ever times when you couldn't control your feelings?"

Alcohol use/abuse: See section 7.25 Substance abuse questions.

Anorexia: See section 7.11 Eating Disorders questions.

7.5 Anxiety: See section 14.3 for descriptors

"Is there something you are very concerned about/afraid of happening?"
"What do you worry about?"
"How does the future look to you?"

"When you get frightened what happens to you?"
"Do you ever have times of great fear or anxiety/panic attacks?" [Inquire about cues/triggers, frequency, duration, whether observed by others, specific physiological symptoms, the sequence of the symptoms, etc.]

"Are there any distressing memories which keep coming back to you?"

"Is there any situation you avoid because it really upsets/scares you?"

Bulemia: See section 7.12 Eating disorders questions

Child behavior disorders: See Chapter 9 Background, and 10.2, 10.4 Reasons for child referral

7.6 Compliance/Non-Compliance:

"What problems have you had in getting treatment/finding an understanding doctor/keeping scheduled medical appointments?"
"What problems have you had in taking prescribed medications?"
"What medications are you taking?" "What medications should you be taking?"
"Have you ever stopped taking medications prescribed for you before they ran out/because of some reason?" "What was the reason?"
"Is there anything which makes you reluctant to take medications/treatments prescribed for you?"

7.7 Compulsions: See also section 7.17 Obsessions and 16.9 for descriptors. Below is partly from Goodman, *et al.* (1989)

REPETITION:

"Are there any words or phrases you feel that you have to say in a certain way or at certain times?"
"Do you ever have to do the same thing over and over, or in a certain way?"
"Is there anything in your house/at work that you have to check on frequently?"
"Are you a person who is especially careful about safety?"
"Do you have to check the doors/windows/locks/kitchen/house/your family's safety?"
"Do you have to wash or clean often?"

BEHAVIORS:

"Do you have any habits/frequent actions/rituals/behaviors that you must/feel compelled to do in a
   particular way or very often?"
"Is there some things you must do in order to fall asleep?"
"Are there any actions you have to do before or while you eat/go to the bathroom?"
"Do you ever have to arrange your clothes in certain ways?"
"Are you very careful about /afraid of poisons/dirt/germs/diseases/contamination?"

EXCESS/IRRATIONALITY:

"Do these actions seem reasonable to you/more than you should/more than a sensible number of
   times a day/take up a long time each day?"
"Do you spend more time on these than you think you would like to?"
"How does doing these things affect your life/routines/job/relationships/family members?"
"Do you feel uncomfortable until these actions are done, even though you may know them to be
   unimportant/even foolish/that they won't really work?"

"How much control do you feel you have over these actions? Do you resist them or yield to
   them?"

Conduct disorders in children: See sections 10.2 and 10.4 Reasons for child referral

---

7.8 Delusions: False (unaccepted by society/subculture/peers), fixed/change-resistant beliefs. See also section 16.11 for descriptors and 7.20 Paranoia

CONTROL:

"Did anyone try to read your mind/use unusual means to force thoughts into your mind/try to
   take/block some of your thoughts away/stop or block your thoughts?"
"Did you ever hear a voice telling you what to do?"
"Have you ever been forewarned/known that something would happen before it did?"

GRANDEUR/SPECIAL ABILITIES:

"Are you an especially gifted person?" (Note reports of a large number of cars or other
   possessions, exaggerated abilities, titles/degrees/education/high positions, dramatic or unlikely
   consumption of alcohol or drugs or history of unlikely or criminal activities)
"Do you have great wealth/unusual strengths/special powers/impressive sexual activities?"
"Are you able to influence others/read people's minds/put thoughts into their minds?"
"Do/did you ever receive personal messages from heaven/God/someone unusual?"
"Have you been in communication with aliens/dead people/God/Christ/the Devil/the Blessed
   Virgin/any Biblical persons?"
"Do you think you are immortal/cannot be harmed/hurt/killed?"

IMPOSTER:

"Are you a fake?" [Separate a delusion from beliefs of inadequacy based on low self-esteem]
"Do you think people recognize who you really are?"
"Are you concerned about being discovered/identified/exposed?"
"What is your real rank?"

MONOMANIA:

Is this person preoccupied with a certain ideas, themes, events or persons? Does all his/her
conversation return to a single topic/false idea?

NIHILISM:

"Do you think everything is lost/hopeless?"
"Do you think that tomorrow will never come?"
"Do you think that the world has stopped?"
"Do you think that things outside no longer exist?"
"Do you still have all the parts of your body?"

PERSECUTION: See section 7.20 Paranoia

REFERENCE:

"Do people do things/do things happen which only you really understand/have special meanings
for you/are designed to convey or tell you something no one else is to know?"
"Are things you see on the TV/hear on the radio/read in the papers especially meaningful to
you/contain special messages just for you?"

SOMATIC/HYPOCHONDRIACAL:

"How is your health? How often are you ill? How often do you see a physician? Do you have
many illnesses/medical or health problems?"
"Do you have a lot of pain or unusual pains?"
"Which medicines do you take regularly? Which medicines do you take regularly that don't need a
prescription for?"

"Is there some illness you are worried about getting or that you already have that worries you?"
"How often do you think about it?"
"How does it make you feel when you think about it?"
"What do you do about it?"

"Do you think you might/have a serious disease like cancer or AIDS or MS?"
"Do you think you might/have some horrible disease which hasn't been diagnosed correctly or has
no cure?"
"Do you think you have a serious disease but haven't been able to find a doctor to treat it?"

SELF-DEPRECIATION: See also section 14.5 Depression

"Do you think you are worthless/sinful/ugly/emitting bad/noxious odors/will be punished because
you have sinned unforgivably?"

7.9 Dissociative Experiences

For standardized evaluation you can use Ross, *et al.*'s (1989, 1990) Dissociative Disorders Interview
Schedule or Bernstein and Putnam's (1986) Dissociative Experiences Scale. They are the experts on
dissociative disorders and multiple personality.

DISSOCIATIVE EXPERIENCES:

"Have you walked in your sleep?"
"Did you have imaginary playmates as a child?"
"Have you noticed that some of your personal possessions were missing?"

"Have you ever suddenly realized that
    you don't remember earlier parts of the trip you are on?"
    you are in a place and have no recall of how you got there?"
    you are wearing clothes you would not choose?"
    there are items in your possession you don't recall buying?
"Have you ever remembered a past event so vividly that it seemed you were actually re-
    experiencing it?"

"Have you ever been greeted by people who call you by another name and really seem to know
    you?
"Have you ever been unable to recall major events in your life?
"Have you ever been unable to decide whether you actually did something or just imagined doing
    it?

DEPERSONALIZATION:

"Are you aware of any significant change in yourself?"
"Do you feel normal/all right/natural/real?"
"Did you ever feel detached from yourself/unattached/divorced from yourself?"
"Did you ever act in so strange a way you considered the possibility that you might be two
    different people."
"Did you ever feel that you have lost your identity/like you were someone else?"
"Are you always certain who you are?"
"Do you ever wonder who you really are?"
"Did you ever feel that you were no longer real/you were becoming someone or something
    different?"

"Have you ever suddenly realized that you don't recognize your face/body in a mirror?"
"Did you ever feel that your self/body was different/changed/unreal/strange?"
"Have you ever felt that your body doesn't belong to yourself?"
"Ever feel like you were/your mind was outside/watching/apart from yourself/your body?"
"Have there been times you felt your mind and body were not together/linked?"
"Do you ever feel like someone else was moving your legs as you walked/ever felt like a robot?"

DEREALIZATION:

"Did you ever get so involved in a daydream that you couldn't tell if it were real or not?"
"Do people, trees, houses, etc. look as they usually do/always did to you?"
"Did you ever feel like you weren't really present?"
"Did you ever feel you were detached/alienated/estranged from yourself or your surroundings/
    everything around you?"

"Have you ever been in a familiar place but found it strange/peculiar/weird/unfamiliar/somehow changed?"
"Did you ever feel that things around you/the world were/was very strange/remote/unreal/changing?"
"Do things seem natural and real to you?"
"Did things or objects ever seem to be alive?"

Depersonalization and Derealization: See above

7.10 Depression: See also sections 14.5 Depression descriptors

SOMATIC/VEGETATIVE SYMPTOMS:

"How is your general health? Has it changed recently?" [Follow up reports of symptoms]

"Has your interest in food increased or decreased?"
"Have you gained or lost weight?"

"How is your sleep? Do you have trouble falling asleep? On how many nights in a week?"
"Do you wake in the middle of the night, other than to go to the bathroom, and then can't get back to sleep?"
"Do you wake up early and can not fall asleep again?"
"Do you regularly nap during the day?" [Count this into total sleep hours which generally decreases with age]

"Have your bowel or bladder habits changed?"

"Has your interest in sex changed?" [Libido is desire not performance]

AFFECTIVE SYMPTOMS:

"How are your spirits generally?"
"How did you feel about (specific event/life in general)?"
"When was the last time you felt really down?"
"Do you get pretty discouraged/depressed/blue? Are you blue/feeling low now?"
"Do you get sad or down for long?"
"Have you felt some personal losses recently?"
"Do you think you are more depressed in the winter than the summer or only in one season?"
    [Consider Seasonal Affective Disorder]
"Have you had a time when you felt very tired or very irritable?"

SOCIAL FUNCTIONING:

"Do you go out less than you used to?"
"Do you find yourself avoiding being with people?"
"Have you given up friendships?"

SELF-DEPRECATION:

"Are you hard on yourself?"
"Do you think you are a wicked person?"
"Do you think that you have sinned and cannot be forgiven?" "Why?"

SUICIDAL IDEATION: See sections 7.27 for Suicide questions and 16.35 for Suicide descriptors

"What do you see for yourself in the future?"
"Do you think you will get well/over this problem? How?"

"When people are depressed they sometimes think about dying. Have you had thoughts like that?"
"Are there times when you wish you would not wake up?"
"Do you feel that life isn't worth living? Do you think you would just as soon be dead/that things/other
    people would be better off if you were dead?"

Optimism/Pessimism:

"What is the worst thing that ever happened to you?"
"What is the best thing that ever happened to you?"
"If you could have three wishes come true, what would you wish for?"

Drug Abuse: See section 7.25 for Substance Abuse questions

ALWAYS ask every client about use and history of medications/street drugs/alcohol/other chemicals.

7.11 Eating Disorders: See also section 16.14 for Eating Disorders descriptors
Evaluate not just weight, fat percentage, and proportion but also self-efficacy, preoccupation, hypervigilance
    around eating, terror over weight gain, typical cognitive dysfunctions, distorted body image, odd eating
    behaviors, etc. See also Garner and Garfinkel (1979) for anorexia nervosa.

"What is your present weight? most you ever weighed? Your lowest weight as an adult?
"Have you gained or lost weight in the last year? How much?"

"How often do you think about your weight or eating or dieting?"
"How do you feel about your current weight?" [Note any disparity between client's statements
    and your judgements of appearance]
"Do you feel you are too fat?" [If yes, ask how long s/he has felt that way]
"Are you afraid of being or becoming overweight?"
"Do you avoid certain foods (foods with sugar, fat, salt, cholesterol, etc.)
"How much control over your eating do you feel you have?"
"How would your life be different if you lost the weight you want to?"

"What kinds of diets have you tried?" [Take a diet history]
"Have you ever gotten so upset or desperate about your weight that you have done something
    drastic?"
"Have you ever: gone on eating binges, vomited after you've eaten, fasted for long periods, used
    diet pills/cathartics/laxatives/diuretics to lose weight, lost a great deal of weight, or felt guilty
    after eating?"

ALTERNATIVE QUESTIONS: The following questions are modified from AA/OA literature:

"Do you think your eating habits are unusual?"
"Is your life dominated by thoughts of food?"
"Is your eating out of your control?"
"Do you have a fear of becoming fat or losing control of your eating?"
"Do you feel fat when your weight is at or below that of your friends?"

"Is your life a series of constant diets?"
"Do you vomit, take laxatives or diuretics or exercise to control your weight?"
"Do you have times when you alternate between eating binges and fasting to control your weight?"
"Does your weight often change as much as 10 pounds because you radically change your eating habits?"

"Do you have "food binges" when you eat a large amount of food in a short time period?"
"If you have binged, was it on high-calorie foods such as sweets, desserts, salty or fatty foods?"
"Have you stopped a binge by vomiting, purging, sleeping or because of pain?"

Fears: A listing of 100 common fears can be found in Braun and Reynolds (1969) with suitable research basis.

7.12 Gay and Lesbian Identity: Normative homosexual identity development[1]: See also section 30.8 Stages of Homosexual Identity Formation

GENERAL QUESTIONS:

"Did you ever have a sense of not belonging or of feeling sexually different from most people?"

"Do you know any gay men? ... any lesbians?"
"What are they like?"
"What images of gay men and lesbians do you have"

"Have you ever thought you might be gay?" "When did you first think this?"
"What was it like to recognize such feelings?"

ATTRACTION:

"Do you find yourself attracted to gay/lesbian relationships or to specific gays/lesbians?"
"Have you ever thought of acting on your feelings?"
"Have you tried to ignore or change these thoughts and feelings and/or convince yourself that you are not gay?"

---

[1] We are grateful to Leslie J. Wrixon, Psy.D., of Cambridge MA, for these questions and guiding us to the stages of identity development.

Understanding:

"Why do you think gay people are that way?" (e.g. They can't help it/are born that way)
"Do you see yourself as gay and accept it without liking it?"

Identity Activism:

"Tell me about the pressures from society you feel/are aware of?"

"Are you out?" ("... of the closet": not concealing one's homosexuality) to friends/family/
    co-worker/the public?"
"Are you considering coming out to them?"
"Are you involved in any gay activities - social, political or otherwise?"

7.13 Hallucinations: See section 16.16 for Hallucinations descriptors

Note: If Subject denies hallucinations note these behaviors which suggest hallucinating: return of gaze to a spot, sudden head turning, staring at one place in room, eyes following something in motion, mumbling or conversing with anyone else, etc.
If there is an indication of the presence of hallucinations ask questions to eliminate those apparently due to entering or leaving sleep, delirium, alcohol or drug withdrawal or abuse, medications, etc. See Chapter 33 Psych./Medical masquerade

General questions:

"Do you have a vivid imagination?"
"Do you dream vividly/so you aren't sure it was a dream?"
"Did you ever think/act in really strange/odd/peculiar ways?"
"Did you ever see or hear things others did not?"
"Have you had any uncanny/eerie/bizarre experiences/anything ever happened to you that you cannot explain?"
"Have you had visions?"
"Has your mind ever played tricks on you?"

Auditory:

"Have you ever heard noises in your head that disturb you?"
"Have you ever heard voices or sounds that other people didn't hear/someone calling your name or talking to you when no one was there?"
"Have you ever heard voices coming from inside your head?" If yes ask "Was this your own thoughts as if a voice were speaking to you or some other voice?"
"Where do the voices come from?"
"Whose voice?"   "Man's or women's?"   "How old were they?"
"What did they say?"   "When does this happen?"   "How often do you hear them?"
"What brings these on?"

VISUAL:

"Have you ever seen anything so unusual that other people didn't believe it?"
"Did you ever have visions/see apparitions/ghosts?"
"Did you ever see anything like in a dream when you were awake?"
"Have you ever seen things that no one else saw?, What?, What did you feel then?, What do you
call these experiences?, What causes these things to happen?"

KINESTHETIC:

"Have you ever felt strange sensations/odd feelings in your body/anything crawling on you?"

GUSTATORY:

"Have you ever felt strange tastes in your mouth?" (metal, electricity, poisons, etc.)

OLFACTORY:

"Have you ever smelled strange odors which you could not account for?" (poisons, death,
something burning, sewage, odd smells from your own body, dead spirits, etc.)

OTHER:

"What was the strangest experience you ever had?, Did you ever visit another planet?, Ever die and
return to life?"
"How/why do you think these things come about?

Homosexual Identity Development: See section 30.8 Gay and Lesbian Identity

7.14 Illusions: misinterpretations or misperceptions of sensory stimuli. See also section 7.9 for
Derealization questions and 16.18 for Illusions descriptors.

"Do things ever seem to change size/look smaller, or larger?"
"Do parts of your body ever seem to change in size or shape or texture?"
"Do things sometimes seem nearer or farther away that they should?"
"Does the world look very different to you?" If yes, ask "In what way(s)?"
"Do any things feel different, in some way, at certain times?"
"Does time ever seem to move very slowly or very fast/telescope?"
"Were you ever surprised that you could hear some sounds other people couldn't hear?" (E.g.
whispering voices, echoes, very loud common sounds, etc.)

7.15 Impulse Control/Violence: See section 16.19 for descriptors.

"Do you find yourself suddenly doing things before you have thought about or decided to do them?"
"Do you feel compelled/driven to do things you don't want to do?"
"Do you feel unable to stop yourself from doing some things?"
"Does 'money burn a hole in your pocket'?"

"Have you ever been involved in sexual behaviors you regretted?"
"Ever steal/shoplift?
"Please tell me about all the times you have had contact with the police."
"Have you ever been fired/evicted/arrested? Why did that happen?"

"What do you usually do when you get very upset and angry?"
"Do you have a bad temper/fly off the handle/flare up?"
"Have you ever lost control of yourself? Ever thrown/broken things? Ever hit/attacked anyone?"
"Do you get involved in more fights than others in your neighborhood?"

Insight: See sections 6.22 Insight questions and 15.17 Insight descriptors

7.16 Mania: See also section 14.7 Mania for descriptors.

"Was there ever a time when you were very excited/talked too much/been restless/did without sleep without having any reason?"
"Have you ever found yourself pacing and couldn't stop/stop for long?"
"Was there ever a time when you were too impatient/irritable/couldn't concentrate/couldn't stop your mind's racing??"

"Were you ever been too happy?"   full of energy?"
                              started things you couldn't finish?"   oversexed?"
                              spent money recklessly/spent money you didn't have/made extravagant gifts?"
"Have you ever overworked/held several jobs at the same time?"

"When did this start? How long did this last? What happened because of this?"
"Were you ever treated for these conditions?"

7.17 **Obsessions:** See also section 7.7 Compulsion questions and 16.22 Obsession descriptors. Differential diagnosis is from depressive ruminations and from delusions. For standardized recording you can use the Y-BOCS (Goodman, *et al.*, 1989) which covers contents, distress, time spent, insight, indecisiveness, avoidance, and resisting thoughts. A children's version is also available.

"Are there any thoughts you just seem unable to forget/get rid of/keep out of your mind/stop thinking about?"
"What do these thoughts revolve around or continually come back to?"
"Are there any phrases/names/dates/slogans/rhymes/titles/music that continually run through your mind/you can't seem to control?"
"Are there any prayers/numbers/names/phrases you feel you have to repeat? Which? When?"

"Is there any possibility you keep thinking about/considering/mulling over/speculating about?"
"Are there any everyday decisions you seem unable to make or spend an excessive length of time making?"
"How often do you think about your health/how your body is working or if it is sick?"

"Do these thoughts seem reasonable to you or more than you should think about/more than a sensible number of times a day/take up a long time each day?"
"How does doing these things affect your life/routines/job/relationships/family members?"
"Do you feel uncomfortable until these actions are done, even though you may know them to be nonsensical/unimportant/even foolish/or that they won't really work?"

"How much control do you feel you have over these actions? Do you resist them?"
"How do you try to get these thoughts out of your head/make them stop?"
"Where do you think these thoughts come from?"

CONTENTS OF THE OBSESSIONS:

Body parts or illness	Cleansing
Contamination: bodily waste, dirt, germs, animals, etc.	Checking
Hoarding or saving	Religious scrupulosity
Repetition, counting, arranging, hoarding/collecting, etc.	
Sexual: "perverse" or forbidden, incest, homosexuality, etc.	Symmetry, precision
Violence: self or other harm, horrific images, blurting out obscenities/insults, etc.	

7.18 **Organicity:**

Ask for a HISTORY of:

Sunstroke	Head injuries	Syphilis
Near-drowning	Head surgery	AIDS/ARC
Electrocution	Apnea	High fevers/delirium
Poisonings	Vertigo/dizziness	Seizures/convulsions/fits

Exposure to toxic chemicals in the workplace
Substance use/abuse/IV drugs/overdoses. See section 7.25, 7.26 Substance abuse questions
Periods of unconsciousness/"knocked out"/having fainted
Episodes of alteration of levels of consciousness, "out cold," "weirded out"
Consider neuropsychological testing and/or neurological evaluations.

7.19 Pain, Chronic: See also section 16.23 Pain disorder descriptors

The usual medical interview asks these questions using the mnemonic OPQRST
Onset: What brings it on?
Palliative or Provocative: What makes if better or worse
Quality or character: E.g. throbbing or steady.
Region or Radiation: E.g. location on one or both sides, etc.
Severity:
Timing and Duration:

For a more standardized and thorough measurement of pain, Hase (1992) offers a revision and improvement of the McGill-Melzak Pain Questionnaire.

"Do you frequently have pain somewhere in your body? Where?"
"Has the pain affected your sleep? How?"
"Has the pain affected your eating? Has your weight changed?"
"Has the pain changed your thinking or concentration abilities? Please explain."
"Do you have to lie down and rest because of the pain or does it force you to keep moving?"
"Do you find that you are thinking about the pain a lot?"

"Tell me about your activities in a 24 hour day such as cooking, laundry, shopping, cleaning, reading, exercise, hobbies, etc. When do you wake up"
"Does the pain affect your ability to take care of your self/your day-to-day needs? Please explain."
"What activities have you had to restrict or stop because of pain?"
"Do you need to use any assistance device? To walk with? When did you start using it? Which physician gave it to you?"

"How often do you get the pain?   How long does it last?"
"Does it affect one area or does it spread?"
"What makes the pain worse?" (Time of day, cold, movement, etc.)
"How has it changed in the last year?"

"What medications do you take for the pain? (Names, dosages, physician, location and phone number.)
"How does the medicine affect the pain?"
"Do you get any side effects?"

"What other treatments have you had?"
"How well did they work?"
"Have you been treated in any Pain Management Program or Pain Clinic? When? Where? To what effect/with what result?"
"Have you ever been referred to a psychologist or psychiatrist to help you to learn to cope with the pain?" (Name, date, phone number, dates of treatment)

"Do doctors seem to have helped or failed you?"
"Has some doctor said your pain was 'imaginary' or 'all in your head'?"
"Do you secretly think you case is hopeless?"

7.20 Paranoia: See section 16.24 Paranoia descriptors

BEING MONITORED:

"When you get on a bus/enter a restaurant/any public place do people notice you/turn around to look at you?"
"Have you ever been singled out for special attention/watched/spied on?"
"Do people sometimes follow you for a while?"

SUSPICION:

"Do you believe you have to be extra careful/extra alert/vigilant around people?"
"Are people doing things which affect you and which you do not understand?"

"Do people talk about you more than they talk about others?"
"Do people say things about you behind your back? What do they say?"
"Are people making insulting/derogatory/critical/negative remarks about you?
"Do people laugh at you?"
"Did people ever think you were homosexual when you weren't?"

"Do you think there is someone or something out to get you?"
"Do you think anyone is against you?" "Do you have enemies?"
"Is there anything about you which has made other people jealous of/prejudiced against/out to get/harm you or damage your property?"
"Does any organization or group of people have it in for you/plotting against you?"
"Would you feel safer if you had a bodyguard/carried a weapon?"
"Have you been attacked/been shot at? Do you need to carry a gun/knife/Mace/hire a bodyguard?"

"Would you say that you are more suspicious than other people, perhaps with good cause?"

BEING CONTROLLED:

"Do people try to trick you/play tricks on you?"
"Do other people seem to know your thoughts? Can other people read your mind?"
"Have you ever had thoughts in your mind which were not your own?"
"Are people controlling your thoughts or your mind? What are they doing? How are they attempting this? Why is this happening?"
"Is your mind controlled by other's/thought waves/electricity/radio or television waves?"
"Are there drugs in your food or drinks?"

7.21 Phobias: See section 16.25 Phobias for descriptors

"Are you afraid of any things that do not frighten most people as much? What are they?"
"Is there anything or any place that makes you very uncomfortable or anxious and so you avoid it?"
"Are there any places/things/activities you must avoid? Why?"
"Do these fears/behaviors seem reasonable to you?"
"What have you tried to overcome these fears?"

7.22 Sexual History: This section is for a non-problem focussed history and is in chronological order. If the subject presents with a problem see sections 9.4 for Sexual History and Adjustment, and 14.9 for Attitudes and Behaviors. See Pomeroy, *et al.* (1982) and Masters and Johnson (1970, chapter 2) or Kaplan (1983) for how to take a very complete sexual history.

ALWAYS ask every client about a history of sexual abuse. See section 7.3 Sexual Abuse questions

CHILDHOOD:

"When were you first aware of the sexes' differences?"
"Did you ever wear the clothes of the other sex as a child?"
"What toys did you play with as child?"
"Were you ever called a 'tomboy' (for females) /'sissy' (for males)?"

"What were your first sexual experiences/feelings? How old were you? What was the situation? What thoughts did you have then?"
"When you first saw someone involved in sexual activity what was your reaction?"

"When did you first masturbate? How did you learn about masturbation? What did it feel like and what did you think when you started?"

"What sexual behaviors did you see between your parents? What were your feelings and thoughts?"

ADOLESCENCE:

"From whom or what did you first learn/learn the most about sex?"
"Did you ever have any sex education classes in school?"
"Did you feel free to ask sexual questions in your home?" "To whom/where did you go with your questions/for information?"
"How do you define puberty?" ("What else?") [breast development, hair - axillary, facia, pubic, leg, menstruation/menarche, voice changes, growth spurt, etc. Tanner stage]
Questions for females: age of menarche, ir/regularities of menstrual cycle, changes in menstrual cycle, pregnancies/miscarriages/abortions/deliveries
Questions for males: age of puberty (voice cracking, nocturnal emissions, body hair, orgasm by masturbation, etc.)

"How and when did you learn about menstruation and pregnancy?"
"How prepared were you for menstruation/wet dreams/the changes in your body?"

"Have you ever engaged in voyeurism/watching someone get undressed, exhibitionism/showing off your genitals, bestiality/sex with animals?"
"What erotic materials (or "pornography") such as books, or magazines or videotapes have you seen?" "What was shown in this material?" (heterosexual, homosexual, intercourse, oral sex, child sex, etc.)

"What sex games did you play with girls and with boys?"
"At what age did you start to date?"
"How many people have you dated and for how long?"
    "What were their ages?"

"What was you first experience with petting like?"

"How old were you when you first had sex with another person?"
    "Was this heterosexual or homosexual?"
    "What were your feelings and thoughts?" [Attend to issues of force]

"What methods of birth control can you name? Which have you used?"
"Do you want to become pregnant/father a child?"
"How often do you have unprotected intercourse?"

"What sexually transmitted diseases can you name? Which have you had?"

ADULTHOOD:

"As you look back over your past history, what have been the sexual high points?"
"What things about your sexual development do you wish could have been different?"

"How often do you have unprotected intercourse?"

"How many sexual partners have you had? How many have been pick-ups/one-night-stands,
    prostitutes/married persons/ of very different age than you/intravenous drug users/bisexual?"

"Have you had sexual experiences with people of you own sex?

"What are your sexual fantasies about?"
"Do any of your sexual fantasies distress or frighten you?"

"Do you have any sexual problems now? Did you in the past? Which?"
    For Men:
        "When have you had difficulty with erection/"getting and staying hard,"
        orgasm/ejaculation/"coming?""
    For Women:
        "When have you had difficulty with arousal/"getting excited/hot," or orgasm/"coming"
        or "climaxing?""
"As you see it, do these affect you alone, mainly you, you and your partner, or is it mainly your
    partner's problem?"
"What have you done to try to overcome this/these problems?"

[As medications and illnesses affect libido and performance ask about medications (prescription and
    over-the-counter, street drugs, alcohol (by referring to sections 7.25) and about intercurrent illnesses
    especially diabetes, blood circulation and alcohol use]

For Women:
    "How does your menstrual cycle affect your mood/attitudes/behavior/sexual desire?"
    "Please describe all your pregnancies."

RELATIONSHIPS:

"In your previous relationships how was the sexual relationship? What was the reason the relationship ended?"

"In your present relationship, how has the sexual adjustment been?"

"How attracted to your partner do you feel?"

"How attractive do you feel to your partner?"

"Are you satisfied with the frequency of sexual relations? Is your partner?"

"What images or fantasies do you think of when you are with your partner?"

"What conflicts do you have with your partner in any aspect of your sexual relationship?" (oral sex, positions, frequency, amount of stimulation, the circumstances of sex, communication of preferences, initiation, etc.)

"What incompatibilities or conflicts exist in other aspects of the relationship?"

7.23 Sexual Identity: Transsexuality [Distinguish Transsexuality from transvestism, cross dressing, dissatisfaction with one's body, and delusions]

"At what age did you first know you were a boy/girl?"

"Did you ever dress in the other sex's clothes/play with their toys?"

"Do you want to look like someone of the other sex?"

"Do you think you really should have been/are the other sex?"

"Are your sex organs normal? Do you dislike them?"

"Do you dislike your sex's clothes or bodies?"

"Have you ever sought to change your sex?"

"Do you want to marry a person of your sex?"

FOR FEMALES:

"Were you a tomboy? Are you still?"

"Do you stand up to urinate?"

"Do you feel like a man trapped in a woman's body?"

FOR MALES:

"Do you ever dress in women's clothes/underclothes/use makeup?"

"When do you do this? How does it make you feel? What do you get from this?"

"Do you feel like a woman trapped in a man's body?"

7.24 Sleep: See also 16.32 Sleep disorder descriptors. Data can also be collected from a sleep/wake diary and questionnaires like Edinger (1985).

GENERAL QUESTIONS:

"Do you have any trouble with your sleep? What kind?" (interruptions, restlessness, parasomnias, nightmares, confusional episodes, seizures, sleep paralyses, awake frightened, vivid images, hypnogogic or hypnopompic illusions, cataplexy, sleep attacks, bruxism, etc.)
"How does this affect your life?"

"Do you wake up refreshed or irritable or tired?"
"What time do you usually go to bed? Fall asleep? Wake up? Get up?" [Compute their total sleep time and compare it with age peers and their own lifelong patterns. This is better than asking 'How much sleep do you usually get each night?']
"Has there been any change in the ways you sleep?"
"Are you sleepy during the day? Do you usually/have to take a nap during the day? For how long?"
"Do you snore loudly?"
"What do you dream about? Do you have bad or unusual dreams? Do you usually have the same dream every night for a while? Are there dreams you dream over and over?"

DIFFICULTY FALLING ASLEEP: Initial insomnia

"What do you just before you go to bed?"
"Typically, what time do you go to bed? What do you do in bed?" (watch TV, read, study, eat, use telephone, have sex, etc.)
"Typically, what time do you fall asleep?"
"How long does it take you to fall asleep after you go to bed?" [15-20 minutes is usual]
"What keeps you awake? (activities, partner, rehearsing the day, conditions of bedroom)
"What do you think about before you fall asleep?"
"Do you see or hear or feel unusual things before falling asleep?"

"Do you do anything to help yourself fall asleep? What do you do to fall asleep?"

SLEEP CONTINUITY DISTURBANCE: Middle insomnia

"How well do you sleep? Are you a very/light/sound/very sound sleeper?"
"Do you awaken in the middle of the night? How many times, on the average?
"Is there anything which wakes you so you can't sleep through the night?" (need to urinate, your bed partner's behavior, a needy child, street noises, etc.)
"How long is it before you fall back to sleep?"
"What do you think about as you lie in bed?"
"What have you tried to return to sleep?"

EARLY MORNING AWAKENING: Terminal insomnia

"What time do you usually wake up/awaken?"
"Do you awaken early in the morning and are unable to go back to sleep again?"
"What do you do then?"
"What do you think about as you lie in bed?"

OTHER:

"How much coffee/cola/tea do you drink each day?, Do you use any caffeine containing
   medications/over the counter medicines/drugs such as Midol, Bufferin, Anacin, etc.?"
"How many cigarettes do you smoke in a day?"
"Do you awaken gasping for air/with leg jerks/cramps/pain?"
"What medications are you taking? Do you use any sleeping aid or sleeping pill?"
"What do you eat before going to sleep?"
"Do you work shiftwork/changing/rotating shifts?"
"Are you under a lot of stress?"
"Did anyone in your family have problems with sleeping/similar problems?"

For a child:

Ask about regular bedtimes, bedtime rituals, reluctance to fall asleep, need for lights/company,
   entry into parent's bed, bad dreams, nightmares, night terrors, sleepwalking, incontinence.

7.25 Substance Abuse/Drugs and Alcohol: See sections 16.33 and 16.34 for descriptors

At present, abuse and misuse issues concern any of these substances[1]:
   Alcohol in beer, wine, liquor, over-the-counter medications, non-potable forms, etc.
   Prescription/legal drugs such as amphetamines, barbiturates, inhalants, opioids, sedatives, hypnotics,
      and anxiolytics
   "Street"/illegal/unidentified/synthetic ("designer") drugs such as cannabis/marijuana/"weed"/
      "grass"/"pot," etc., cocaine, crack, hallucinogens, narcotics
   Over-the-counter medications
   Caffeine containing beverages and foods,
   Tobacco
   Substances inhaled and smoked such as chemical thinners, gasoline,

The CAGE criteria are a simple set of questions which can and should be asked of every new patient:
   "Have you ever felt the need to   **C**ut down your drinking?"
      "Have you ever felt   **A**nnoyed by criticism of your drinking?"
      "Have you ever had   **G**uilty feelings about your drinking?"
   "Have you ever taken a morning   **E**ye-opener?"

There are no sharp demarcations or agreed upon criteria between use, misuse, abuse, being an 'alcoholic',
   'problem drinker', or 'alcohol addict' because people now enter treatment at all stages.

---

[1] Bernard (1991) provides a very complete checklist of substances-by-when-used which can be used for screening.

GENERAL QUESTIONS ABOUT EFFECTS:

"What happens to you when you drink/use drugs? Do you change a lot/act very differently/do strange things/have other parts of your personality come out?"

"Has drinking/drug use affected your school/work/job/career, friendships/family/marriage, health, or any other area of your life?"

"What problems has the use of alcohol/drugs caused in your life at any time? Has drinking/drug use caused you any problems in the last month?"

"Which of these have you had (these may need to be rephrased and repeated): shakes, blackouts, hallucinations, cramps, rhinorrhea, headaches, seizures, delirium tremens, thoughts of suicide, body aches, diarrhea, cold sweats, dry heaves, injuries from falls/fights/motor vehicle accidents, etc.

"Are you or other people concerned/worried about your drinking/drug use? Have people tried to get you to stop drinking/using?"

"What have you tried to stop/control your use?" "How did this work out for you?"

CONSUMPTION PATTERNS:

"What is/are your drugs of choice/preference?"

Because the individual's patterns of use/overuse/misuse/abuse change with availability, resources, setting, choice, treatment and aging, and may involve cross-addictions, temporary substitutions or preferences, and many other factors, a detailed and individualized history is desirable. However, such tailoring is not possible in the format here. Therefore follow your clinical intuition and the client's lead (or avoidances) in history taking to get all the relevant facts and experiences.

It may be useful to construct a table like this as you obtain the history especially if the history is complex.

Drug name/type	Route	Age started	Amount	Frequency	Use out of control?	Last dose

Alcohol:

"Do you think you drink about the same as most other people?"

HISTORY

"When and where did you first drink any kind of alcohol?"
"When and where did you first drink to excess/drunkenness?"
"When did you first start drinking regularly?"
"Do you drink more now?"
"How did you progress to the quantity you now drink?"

"What is your preferred drink?" "What else will you drink?"
"Do you ever drink alcohol substitutes such as shaving lotion or hair tonic?"
"Do you drink every day or every other day?"

"When you drink *how much* do you consume? Do you drink more than a case of beer/fifth of whiskey[1] in a day/drink for two days in a row?"

"At what time of day do you start drinking?" (as soon as awaken/all day long/no particular time/at lunch/after work/with dinner/late at night/weekends only)

"Do you stay drunk during the day? Most days? When?"

"Do you ever feel you *need* a drink to get going/can't get through the day without a drink?"

"What are the usual *situations or moods* just before you start drinking?"

"Do you ever drink heavily after a fight or disappointment?" (other precipitating emotions: angry, frustrated, lonely, bored, to calm down)

"Do you drink more when you feel under a great deal of pressure?"

"Where do you get your alcohol?" (from peers/dealers/bartenders/steal it/sneak it from others)

"Where do you drink?" (at work/home/parties/bars)

"With whom do you drink?" (alone/with buddies/friends/spouse)

"Do you drink now without eating anything?"

"When you are drinking at a party or social occasion do you sneak a few extra drinks?"

"Have you gulped your drinks to get drunk quickly?"

"Have you concealed/lied about the amount of your drinking?"

Drugs:

"What drugs have you used?" (street drugs like marijuana/cocaine/crack/heroin/"ice"/ hallucinogens/LSD/"Ecstasy"/"uppers"/"speed"/"downers"/pain killers/"ludes"/"Reds"/ "Black Beauties"/ tranquilizers/etc.?)

"What chemicals have you used?" (glue sniffing, inhalants such as gasoline, butane, naptha, etc.)

"What drugs or medications have you used in the last month/6 months? How did you get them?"

"Have you ever used drugs prescribed for you (such as pain killers/sleeping pills/tranquilizers/ barbiturates/etc.) in a way that the doctor didn't prescribe?"

"Have you ever taken medications prescribed for someone else?"

"When did you first use street drugs/misuse medications/sniff chemicals?"

"What effects did they have on you?"

"What did you use at first?"

"When did you first start using it/them regularly?"

"How did you progress to the quantity you now use?"

"What are the usual situations or moods just before you start using?"

"How often do you use? When do you start using? Do you ever feel you *need* to do some drug just to get going/get through the day or night?"

"Where do you use?" (at work/home/parties/houses)

"With whom do you use?" (alone/with buddies/friends/spouse)

"How do you take each drug/chemical? What is the usual/maximum amount you take?"

---

[1] Starting with a large amount may reduce defensiveness and untruthfulness.

The following sets of questions apply to both alcohol and drugs:

EFFECTS:

"What are the positive and negative effects of your drinking/drug use? What are the effects you
like best?
"What kind of person are you when you are drunk/high?"

CONTROL:

"Once you start drinking what stops you? (no money, self-control/decisions, self created rules as to
location or time, intoxication, unconsciousness, lack of money, etc.)"

"Do you think you need to drink to function normally/get through the day?"

EMOTIONS:

"Do you feel guilty/embarrassed/remorseful/apologetic about the way you drink/use drugs?"
"Do you ever lie about/conceal/justify/avoid discussion of your actual drinking/drug use?"
"When was the first time you became concerned about your use of drugs or alcohol?"
"Have you ever regretted what you have done or said when you were drunk/high?"
"Have you failed to keep promises to yourself to cut down on your drinking/drugs?"

"Why do you stop? What stops you?" (Internal or external forces)
"Have you ever tried to cut down or stop and couldn't? What thoughts/feelings/urges did you have
when you tried to stop or refrain?"

"What means have you tried to control your drinking/drug use?" (relocating, prayer/religion,
switching to (beer), willpower, detoxification, rehabilitation programs, Alcoholics Anonymous,
new friends, isolation, etc.)
"What was the longest period of sobriety/staying clean you have had?"
"Do you think you have lost control of your drinking/drug use? When?"
"Have you ever attended an Alcoholics Anonymous meeting?"

HEALTH CONSEQUENCES:

"Did a doctor ever tell you to stop drinking/using drugs for your health?"
"Is your drinking worsening a health problem you have?"
"Have you ever received treatment/medication/been in a hospital/drug program/rehabilitation
program because of your drug use/drinking/drinking too much/for detoxification from
drinking/drug use?"

"Has using drugs or alcohol ever changed your eating/weight? Your sleeping? (irregular patterns,
day-night reversal, interruptions, been up 24 hours when using)
"Have you ever had any of these when you drank or stopped drinking: shakes/morning tremors,
visions, hearing voices, feeling things on your skin, D.T.'s (Delirium Tremens), cirrhosis,
gastritis, pancreatitis, convulsions, jaundice, or any other disease or problem?"
"Have you ever had blackouts/times where you couldn't remember what you did or how you got to
where you were? When did these first happen and when most recently? How often?"
"Have you ever become very drunk when you had only one or two drinks?"

FAMILY/SOCIAL CONSEQUENCES/IMPACTS:

"Have your friends/family members complained/showed concern about your drinking/drug use?"
"Have you ever gotten into a serious fight with/hit/beaten/been beaten by your spouse/children/
    relatives/friends when drunk/high?"
"Is your partner also a problem drinker/alcoholic/drug abuser?"
"Do any family members like your brothers or sisters/parents/children have a problem with alcohol
    or drugs?"
"Does or did chemicals cause strained relations with you children or family/neglect/verbal/sexual/
    physical abuse?"
"Is there any physical/sexual/emotional abuse in your current family or the family you came
    from?"
"Does drinking ever spoil family gatherings/make for a atmosphere of tension/make your children
    afraid of you/cause others to talk about you?"
"Do you avoid your family when you are drinking/high?"
"Has drinking/drug use caused you any sexual problems?"
"How would you describe the overall effect of drinking/drugs on your marriage/children/family/
    friends?"
"How do you spend your leisure/free time and with whom?"

VOCATIONAL/FINANCIAL CONSEQUENCES:

"Did your drinking/drug use ever cause problems when you were in school?"
"How much work have you missed because you were drunk/high/hung over?"
"Did you ever get into fights at work?"
"If you were in the military did you drink there? Did your drinking cause problems in the
    military?"
"Have you ever been disciplined/fired/damaged anything/hurt anyone because of your drinking/
    drug use?"
"How did/do you get the money to buy drugs?"
"How much dealing in drugs have you done?"

LEGAL CONSEQUENCES:

"Have you been arrested for being drunk/disorderly conduct, Driving While Intoxicated/Driving
    Under the Influence, assault or other crimes/destructive behavior when you were drunk?"
"Have you gotten into fights while you were drunk/high?"
"Have you run up large debts/been evicted because of drinking or drug use?"

IDENTITY

"Would you say you are a "social drinker" or "have a drinking problem" or how would you
    describe your use?"
"Do you think you are an alcoholic?" "Do you think you are addicted? Why or why not?"

OTHER ASPECTS:

"Has your drinking/drug use caused you any spiritual problems?"

The following are from AA and can form a simple and usable **checklist for relatives** of users:
> Does someone in your family undergo personality changes when he/she drinks or uses drugs?
> Do you find yourself bewildered by what is happening in your life?
> Do you believe that alcohol or drugs are more important to this person than you are?
> Do you feel sorry for yourself and frequently engage in self pity?
> Has alcohol or drugs ruined special occasions?
> Do you find yourself covering up for someone else's drinking or drug use?
> Do you often feel guilty or apologetic?
> Is drinking or drug use involved in many of your family's activities?
> Do you feel you are different from other people in some negative way?
> Do you often feel depressed?
> Have you ever tried to fight the drinker or user by joining in the drinking or drug use?
> Do you have an unhappy home life?
> Is your family having financial troubles because of drinking or drug use?
> Have you ever tried to control the drinker's behavior by hiding the car keys, pouring liquor down the drain, etc.
> Do you find yourself doing things out of character?
> Do you get distracted from your responsibilities because of this person's drinking or drug use?
> Do you find yourself responding inconsistently to other members of the family?
> Have you ever feared for your safety or the safety of other family members because of drinking or drug use?
> Do you no longer feel good about yourself?
> Have you ever been embarrassed or felt the need to apologize for the actions of a family member who has been drinking or using drugs?

The following are from <u>A</u>lcoholics <u>A</u>nonymous and can form a simple and usable **checklist for users**:
> Do you ever lie about how often you use drugs of alcohol?
> Do you drink or use drugs to overcome shyness or feel more confident?
> Do you make promises to yourself or others about stopping or cutting down your use of alcohol or drugs?
> Do you drink too much at the wrong time? (at weddings, when there are important guests)
> Do you drink or use drugs in the morning?
> Is drinking or using drugs causing you problems getting along with members of your family?
> Have you ever stayed home from school or work because you were too hung over to attend?
> Do you drink or use drugs to escape from your problems?
> Has anyone told you that you are using drugs or alcohol too much?
> Do you hide alcohol or drugs from your family or school officials?
> Have you ever been in trouble with the police because of drugs or alcohol?
> Have you ever been treated by a doctor or in a hospital because of using drugs or alcohol?
> Do you have to keep on using drugs or drinking once you start?
> Do you need to drink or use drugs at a definite time every day?
> Have you changed friends or switched social groups to hang out with those friends who like to get high?
> Are you participating less in extracurricular activities such as sports, clubs and hobbies because of your drinking or drug use?
> Does any member of your family have a drug or alcohol problem?
> Have you tried unsuccessfully to stop using drugs or alcohol?
> Have you ever had a blackout? (lost memory of for events that happened or actions you performed while drinking or using drugs)
> Do you drink or use drugs when you are alone?
> Is drinking giving you a "bad reputation" in your school or your neighborhood?
> Has drinking or using drugs affected your health?
> Are you less productive in school (getting lower grades, putting less effort into your schoolwork) than you were before using drugs or alcohol?

Do you drink or use drugs to relieve the pain of living your life?
Do you ever go to school or work under the influence of drugs or alcohol?
Do you ever feel guilty or sad (or remorseful) about your use of drugs or alcohol?
Are you having money troubles because of your use of drugs or alcohol?
Are you less ambitious than you were when you drank less or used drugs less?
Are you less efficient than you were?
Are drugs or alcohol making it hard for you to sleep?
Have you had any accidents because of using drugs or alcohol?
Do you have trouble getting rid of cans or bottles or paraphernalia?
Are you less particular about the people you are with or the places you go when you are drinking?

7.26 Substance Use: Cigarettes and Caffeine

TOBACCO

"Do you smoke cigarettes/cigars/a pipe? Do you chew/use smokeless tobacco/snuff?"
"How many cigarettes/cigars do you smoke each day?"
"When did you start smoking?"
"Did you ever smoke more or less than you do now?"
"Have you changed the brand you smoke to cut down?"
"Have you tried to stop smoking? How? How many times? What has and hasn't worked for
    you?"

CAFFEINE:

"How many cups of coffee (except decaffeinated/Sanka) or cola drinks (Coke, Pepsi, Dr. Pepper,
    etc. diet or regular) do you drink in a day?" [Note: some non-cola drinks contain caffeine]
"How often do you take APCs/Anacin/Bufferin/(for pre-menopausal females) Midol?"
"How often do you eat chocolate?" "Do you have some chocolate when you feel down?"
"How much tea/iced tea do you drink each day?

7.27 Suicide: Aspects of self-destructive behavior: See also section 16.35 Suicide descriptors

INITIAL INQUIRY:

"You have told me about some very painful experiences. They must have been hard to bear and
    perhaps you sometimes thought of quitting the struggle/hurting yourself or even ending your life."
    If this idea is accepted by the client ask the about the following areas:

DEATH WISH:

"When was the last time you wished you were dead/thought you/others/the world would be better
    off if you were dead?"
"Has it crossed your mind that death would relieve you or end the pain you feel?"
"Have you thought this way before?"

IDEATION:

"Have you recently said to yourself or others words like: 'I can't take any more of this', 'Who needs this crap/pain?', 'You won't have to worry about me much longer', 'Soon it will all be over'?"

"When was the first time you thought of/considered ending it all/hurting/killing yourself?"
"When was the last time you thought of/considered ending it all/hurting/killing yourself?"
    (Less preferred version -"Have you ever seriously thought about ending your life/killing/doing away with yourself?")
"Do you feel that you want to die now?"
"Have you recently/in the last month made any plans to hurt or kill yourself?"

"Have you thought about how/where/when you might kill yourself?"
"Have you thought about what you would say in a suicide note?"
"Have you thought about how easy or difficult it would be to kill yourself?"

"When you have suicidal thoughts how long do they last?"
"What brings on these thoughts?"
"How do you feel about these thoughts?"
"Do you feel you have control of these thoughts?"
"What stops/ends these thoughts?"

AFFECTS AND BEHAVIORS:

"How often have you felt lonely/fearful/sad/depressed/**hopeless**[1]?"
"Are there more themes of despair in your writing/what you are reading/art work/music/what you listen to than there were before?"
"Are you suddenly very happy after a depression?"

"Have you lost someone close to you?" (through breakup, divorce, death)
"Have you lost interest in/given up some of your interests/hobbies/activities?"
"Have your grades dropped/your work performance fallen off?"

"Because of a bad mood, have you ever ...?"
    not Eaten   Slept poorly   gotten Drunk or High   Run away
    gotten into a physical Fight or trouble in/kicked out of school   Damaged property
    gotten into Trouble with the Police or arrested
    been involved in physical or sexual Abuse or actions you have regretted later
    gotten Pregnant/gotten someone pregnant
    increased your use of Alcohol or Drugs?
"Are you more careless with/have changed for the worse your grooming, eating and sleeping?"
"Are you taking more risks than you used to?"

MOTIVATION:

"Why are/were you thinking of killing yourself?"
"Have you felt "My life is a failure" or "My situation is hopeless?"
"What would happen after you were dead?"
"Under what conditions would you kill yourself?"
"Did you know anyone who killed him/herself? Who, when, where, how, why, closeness?"

---

[1] Hopelessness seems to be the crucial factor in suicide, not depression.

DETERRENTS/DEMOTIVATOR:

"Do you have any reasons to live?"
"What would prevent you from killing yourself?" (e.g. "I'm a coward/no courage", my children, religious convictions, shame, "I wouldn't give her the satisfaction", wish to live-enjoyment, hope for change)

GESTURE/ATTEMPT:

"When was the first time you tried to hurt or kill yourself?" [Less preferred version - Have you ever tried to hurt or kill yourself?]
"Have you tried more than once?"
"When was the last time you tried to hurt or kill yourself?"

"What were you thinking at the time about death or dying?"
"Did you intend to die then?"
"How did you try to do it?" Were you alone?, Were you using drugs or alcohol?"
"What happened before each attempt?" (an argument, conflicts with family, a humiliating experience, disappointments, school difficulties, incidents with police, a pregnancy, an assault, physical/sexual/abuse, you were told "I wish you would die")
"What happened afterward?" [hospitalization (intensive care unit, psychiatric, general medical), effects on family and friends, on yourself, counseling or therapy?]

PREPARATIONS:

"Have you given away any (prized) possessions of yours/written a will/checked on your insurance/made funeral arrangements?"
"Have you told anyone about your plans?"
"Have you written a suicide note?"

PLAN/MEANS/METHOD:

"Have you made any plans to hurt or kill yourself?" [degree of practicality/care]
"How would you do it?" "Do you have the means?" [availability, opportunity] [lethality]
"Are you making preparations?" [collecting pills, loaded gun]

OTHER:

"Has any relative or friend of yours ever tried or succeeded in killing him or herself?" (number, time when tried, most recent attempt)

A most interesting approach to the evaluation of suicidal intention is the Firestone Voice Scale for Self-Destructive Behavior (Firestone, 1991) which ranks the thoughts on a 11 level scale from self-critical to cynical, vicious, urging substance abuse, withdrawal, self injury, and suicide.

8. Introduction to the Report, Identifying Information, and Reliability

Reasons for referral can be found in Chapter 10.

8.1 The Evaluation report:

Use a complete heading or stationery for identification of the evaluator by name, degree and title, agency address and, where appropriate, affiliation, supervisor, license number, phone number

Dates and location (e.g. in the hospital room, school's office, private office, home visit) of examination/evaluation/interview(s)/testing, time of day, total time of testing, duration of interview, etc. as relevant.

ALWAYS DATE the report.

8.2 The Evaluation Process Consisted of/is Based on/Sources of Information:

Review of reports furnished/case histories/treatment summaries and reports/school records/previous evaluations, etc.
Collateral interview with the client/friend/spouse/parents/family/relatives/care-giver/child, interpreter, collaterals.
Testing: List separately each test or questionnaire by its full name and use abbreviations/acronyms in the body of the report.
Consultation with other professionals.
Observational interview of the client/child/family.

"All tests were administered, scored and interpreted by this report's author without the use of assistants or supervisees."

8.3 The Client:

The description should be so detailed as to enable the identification of the unique individual. See Chapter 11 Behavioral Observations for specific language

NAME:

Given, Christian, married, family of origin, maiden, changed, aliases, Also Known As

For a Child: nickname(s), Prefers to be known as ...

IDENTIFICATION:

address, case number, client of ___ , etc.

GENDER: [not sex]

AGE: Only as of demonstrable relevance:

For a Child: Use 9 years and 3 months, or 9 3/12, 9' 3," or 9 years and 3 months, not the ambiguous 9.3 years

MARITAL STATUS: Note: Be consistent in reporting marital status for males and females

Current: never married [preferable to "single" because it is less ambiguous]/living with a paramour/partner/married, common law marriage/separated/divorcing/divorced/widow/widower/ unknown
Number and duration of marriages, common-law marriages, separations, divorces, etc.

OCCUPATION:

Employed/unemployed, underemployed, other occupations, part-time work, previous occupations, etc. See Section 28.0 Vocational

NATIONALITY/ETHNICITY: and language used in the home

RACE: Note: Be consistent across reports in reporting race; do not report it only for minorities. If in doubt about a person's race or what are currently, locally or personally acceptable terms, ask.

African-American (preferable to Black and consistent with similar hyphenated usages), white/ Caucasian/"Anglo," Asian or Asian-American (preferable to Oriental[1]), Hispanic, Latino, Raza,[2] Native American, Inuit ("Eskimo"), Oceanic, etc., biracial/multiracial/of mixed races

RESIDENCE/LIVING CIRCUMSTANCES: born into, recent if changed, current

---

[1] My thanks to Fay Murakawa, Ph.D. of Los Angles for clarification and correction.

[2] Be wary of using any global term to describe the psychological/cultural diversity of this or other large population groups.

RELIGION: Only as relevant
> Parental/baptized into/raised in/rejected/atheist/agnostic/non-practicing/unaffiliated/ unimportant to this person
> Preference: converted to/practicing/pious/devout/righteous/zealous/proselytizing/evangelizing/ preoccupied/delusional

For Disability Examination: Date of alleged industrial/other injury, date last worked

Referral Reason: See Chapter 10. Reasons for Referral

8.4 Other Identifying Information:

In preparation for/advance of the interview I received and reviewed the following records: ___ .
Records were destroyed/unavailable/scant/unhelpful/scattered/adequate/pertinent/voluminous

I saw (name of client) on (date) (and total time and time of day if relevant) following your kind referral.

Legal mental health status: in/voluntary treatment/commitment (give the number or name of the applicable section of the local law)

8.5 Self-sufficiency in appearing for examination:

Came to first (or second, etc.) appointment, late by ___ minutes/excessively early/appropriately early for examination/on schedule/exactly on time for examination

Came alone/without escort or accompanied, role of companion in examination. Came with friend, spouse, children, escort, caseworker, etc.

Degree of difficulty finding the office

Drove/driven/mode of transportation

8.6 Chief Complaint/Concern: Patient's view of illness in his or her own words, and beliefs about the source(s) of the complaints.

Onset, circumstances of onset, triggers/cues/precipitates/stimulants

Duration, progression and severity of presenting complaint

Effects of the complaint on the functioning of the patient

Effects of treatments on complaint

Reasons and goals for seeking treatment at this time

Formal/chief/presenting complaint

Evaluator's clarification or reformulation or elaboration of complaint

For a Child: parental/teacher's/authority's perception of problem(s)

For a Disability examination: Claimant's view of the impairment created by the injury/complaint/disorder

8.7 Consent Statements:

INFORMED:

We discussed the evaluation/treatment procedures, what was expected of both the client and the evaluator/therapist, who else would be involved or affected, the treatment's risks and benefits, and alternative methods's sources and costs and benefits.
The client knows that the results of this evaluation will be sent to ... and used for ....
In a continuing dialogue these have been explained in language appropriate to his/her education and intellect.
S/he understands the procedures, their consequences/effects, alternative procedures and their consequences, and the decisions involved which s/he is being asked to consent to.

VOLUNTARY:

S/he understands and willingly agrees to fully participate.
S/he understand that s/he may withdraw his/her consent at any time and discontinue the evaluation/treatment.

COMPETENCY TO CONSENT:

I have no reason to suspect that this person in not competent to consent to the evaluations/procedures/treatments being considered.
S/he is not a minor, nor mentally defective, nor does s/he have any limitation of communication, psychopathology or any other aspect which would compromise his/her understanding and competency to consent.

8.8 Reliability:

RELIABILITY:

On the basis of ...
 observations of this person for __ hours on __ occasions in (settings)
 internal consistency of the information and history
 absence of omissions/deletions of negative information, contradictions
 the character and cohesiveness of the client's responses, spontaneous comments, and behaviors
 consistency of information from different sources
 client's ability to report situations fully
the data/history are felt to be completely/quite/reasonably/rather/minimally/questionably reliable.

I consider her/him to be an adequately reliable informant

VALIDITY/REPRESENTATIVENESS:

Results are believed to be a valid sample of his/her current level of functioning/typical behavioral
 patterns/accurately represent his/her behavior outside the examination setting because he/she
 refused no test items/questions, he/she worked persistently/was most cooperative/had no
 interfering emotions such as anxiety or depression
Test findings/results of this evaluation are representative of his/her minimal/usual/optimal level of
 functioning
S/he attempted to be cooperative with the interview and indeed was helpful.
S/he is not an astute observer

ACCURACY:

Her/his appraisals tended to be supported/corroborated by my observations/others records.
(<->) Complete/quite organized presentation/accurate recall of details/names and sequences/sparse
 data/stingy with information/only sketchy history/nebulous/vague/ambiguous/illogical/contradictory
S/he presented personal history in a spontaneous fashion, organized in a chronological sequence
 and with sufficient detail, consistently, and logic and attention.
Poor/adequate/good/excellent historian
His/her response to questions appeared to be free of any deliberate attempts to present a distorted
 picture.
Although somewhat dramatized, the core information appears to be accurate and valid for
 diagnostic/evaluative purposes.

Despite allegations of pain and deficiency he is able to get up and down from a chair without difficulty

S/he had difficulty presenting historical material in a coherent and chronological manner.
The information offered is disorganized/haphazard/factitious/scattered.
Client was questioned extensively and creatively but it was not possible to determine/get a clear
 picture of/more information on _____
Impossible to obtain any delineation of symptoms other than his/her informal description of "I lost
 it"
S/he becomes tangential when pressed for specifics.

It should be noted that in each of these complaints his/her description was vague, self-contradictory and not completely consistent with any recognized clinical pattern.

The above information was provided by the informant/name/client/claimant and should not be considered as the opinions of the writer.
The patient gave what she seemed convinced was an accurate account of her personal situation although she seemed unaware of her many limitations and deficits
Ganser's syndrome/hysterical pseudodementia/*vorbeireden*

TRUSTWORTHINESS/HONESTY:

S/he seemed to be honest in her/his self-descriptions of her/his strengths and weaknesses.
S/he appeared to be a truthful witness and an accurate historian.
She did not appear to be fabricating any of her history.
S/he tries hard to be accurate in recalling events but ....
S/he tried to provide meaningful responses to my questions but ....

I believe s/he has been honest/truthful/factual/accurate.

Responded eagerly to leading questions endorsing the presence of symptoms or problems if suggested
The history offered should be taken with a grain of salt/was fabricated/grandiose
Was a willfully poor historian
S/he lies with panache

Client is deliberately deceptive, malingering, faking good/bad
Motivated only to obtain benefits/malingering
Client's attitude toward his/her illness/disability suggests indifference/tolerance/acceptance/transcendence
S/he indicated a sense of righteous entitlement to his/her ... (e.g. alcoholism, violence, irresponsibility, etc.)

9. Background Information - History
This Section consists of HISTORY and ADJUSTMENT in many areas.
REFERRAL REASONS are in Section 10.0

This Chapter's Sections Include:

9.1 History/Course of the Present Complaint/Problem/Illness:

ONSET DATE AND CIRCUMSTANCES:

Precipitating stresses/situations/events, anniversary reactions, pre-morbid personality and functioning levels, development of signs/symptoms/behavioral changes, longitudinal/chronological/biographical sequence, periods of/attempts to work/return to functioning since onset, current status

COURSE:

Single episode
Remissions:
> Therapeutic, spontaneous
> Duration of episodes and remissions
> Return to what level of function/symptomatology: decompensation/damage/recompensation/recovery/adjustment/overcompensation/growth
Recurrences/relapses/exacerbations/worsenings/flare-ups/fluctuating course

For a Disability Examination:

Applicant's description of industrial stressors, onset of complaints, and (alleged) injuries or illness associated with onset.
Psychological response to (alleged) injury situation
> History of mental health problems since (alleged) injury
> History of treatment(s) since (alleged) injury;
Current treatment and medication, including medication taken on day of examination.

9.2 Pertinent Medical History or Findings:

PSYCHIATRIC :

Psychological difficulties in the past, treatment(s)/professional help sought
Hospitalizations: date(s), name(s), location(s), condition on admission(s), therapies instituted and response to treatment(s), duration(s) of hospitalization(s), condition on discharge(s), time(s) before next hospitalization, intercurrent illnesses
Current and past medications/therapies/treatments received, effects of/response to/treatments, side effects, condition(s) on discharge(s) from treatment
Discharge/follow up/referral/lost to follow-up

Reason for current admission/is result of ....
Suicide: ideation/gestures/attempts: See section 16.32 Suicide descriptors
Precautions needed to prevent: sexual misbehavior, suicide, elopement, assault, homicide

PREVIOUS TESTING OR EVALUATIONS:

Methods of evaluation: History and Physical, neurological, intellectual, educational, neuropsychological, personality, projectives, organicity, vocational

Availability, results/findings, scores, comparisons with current results, omissions and contradictions, "rule-out"s (r/o)

PREVIOUS PSYCHOTHERAPY OR COUNSELING:

Dates, nature of problems, providers and nature of services, outcome

Types of treatments: see Chapter 21. Recommendations

MEDICAL:

Childhood illnesses
Symptoms: Consider using a checklist such as the Symptom Check List-90 for completeness
Diseases/disorders with known psychological aspects: e.g. thyroid, Mitral Valve Prolapse, AIDS, diabetes, cancer of the pancreas, alcohol abuse, etc.
Surgeries:
Pregnancies: gravida (#), para (#), abortio (#)
Injuries/accidents: especially traumatic brain injury, closed-head injury, and unconsciousness-producing incidents
Drug treatment, use and abuse, street/illegal/illicit drug use: See sections 7.25 for questions and 16.33 Substance abuse descriptors

9.3 Personal, Family and Social Histories and Current Social Situation:

FAMILY OF ORIGIN: Construction of a genogram (See section 9.7 Genogram) may be useful to guide inquiries and to record findings

Composition of family during his/her childhood and youth
Family's response to patient's behavior/problems/illness
... present in his/her bloodline/consanguinity/relations/family tree

S/he has a most unfortunate history.
Has a history of having lived for (#) years in an agonizing/tormenting/abusive/sociopathic/criminal/ chaotic/pathogenic family.
The family environment was unstable, unstimulating, and unstructured
Her/his early life situation was chaotic, victimizing, traumatic, tumultuous, tragic, disastrous

For a child:

Present family problems: marital conflict, separation, death of a parent/sib, relative, criminal victimization, work difficulties, financial concerns, drug/alcohol abuse, medical illness, disabilities, etc.

PARENT'S QUALITIES:

Personality characteristics, manner of relating to client, disciplinary methods, client's perception of parent's influences
Marriages and divorces, separations, severe illnesses
Qualities of the marital relationship: stormy, close, distant, warm, functional, abusive, demonic, etc. See also Chapter 27. Relationships
Other: larger family, patterns, obligations, familial 'debts and credits'
Occupation(s), effects of employment/career on client
General physical and mental health during client's childhood, present health, chronic illnesses, disabilities

Parental history of substance abuse or misuse, physical or sexual abuse, traumas
Age/birth date/year and cause of death, client's age and reaction to death and its consequences

DEVELOPMENT AND HEALTH/MEDICAL HISTORY:

Pregnancy: product of an unplanned but accepted pregnancy, full term, premature by __ weeks, difficulties/illnesses before/during pregnancy
Delivery: natural/prepared/unprepared/difficult/uneventful/easy, duration of labor was __ hours, birth weight, Apgar scores, birth defects
Exposure to toxins/drugs/alcohol/diseases/insults pre/peri-/post-natally
Development:
    Post-natal difficulties, weight gain, eating, sleeping, daily routines
    Milestones: timing/delays in development in _____ area(s)/advanced/gained and later lost, crawling, sitting up unaided, walking, toilet training, speech and language, immature behavior patterns
Present health situation: illnesses, medication(s), disabling/handicapping conditions, observable symptoms such as cough, runny nose, flu

SIBS/STEP-SIBLINGS/HALF-SIBLINGS:

> Ages, sex, location in a birth order/sibline/sibship/confraternity/constellation of (#) of children/sibs/siblings, Client has (#) brothers and (#) sisters of whom s/he is the (#th). relationships among sibs in past and at present
>
> General physical and mental health during client's childhood, present health, chronic illnesses, disabilities

Social Context for a Child:

> Living arrangements: with both parents, step/remarried parents, single parent, grandparents, foster homes, institutions, relatives, adoption, lives with whom, relationship, language in the home, legal issues
>
> Location: city/metropolitan/urban/suburban/rural/institutions/military bases
>
> Home supports: destitute/homeless/poverty, working poor, welfare/Aid to Families with Dependent Children/Social Security (Supplemental Security Income, SS Disability Income)/working class/middle class/upper class, disrupted/consistent, many/few/no moves
>
> Social relationships: many/few/no friends, close/best friends, organizational memberships, cultural interests, friends/buddies/clique/peer group membership/ or isolation/exclusion/rejection/ "loner." See also Chapter 26 Social/Interpersonal Functioning

SOCIAL HISTORY AND SITUATION AS AN ADULT:

> Marriage(s): age/date/termination reason, number/age/sex of children, relationship with ex-spouse/spouse/children, adultery/extra-marital relations/exclusivity/monogamy
>
> Living circumstances: lives alone/with family/other persons/alone but with much family support
>
> Vocational/occupational: See also Chapter 28. Vocational Evaluations
>> Previous job's nature/demands/durations
>>
>> Present occupation- chosen?, duration, satisfaction?, intellectual demands, social-behavioral requirements/demands, aspirations, frustrations
>
> Military service: none/rejected/alternate service/avoided/enlisted/volunteer/draftee, training, work performed, promotions/demotions, branch, duration, adjustment, combat/combat zone/non-combat/location, reenlistments, length of service, final grade, kind of discharge
>
> Legal/Criminal history: warnings from police, charges as a minor, charges/indictments, arrests, prosecutions, convictions, incarceration/probation/parole, civil suits, current litigation/lawsuits, bankruptcy, violence directed against anyone
>
> Exposure history to toxins and risks
>
> Other: special skills, career goals, debts/burdens/adequacy of income to meet responsibilities/needs
>
> Recreational activities: see chapter 29. Recreation

For Disability Examination: Distinguish baseline, injury concurrent and post-injury events in each area
> Educational level and training: professional, technical, etc.
>
> Sequential description of occupations pursued (including military service)
>> Training and skills required
>>
>> Supervisory responsibilities
>>
>> Career mobility: upward, downward, lateral, static
>
> Difficulties and/or accomplishments in each occupational setting
>
> Previous occupational injuries, time lost, and outcome

SEXUAL HISTORY AND SITUATION: See section 7.22 Sexual History questions

EDUCATIONAL SITUATION:

Level: pre-school/kindergarten/elementary/middle/junior high/high school/ 2 or 4 year college/graduate school

Rural/suburban/urban/inner city

Day/full time/part time

Public/private/parochial/religious/sectarian/special (indicate needs met)

Teacher, relationship(s) with teacher(s), teacher's report/description of problems

Class assignment/level: grade/freshman/sophomore/junior/senior, age-grade differential
   Regular classes, Special Education: Trainable Mentally Retarded, Educable Mentally Retarded, Learning Support, Learning Disability classes, Socially and Emotionally Disturbed, Mainstreamed, Scholar's program, Gifted in (subject(s))

Overall level of academic achievement/performance/grades, Quality/Grade Point Average, standing in class, major area of study and its relationship to present employment

Grades completed, "social promotion" or earned advancement, dropped out of school in grade (#) at the age of (#)

Degree obtained: Academic/Technical/Vocational/ General Equivalency Degree/College Preparatory, etc.

Extracurricular activities, athletics, social service, music, scholarly, religious, political

Other aspects: favorite subjects, peer and teacher relationships, position in peer group, aspirations

Are there behaviors inimical to the welfare of other pupils?

Summary Statements:

S/he has received special services/educational support through her whole school history/since the ___ grade/in grades ___ .

Referral Reason: See Chapter 10 Referral Reason

Sexual History - Non-Symptomatic: See section 7.22 Sexual History questions and section 7.2 and 7.3 for Child Abuse questions

Substance Abuse History: See section 7.25 Substance abuse questions

:::

9.4 Adjustment History:

IN EDUCATION/MILITARY SERVICE/OCCUPATION(S):

Able to conform to social standards, hold employment, advance in a career, adjust to superiors/peers/ co/fellow workers, schedules, work load and task changes

SEXUAL ADJUSTMENT: See also section 7.22 Sexual history questions

Disturbed sexual performance/dysfunctions: loss of desire, inhibited arousal, primary/secondary/ occasional difficulty getting or keeping an erection/"impotence," fast/premature/delayed ejaculation, inhibited orgasm, dyspareunia, vaginismus

History of physical and or sexual abuse, molestation, violence/victimization, traumas

Orientation and object choice: celibate, "sex addict", heterosexual, homosexual, lesbian, bisexual, asexual, etc.

Paraphilias/variations: sexual minorities/variations/special interests: pedophilia, exhibitionism, voyeurism, pornography, prostitution, sadism and masochism, zoophilia, frottage, bondage and domination/discipline domination and submission, fetishism, transvestism (TV), "water sports"/"golden showers"/"toilet service"/urolagnia, Greek (anal)/French (oral)/English (whipping) sex, transsexualism, etc.

The patient was not questioned about sexual preferences/orientation, history or interests.

SOCIAL ADJUSTMENT:

Acquaintances, clique membership/exclusion, friends, buddies, best friends, relationship with sibs/friends/enemies

Able to adjust to marriages, child birth/parenthood, losses, aging, illness, health care/services/ treatments

:::

9.5 Social History for a Disability Examination: See Chapter 28. Vocational Evaluations

Interpersonal relationships

Previous life changes (external stresses and losses) and response to these

Educational history

Legal history, when applicable. Include previous Worker's Compensation and other personal injury claims, with the circumstances and outcome.

Criminal history if relevant to diagnosis and/or disability

Substance use and abuse

Applicant's description of a typical day

:::

9.6 Summary Statements

S/he denied the presence of any environmental or circumstantial, precipitating or contributing event which could have thrown her/him out of balance/destabilized her/his normal adjustment

His/her history is remarkable only for ... (findings).

9.7 Family Genograms/Family Tree/Pedigree

Enter any relevant information in spaces next to symbols. Use as many copies of the genogram as necessary. Some typical information might be demographics [name, gender, date of birth, marriages, separations, divorces, deaths (cause of death)], current health/psychological status, nodal events (moves, separations, financial changes, illnesses), functioning levels, and critical events, ethnicity, religion or religious change, education, occupation, legal difficulties, medical risk factors/illnesses/conditions, dates left home, triangulations, and balances.

Listing the main events in chronological order on another page may help understand the history better.

Other Family information for evaluations can be found in Chapter 27. Evaluation of relationships.

The construction and use of genograms[1] in family therapy is fully explored in McGoldrick and Gerson (1987).

Here are the conventions for recording a genogram:

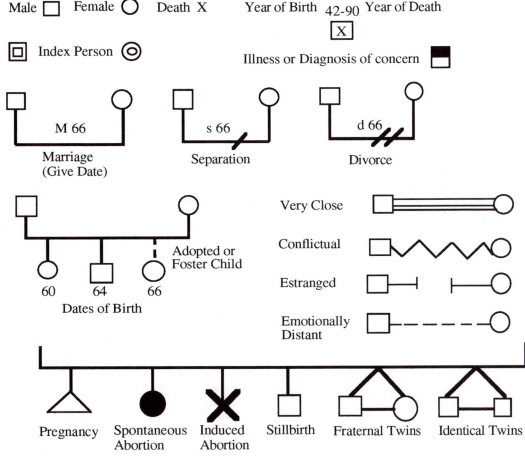

---

[1] If you do a lot of these or want to use them in family therapy there are programs for IBM and Macintosh computers available, including paper forms, checklists and other quite useful materials available from Randy Gerson, Ph.D., Humanware, 2908 Creek Road, NE, Atlanta, GA 30327.

OTHER SYMBOLS:

Dotted line in a relationship means that they are living together/in a liaison
Stillbirth: small square with x in it
Draw a line around those members of the current household.

9.8 Sociogram:[1] This is a diagram of associates, friends and enemies and indicates the kinds, frequency and qualities of the contacts.

"Who do you talk to most in your family/at school/at work/etc.?"
"Whom do you spend time with the most?"
"How important are you in your family?"
    "Has this changed?"

---

[1] This was suggested by Dolores Arnold of Lawton, OK.

10. Referral Reasons and Typical Problems

10.1 Referral Reason:

Client was referred by ___ (referral source - person and agency)

ON: (date of referral)

FOR: (rationale/purpose):
    mental status evaluation
    clinical interview
    diagnostic determination
    forensic evaluations
    custody evaluation
    pre-treatment evaluation and recommendations
    educational placement
    vocational recommendations
because of your acute consideration of ___ (diagnosis)

IF NO SPECIFIC REASON:

    To ...
        determine the nature and extent of psychiatric/psychological disabilities
        assist with the development of a treatment/rehabilitation/education program
        evaluate suitability for entry into ____ program
        assess extent of neurological damage
        determine benchmarks of current functioning
        meet organizational needs for evaluation
        assist with legal/forensic decisions

10.2 Typical Problems of Children at Home: For problems at school see secation 10.3

These are in alphabetical order as no theory provides an agreed upon structures. See also parallel parts of the adult symptoms listed in Chapter 16 Abnormal Signs and Symptoms.

Abuse: physical, suspected, being investigated, confirmed, by whom/relationship, duration.

Aggression/violence: verbal aggression, repeated threats, throwing things, destroys toys, property of others, physical fights/attacking/violence. See section 16.19 Impulse Control.

Anxiety, fears, phobias: see section 14.3 Anxiety

Attention seeking behaviors: tattling, baiting, lying, provoking others, overly demanding of attention from teachers/peers/adults, craves ___ 's attention, tantrums, disruptive noises, "clowning around," pranks, "daredevil," interrupts, "class clown," talks out, compulsive talking, manipulates

Autistic withdrawal: lack of responsiveness to people, resistance to change in the environment

Non-Compliance: disobedience, negativism, noncompliance, argues, "sasses/talks back/mouthy," defiance of authority, lying around chores/house rules, complies only when threatened, independent/autonomous/"stubborn,"

Low Concentration, distractible. See section 16.5 ADHD

Conflicts with parents over: persistent rule breaking, spending money, doing chores, doing homework, choices in music/clothes/hair, school grades, friends

Cries easily, whines,

Dawdles/lingers in dressing, eating, bedtimes

Daydreaming

Dependency

Depression

Drug abuse

Eating: poor manners, refuses, appetite changes, pica, weight gain/loss, anorexia, bulemia, obesity

Elective mutism

Encopresis

Enuresis

Fire setting

Hyperactivity

Hypochondriasis

Imaginary playmates/fantasy

Isolation, withdrawal

Legal difficulties: truancy, runs away, loitering, panhandling, hangs out with peers, steals/shoplifts, underage drinking,, vandalism, fighting, drug sales

Lying

Need for __ degree of supervision at home over play/chores/schedule.

Neglected, berated, belittled, humiliated

Overactive/restless

Relationships with sibs/peers: loving, supportive, rivalry, competition, fights, teases/provokes, assaults

Running away/wandering off

Sleep problems: parasomnias: refusing to go to bed, nightmares, night terrors, sleepwalking, excessive drowsiness, refusal to get out of bed. See section 16.32 Sleep disorders

Steals

Self-abusive behavior: tattooing, self-mutilation, scarring, cutting, burning, insertion of objects into the body, biting or hitting self, head banging, nail biting

Sexual:

>> sexual preoccupation, masturbation, inappropriate sexual behaviors, obscenity/swearing
>> molests/molestation/molested, threatens, fondles, touches, battery
>> intercourse/entry: oral/vaginal/anal/femoral
>> repeated/single episode/recurrent
>> assault, rape, force used, damage
>> medical attention/surgery, school/family/Mental Health - Mental Retardation Center/Child
>>> Protective services/police/court interventions

Shyness

Speech difficulties, stuttering. See section 11.5 Speech behavior

Swearing/blasphemy

Temper tantrums: falls to floor and bangs heels/head, breath holding episodes, throws objects,
> screams, weeps, destructive, duration, how handled (Time Out, spanking, ignored, punished,
> mocked)

Thumb-sucking

Tics: involuntary rapid movements, noise or word productions

Violence: hits parents, destructive, See section 16.19 Impulse Control/Violence

CHILD'S PERCEPTIONS OF:

The parent's role of disciplinarian: uses lectures/threats/guilt inductions/force/spankings/groundings/
> allowance reductions/privilege losses as a consequence irregularly/arbitrarily/regularly, with
> good/mixed/poor success at control

Feels closest to mother/father/sib/uncle/aunt/grandparent/no one in the family

10.4 Typical Problems of Children at School:

ACADEMIC:

Performance: passes/fails tests, difficulty with _____ (subject), subject matter appears too difficult, extracurricular activities interfere with academics

Failure in subjects, kept back, social promotion, retention in grade, underachievement

Completes daily assignments/homework, in class assignments

Lacks order and system in work and method of study

Sloppy, lacks organization, precision, neatness

Does not seek help when appropriate (may copy from peers)

Cheating

Dropping out

SOCIAL:

With peers:

Loner; relates to few students, relates to adults only on request

Clique membership/exclusion, isolates self, "different," doesn't belong/fit in

Timid/shy/dependent/anxiety prone, is an object of scorn/ridicule/mockery/teasing/name-calling/insults/ threats/physical attacks, is scapegoated, picked on, does not defend self when attacked, ostracized

Violent, aggressive, hostile, inflicts pain on others, intimidates, bullies,

Is easily influenced/led, suggestible, engages in risky activities

Sexual inappropriateness

Prejudice, bigotry

Verbally criticizes/abused/insults peers, name-calling, unprovoked attacks, fights with ___, bullies

Gets along/is accepted/valued as friend, adept, does/doesn't sustain friendships,

Follows classroom rules and procedures, disrupts

Respects rights and property of others

Participates/does not participate in group activities

Interacts appropriately with peers

With teachers:

Non-compliant, disobeys, refuses to complete work assignments, seldom prepared, unmotivated, reluctantly participates, requires 1:1 supervision,

Attention seeking behaviors: tattling, baiting, lying, provoking others, overly demanding of attention from teachers/peers/adults, craves ___ 's attention, tantrums, disruptive noises, "clowning around," pranks, "daredevil," interrupts, "class clown," talks out, manipulates

Overly dependent on teacher

Lacks respect for authority, insults, dares, provokes, acts out,

Maturity: impaired judgement, does not take responsibility for own work/belongings, accepts responsibility for own behavior and consequences, demonstrates positive/resilient self-concept

CONDUCT/DEPORTMENT:

Uncooperative/non-compliant
Oral aggression/resistant
Disruptive: agitates students/disturbs/disrupts other kids, low respect for authority/confronts
        teachers/defiant, insults, defies, lies, troublemaker,
Bullies/intimidates, teases
Aggressive, steals, destructiveness of own/others/peers/teacher's/school property
Must always be first
Does not take responsibility for own words/actions

ATTITUDE:

Antagonistic, smart-aleck

COGNITIVE:

Distractible, inattentive, handles new or exciting situations poorly, lacks foresight, low frustration
        tolerance, gets confused in group, does not finish his/her work, daydreams. See section 16.4
            ADDH.
Dysgraphia
Dyslexia
Eye preference
Hand preference

BEHAVIORAL:

Slow moving or responding, lethargic, hypo-active, < normal > impulsive/hyperactive/overactive
Overactive: See also section 16.5 ADDH
Inappropriate out-of-seat behaviors, in-seat behaviors, restlessness, fidgety
School's response to behavior problems: suspensions, truancy, expulsions/suspensions/
        disciplinary conferences

AFFECT

Depressed, sad, unhappy, cries, hurt, low energy, easy fatigue, apathy, withdrawn, suicidal
Anxious, fearful, nervous habits (tics, tapping, restlessness, mannerisms, drums), avoids certain
        things/actions/situations, "freezes" in these situations
Angry, irritable, outbursts, rage, tantrums

Emotional constriction: has full/limited range of emotions, expresses only high intensity feelings
Self-harming: bites, hits, scars, lacerates self
Pouts, easily hurt, "thin-skinned"

MOTIVATION:

Does not try, makes little effort, content to "get by,"
Has ability to do better work, but lacks interest to do so, gives up too easily, "That's too hard,"
Does not persevere, needs great encouragement, gives up too easily/at first sign of difficulty, low
        frustration tolerance

Pays attention/doesn't, daydreams, preoccupied, daydreams, stares out of window,

Completes assignments: homework, in-class,
Makes up missed assignments
Turns in assignments on time/late
Shows interest in subject matter, in learning
Attendance: misses excessive days, absenteeism, tardy, tardiness, cuts classes, truancy

Alert/sleepy in class
Careless/meticulous work
Does not spend enough time on work
Copies assignments from others, does own work
Comes to class with/without necessary work materials
Forgetful

School phobia/avoidance

PHYSICAL:

Fine motor coordination: cuts, draws, ties, writes, dextrous, alternates right-left, ambidextrous
Gross motor coordination: walks, runs, jumps, hops, skips, climbs, balances, falls, catches
Many physical/medical complaints, accident prone

STUDENT'S PERCEPTIONS:

of grades, source of problems, other problems, fairness of system, attitude of peers/teachers/
administrators

Identity, self esteem, confidence, self-derogates, self-critical, suicidal statements

OTHER ASPECTS:

Behavior deteriorates when confronted by academic demands
Appropriate behavior in structured/unstructured situations
Is too tired during the school day to put forth best effort
Hearing, sight, coordination problem

11. Behavioral Observations

THIS CHAPTER covers the following areas: APPEARANCE including clothing

MOVEMENT of all kinds, and

SPEECH behaviors.

How the client   RESPONDED TO THE EVALUATION INTERVIEW and how s/he

PRESENTED HIM/HERSELF in the examination

are covered *IN THE NEXT CHAPTER* 12. Relating to the Examination

Speech behaviors which reflect abnormal cognition can be found in Chapter 15.9 Stream of Thought

11.1 Communication barriers present:

Near/farsightedness, astigmatism, cataracts, hemianopsia, blindness, etc. Totally/partially/not compensated for with glasses

Hearing impairment: total/partial deafness in left/right/both ears compensated for/with aids/lip reading/signing/total communication/American Sign Language, understands amplified/ simplified/repeated conversational speech

Impaired speech: See section 11.5 Speech behavior

Unfamiliarity with the English language, English as a second language

11.2 Physical Appearance:

Note: Because, in the American culture, physical beauty is so tightly associated with goodness and health and so impactful on a person's life course all clinicians should be fully informed about the distortions these judgements cause and be cautiously circumspect.

OVERALL APPEARANCE:

Hygiene is managed independently, effectively and appropriately.
No unusual physical features, unremarkable, clean, well groomed, well dressed
In No Apparent Distress

Appears older/younger than chronological/stated age His/her appearance is not unusual.
Disfigured, maimed, disabled, crippled

Evidence of current drug use/physical dependence: See also section 16.4 Alcohol intoxication

Recent needle marks, needle tracks, thrombosed veins, piloerection/"goose bumps." sweating, lacrimation/tearing, diarrhea, rhinorrhea/"post nasal drip", pupils dilated/constricted

For a Child:

Appears to be well cared for/well trained in self care/assisted/supervised/ignored/neglected

Vocational evaluation:

Employable appearance
S/he would not be identified as unusual in a group situation on the basis of physical appearance alone.

BUILD: (<->)

Emaciated	Thin	Average	stocky	formidable
sickly	lean	well-developed/built	chubby	hulking
malnourished	wiry	weight proportionate	heavy set	enormous
under-nourished	slender	to height	husky	
underweight	lanky	well nourished	heavy	
cachectic	skinny	within usual range	robust	
gaunt	bony	healthy	chunky	
frail			portly	
		large-boned	beefy	
petite		rangy	burly	
small-boned		large-framed	overweight	
diminutive		rugged	pot-bellied	
			barrel-chested	
			rotund	

Somatype- Sheldon	Ectomorph	Mesomorph		Endomorph	
- Kretschmer	Aesthenic	Athletic		Pyknic	(Diplastic)
Temperament	Cerebrotonia	Somatonia		Viscerotonia	

Height: It is preferable to state height objectively rather than in the "short/average/tall" relative
terms unless you also include your own height.

Weight: Ask: "What do you now weigh?" and "Is this your usual weight?"

N. B. 'Obesity': "hardly/mildly/moderately/extremely/massively/morbidly" are all misleadingly
subjective and subject to changing tastes and styles. It is far more preferable to report measured
height, weight and general "build" or to weigh the person, and look in the Metropolitan Life
Insurance Company's Table of Desirable Weights and report, say, "10% overweight."
Obesity is not a psych. diagnosis.
Common 'diagnoses': Mild = 20-40% over, moderate = 41-100% over, and severe = more than
100% over the published in height to weight tables.
Android/abdominal/"Apples" or gynoid/femoral/"Pears"

For a Child:

Stature in relation to age is short/normal/tall, at the __ percentile of the standard tables for height and
weight for children, Tanner stage (of sexual development) #

COMPLEXION:

Dark/light skinned/complected, swarthy, olive-skinned, florid, ruddy, red-faced, "peaches-and-cream,"
tanned, sunburned, mottled, wan, sallow, jaundiced, sickly, pale, pallid/pallorous, leathery, weather-
beaten, worn, wrinkled, pimply, warty, scarred, poorly complected, shows negligence, birthmarks,
Port-wine marks, scars

FACE:

Pinched, puffy, washed out, emaciated, old/young looking for chronological/true age, baby-faced,
long-faced, moon-faced, dark circles under eyes, bulbous/red/richly veined nose, delicate/coarse
features
Movement: tics, twitches, drooping, mobility during interview/over topics

Head: odd shaped, microcephalic/macrocephalic, dolichocephalic/mesocephalic/brachycephalic,
normal, cretinous, damaged

Teeth: unremarkable hygiene, dentures, gaps and missing teeth, edentulous, unusual dentistry, bad
breath/breath odor/"halitosis"

Notable features: ears, nose, cheeks, mouth, lips, teeth, chin, neck

FACIAL EXPRESSIONS: See also Chapter 14. Affects

Attentive, alert, tense, worried, indrawn, frightened
Sad, frowns, downcast, in pain, grimaces in pain, forlorn, drawn
Tearful/watered/tears up/tears falling/open crying/sobbing
Apathetic, preoccupied, inattentive, unspontaneous, withdrawn, vacuous, vacant, absent, detached,
Mask-like, did not smile/change expression during the long interview, lacks spontaneous/
     appropriate/expected facial expression, flat, expressionless, lifeless, frozen, rigid, head bobbed as
     if nodding off
Calm, composed, relaxed, dreamy
Smiling, cheerful, happy, delighted, silly/sheepish grin, beaming
Angry, disgusted, distrust, contempt, defiance, sneering, scowling, grim, dour, tight-lipped, hatch marks
     between his/her eyes, has a chronic sour look
Quizzical
Face, mien

EYES: See also section 11.4 Eye Contact

Large, small, close-set, almond-shaped[1] (preferable to "slanted"), sunken, bloodshot, red, pink,
     bleary-eyed, bulging, cross-eyed, wide-eyed, "wall-eyed"
Staring, unblinking, glassy-eyed, vacant, penetrating, vigilant, nervously/frequent blinking, darting,
     squinting, tired, "eyes twinkled," limpid, unusual

Brows: beetling brows, massive, raised, pulled together, pulled down, shaven, plucked

Glasses: regular corrective lenses, half lenses, bifocals, reading glasses, contact lenses, sunglasses,
     needed but not worn, broken/poorly repaired

HAIR:

Hairstyle: of a fashionable length and style, long, pony-tail, pig-tails, corn-rows, braided, crew/brush
     cut, natural/"Afro", frizzy, curly, finger curls, dredlocks, wavy, straight, uncombed, tousled,
     Punk, "Mohawk", pageboy, currently popular haircut, stylish, unusual hair cut/style/treatment,
     moused, permed, "relaxed," unbarbered, simple/easy to care for cut, unremarkable
Color: bleached, colored/dyed, frosted, streaks of color, different color roots, salt-and-pepper,
     gray/color, faded color, fair-haired/blonde/platinum, brunette, brown, auburn, chestnut, black, red
     haired, albino
Other: Clean, dirty, unkempt, greasy/oily, matted.
     Thinning, receding hairline, high forehead, widow's peak, male pattern baldness, balding, bald spot,
          bald, head shaven, alopecia
Wig, toupee, hairpiece, "a rug", implants, transplants, an obvious hairpiece

Beard: clean-shaven, unshaven/needs a shave, had the beginnings of a beard, wispy, scraggly, stubble,
     stylish, cultivated/deliberate stubble, grizzled, poorly/well maintained/groomed, neatly trimmed, full,
     closely trimmed, mutton chops, Goatee, unbarbered, Van Dyke/ZZ Tops/Santa Claus style
Moustache: wore/sported a moustache/moustached/moustacioed, oriental, handlebars, pencil thin, neat,
     scraggly, just starting

---

[1] My thanks to Fay Murakawa, Ph.D. of Los Angles for this clarification and correction.

OTHER ASPECTS OF APPEARANCE:

Grooming/hygiene/cleanliness: excellent/good/unremarkable/fair/marginal/poor/awful, haggard, scruffy, bedraggled, unremarkable/as expected, neglected, indicating indifference, acceptable but not optimal, neat, tidy, meticulous

His/her personal grooming and hygiene while relatively neat and clean does reflect impoverishment/ very limited resources/cultural background/physical limitations/cognitive limitations.

Odor: body or clothing, musty, noticeable, offensive body odor, excess perfume, smells of alcohol, ineffective deodorant

Nails: cleanliness, tobacco-stained, dirty, grimy, bitten down to the quick, overlong, broken, polished, manicured

Skin: bruises, cuts, abrasions, scabs, sores, damage, tattoos, acne, *acne vulgaris* scars, scars, Port-wine stains, mottled

Other: jewelry (rings, earrings, bracelets, pins, etc.), makeup, hearing aid, prosthesis, colostomy, catheter, other device

Notable aspects: shoulders, chest, breasts, back, pelvis, genitals, legs, feet, hands, fingers, swollen/wasted ankles/hands/parts

Breathing: noisy, wheezed, Shortness Of Breath, assisted, usual

Shows some signs of self-neglect.

Shows the ravages of drug/alcohol/illness/stress/over-work/age/disease, dissipated, ill-looking, out of shape

Tired, pathetic, pale and wan, frail, sickly

BEARING:

Suggests chronic illness, appeared weak/frail, low stamina/endurance/easily winded, listless, labored, burdened

Erect, "military", proud/arrogant, overly proper, deferential

11.3 Clothing/Attire:

The relevant perspectives are not fashion or newness but what clothing means about the client's ability to care for him/herself and his/her judgement of appropriateness.

APPROPRIATENESS:

For situation/occasion/weather, nothing unusual for a visit to a professional appointment/office

Presentable, acceptable, suitable, appearance and dress appropriate for age and occupation, business-like, professional appearance, presents an employable appearance, nothing was attention-drawing, modestly attired

His/her idea of suitable, not suitable for age/suitable for a younger person, not suitable for his/her station in life, too casual to be acceptable, care of person and clothing was only fair

(<->) Institutional, odd, unusual, eccentric, peculiar, unique combinations, carefully disordered, dressed to offend, un/conventional, attention seeking/drawing, outlandish, garish, bizarre

QUALITIES OF CLOTHING: (<->)

filthy	seedy	needing repair	plain	neat	stylish
grimy	disheveled	threadbare	out of date	careful	fashionable
dirty	neglected	rumpled	old-fashioned	dresser	elegant
smelly	wrong size	clean but worn	old	overdressed	dandified
dusty	ill-fitting	worn		clothes	
oily	unkempt	shabby		conscious	natty
greasy		tattered		in good taste	dapper
food spotted	messy	torn			
	slovenly			seductive	
	sloppy	shows unilateral	regional/	revealing	
	baggy	neglect	foreign	flashy	meticulous
	bedraggled	unzipped	designs	too tight-	immaculate
	raggedy	unbuttoned	eccentric	fitting	
			overly somber	tasteless	
				design	

OTHER:

Dressed in a manner typical of today's youth/of the 1940's/1950's/1960's
Attired in the style of her/his contemporaries
Overly prim

11.4 Movement/Activity:

SPEED/ACTIVITY LEVEL: (<->)

Almost motionless, little animation, psychomotor retardation, slowed, slowed reaction time to
   questions/latency, < normal > normokinetic, restless, squirming, fidgety, fretful, constant hand
   movements, continual flexing of ___ , hyperactive, agitated, frantic, frenetic

For a Child:

High activity level: motorically active, fidgets, difficult to redirect/redirectable, difficulty remaining in
   his/her chair/seat, many out-of-chairs, restless and distractible, investigated all the contents of the
   room/desk/testing materials, overactive/hyperactive/aggressive, a darter, tantrums/tantrumming
See section 16.5 ADDH

COORDINATED/UNCOORDINATED: (<->)

Awkward, clumsy, "klutzy", often injuries self, inaccurate/ineffective movements, jerky, uncoordinated,
   < normal >, purposeful, smooth, dextrous, graceful, agile, nimble
Degree of body awareness, body ego, body confidence

For a Child:

Coordination: delayed by __ months/years, gross and fine motor, noticeably poor manual dexterity, held objects such as pencils awkwardly, difficulty coordinating hands and fingers when asked to copy designs, hands were shaky on tasks

PRAXIS:

Handedness/preference/dominance/astereognosis
Handshake: (<->) avoided, fishy, moist/sweaty/nervous, limp, tentative, weak, delayed, < normal >, firm, exaggerated, painfully tight
Handwriting: (<->) elegant, precise, stylized, legible, sloppy, primitive, prints, scrawl, illegible, no recognizable letters

Ask client to walk, write a sentence, tie shoes/tie and observe skill, difficulties

For a Child:

Grip: The student held the pencil in a grip considered correct/improper/in a fist-like grip/atypical/awkward/in a palmar grasp/perpendicular to the table/down by the graphite/with fingers too close to the point/thumb overlapping the forefinger/forefinger overlapping the thumb/with two fingers and the thumb/with three fingers and thumb/between the forefinger/index/pointer and third/middle finger, tensely
Slight problems in fine motor coordination were noted in making wavy/irregular/straight/heavy/light/wild/uncontrolled lines

MANNERISMS/ODDITIES of motor behavior/automatisms/use of hands/body: See also Symptomatic movements, below

Aimless/stereotyped/perseverative/repetitious/unproductive/counter-productive movements, head-bobbing, wriggles, hand or finger movements, bounces leg, posturing, picks/pulls at clothing, pulls lips into mouth, rocking, walking on tiptoe/heels,
Perseverates: pauses and repeats movements at choice points as when leaving the room/in doorway
Stereotyped movements such as twirling, rocking, engaged in self-stimulation, hand flapping,
Manneristic mouth movements such as tongue chewing, lip smacking, whistling, made odd/animal/grunting sounds, belching,

Squints, covered face with hands and peeked out, made faces/grimaced

Childlike gestures/facial expressions/speech (e.g. "Gol-lee")
Sniffles repeatedly/loudly, uses/needs but does not use tissues/handkerchief, freely and frequently picks his/her nose, repetitively "cleans" ears with fingers
Yawned excessively/regularly/elaborately, appeared sleepy/tired, rubbed eyes
Made audible breathing sounds

Needed to stretch/get up and walk periodically

Smoked incessantly/carelessly/dangerously/compulsively/selfishly
Effeminate, overly feminine, mannish, "macho/a"

SYMPTOMATIC MOVEMENTS:

Waxy flexibility *(cerea flexibilitas)*, tardive dyskinesia, dysiadochokinesia, Parkinsonian/Extra-Pyramidal Symptoms/movements, athetoid, athetotic, akathesias, choreiform, akinesia, "pill-rolling", "chewing", "Restless Leg Syndrome", opened and closed legs repeatedly, paced, restlessness, hyper/hypotonic, hyper/hypokinetic, echopraxia, cataplexy, denudative behavior. See also section 16.31 Side effects of medications
Tremor: none/mild/at rest/of intent/familial, quivers, shivers, twitches, tics, shakes
Autonomic hyperactivity. See section 14.3 Anxiety

MOBILITY: (<->)

Confined to bed, bedfast, uses wheelchair, adaptive equipment, requires support/assistance/supervision, uses a gait aid (cane, brace/leg/back, walker, crutches/Canadian, wheelchair, geriatric chair), slow, careful, avoids obstacles

GAIT, CARRIAGE AND STATION: (<->)

Astasia, abasia, shuffles, desultory, effortful, dilatory, stiff, awry, limps, drags/favors one leg, awkward, walks with slight posturing, lumbering, leans, lurching, ataxic, collides with objects/persons, broad-based, knock-kneed, bow-legged, < normal >, ambled, no visible problem/no abnormality of gait or station, fully mobile including stairs, springy, graceful, glides, brisk/energetic, limber
Mincing, exaggerated, strides, dramatic/thespian/for effect, unusual, able to locomote and navigate under his/her own power

For a Child:

Uncoordinated, e.g. difficulty climbing stairs, brushed ankles against each other, unsteady forward gait, stumbled at intervals. Note the wear patterns on shoes

BALANCE:

Dizzy, vertigo, staggers, sways, fearful of falling/unsure, unsteady, positive Romberg sign, complains of light-headedness, < normal >, no danger of falling, steady

POSTURE: (<->)

Hunkered down, hunched over, slumped, slouched, stooped, round-shouldered, limp, cataplexy, relaxed, < normal >, stiff, tense, guarded, rigid, erect, upright, sat on edge of chair, odd, leans, peculiar posturing/atypical/inappropriate. Sat sideways in the chair, reversed chair to sit

EYE CONTACT: (<->)

None, avoided, stared into space, stared without bodily movements or other expressions, kept eyes downcast, broken off as soon as made/passing/intermittent, wary, alert, looked only to one side, brief, flashes, fleeting, furtive, appropriate, effective, < normal >, expected, modulated, lingering, staring, glared, penetrating, piercing, confrontative, challenging

OTHER:

Pain behavior accompanying movements: degree of difficulty getting down into and up from a chair, sighs, groans, grimaces, winces, sits/walks rigidly, splinting/braces. See also section 16.20 Pain disorder

For a Child:

Dominance: mixed, right/left, as seen in hopping on a foot/preferred hand/use of one eye to sight/flipping a coin/catching a thrown object

11.5 Speech Behavior: Give quotes/verbatim/examples. See also section 15.9 Stream of thought

ARTICULATION:

Unintelligible, stammer/stutter, stumbles over words, mumbles, mutters under breath, lisp, sibilance, slurred, juicy, garbled, understandable, clear, clipped, choppy and mechanical, poor diction, poor enunciation, pace/cadence/rate, too slow/fast, rhythm, misarticulated, unclear, dysfluencies, dysarthrias (spastic, flaccid, ataxic), aphasias
Accent: foreign, regional, odd, intense, confusing, drawl, burr
Misspoke: confused word (e.g. wall for while) requiring repetition and inquiry for clarification

For a Child:

Immature: simpler sentences/formation than expected, articulation errors, difficulty in speech articulation: especially sounds such as r, sh, th, z or ch, slid over some consonant sounds

VOICE'S QUALITIES:

Loud/noisy/almost screaming, brassy, gravelly, hoarse, raspy, throaty, nasal, screechy, squeaky, shrill, staccato, strident, harsh, mellifluous, quiet, soft, weak, frail, thin, "small" voice, barely audible, whispered, affected, tremulous, quavery, low/high pitched, sing-song, whiney, odd inflection/intonation, monotonous pitch/tone, sad/low tone of voice, muffled,
Bass, baritone, alto, soprano
Whispered to him/herself, talks under breath

PHRASEOLOGY: (see also Content below)

Spoke in almost "babytalk"/infantile/childish/immature style, mispronounced words, uneducated vocabulary/uncultured language/reflective of cultural deprivation, slang words, grammatical mistakes, non-standard/substandard English
Dialect, regionalisms, provincialisms, foreign words/idioms
Cliches, habitual expressions, repetition of catch phrases, many "You know"s
Pedantic, pseudo-intellectual, stilted, excessively formal, jargon
Inappropriately familiar
Punning, rhyming, contrived language
Casual and familiar swear words, epithets, hostile cursing, racial/ethnic/religious slurs
Anomia, agramatism
Syntactical/syntactical errors

For a Child:

Underdeveloped vocabulary for his/her age
Conversation consisted of 3-4 word phrases rather than sentences

SPEECH AMOUNT/ENERGY/FLOW/RATE/PRODUCTIVITY/RHYTHM: (<->)

halting	Slowed	Normal	Pressured	Verbose	Flight of ideas
hesitant	minimal response	initiates	loquacious	over-prod-	
delays/ed	unspontaneous	alert	garrulous	uctive	
inhibited	unresponsive	productive	rapid	bombastic	
blocked	terse	animated	excessive	non-stop	
lags	sluggish	talkative	wordy	vociferous	
slowed	paucity	fluent	exaggerated	over-abundant	
reaction time	sparse	well-spoken	hurried	over-responsive	
	hesitant	easy	fast	excessive detail	
mute	laconic	spontaneous	voluble	voluminous	
elective	impoverished	smooth	rushed	hyperverbal	
mutism	economical	crisp	talkative	long-winded	
only nods	taciturn	even	expansive		
single words			blurts out		
			run-together		
word-finding			raucous		
difficulties					
word					
searching					
difficulty gener-					
ating thoughts					

SPEECH MANNER:

distant	Normal	candid	empathic
hurried	warm	open	touching
pedantic	sincere	frank	insightful
somber	well modulated	guileless	wise
inarticulate	articulate	free	charming
whiney	gets ideas across well	untroubled	witty
	good natured	easy	jovial
expressionless	engaging		
monotone	well-spoken		
mechanical	eloquent		
	realistic		
	measured		
	thoughtful		
	responsive		

SUMMARY STATEMENTS FOR NORMAL SPEECH BEHAVIORS:

I noted no impairments in language functioning reflecting disordered mentation.
S/he could comprehend and carry out the test/evaluation instructions and tasks, and didn't
misinterpret or misunderstand the test materials or questions.
No language impairment receptively or expressively
Communication was not impeded in any way, satisfactory/adequate/normal expressiveness
No abnormalities of audition/hearing
Without articulatory deficit
Comprehension of English/spoken words was normal/defective/abnormal.
His/her ability to understand the spoken word was adequate within the context of this examination
but might not be in ___

Did not have to have the **questions/instructions** rephrased/simplified/repeated
Auditory comprehension was adequate and oral delivery was effective.
His/her speech was sophisticated with considerable emphasis on intellectual/personal/medical/
historical/family matters

S/he is a **reciprocal conversationalist**/dialogued spontaneously/is able to carry on a conversation
S/he is able to initiate topics appropriately.
S/he follows the conventions/social rules of communication including appropriate phrasing, turn-
taking, and understood the suppositions and expectations of native speakers of American
English
Participated/did not engage in appropriate social dialogue
Little/normal/expected/excessive small talk

Hearing was normal/normal with use of hearing aid/hard of hearing/partially deaf/read my
lips/required me to raise my voice/shout/completely deaf

CONVERSATIONAL STYLE: See also Section 12.8, Other Statements

Used a paragraph where a word would do
An excessively verbal person who needed more braking than prompting

Assumed that I, the listener, knew more than I did about his/her history/ideas/the subject of the conversation

Speech was slow, deliberate and, at times, evasive
All of his/her speech was defensive/designed to emphasize his/her degree of disability
His/her answers were not to be relied upon, but were pertinent and to the point. (See also Sections 8.9, Reliability and 12.2, Rapport)

Uses vulgarity/blasphemy/scatology/sexuality to shock
Preoccupied (See Section 15.9, Stream of thought, Preoccupations)
Rote re-telling of an often-told story
Uses psychiatric language sophisticated enough to suggest a person who is system-wise
Excessively colloquial for our relationship
His/her language choices were, in reality, more odd than I am able to reproduce here.

For a Child:

Perseverative, echolalic, mimicked examiner's speech, delayed language acquisition, difficulty in comprehending or expressing oral language

---

11.6 Other Behavioral Observations/Demeanor:

NORMAL:

Took good care of his/her appearance in regard to dress, hygiene, and grooming
Nothing unusual/remarkable/noticeable about his/her posture, bearing, manner, or hygiene.
No deformities

ABNORMAL:

Brought to the examination: possessions, cigarettes, presents, papers, briefcase, coffee/refreshments/candy/food
Fidgety, nervous and inappropriate laughter/smiling, titters, giggles, nervous habits. (See also section 14.3, Anxiety
Audible sighs, tearful, tears, crying, sobbing, hand wringing. (See also section 14.5, Depression)

For a Child:

Tantrum: assaultive, destructive to property, aggressive to others, redirectable

12. Relating to the Examination

This CHAPTER and the next describe FACE-TO-FACE or one-on-one, INTERPERSONAL BEHAVIORS

THIS CHAPTER covers:　　1.　RESPONSE TO ASPECTS OF THE EXAMINATION including
　　　　　　　　　　　　　　　RESPONSE to the PROCEDURES of evaluation
　　　　　　　　　　　　　　　RAPPORT
　　　　　　　　　　　　　　　RESPONSE to the METHODS of evaluation
　　　　　　　　　　　　　　　CONCENTRATION, MOTIVATION, RESPONSE TO FAILURE
　　　　　　　　　　　　　　　APPROACH TO THE TASKS OF THE EXAMINATION

The NEXT CHAPTER covers: 2. SELF-PRESENTATION of the client to the evaluator.
Other Chapters of relevance are 26. Social Functioning and 27. Relationships

12.1 Relating to the Evaluation's Context: (<->) See also Sections 12.2 Rapport , 12.5 Effort/ Attention/Concentration

Unable to recognize the purposes of the interview/the report to be made, unaware of the social conventions, did not understand or adapt to the testing situation, s/he was not able to comprehend or respond to questions designed to elicit ____ or symptoms of ___, low attending skills, just able to meet the minimum requirements for appropriate social interaction, misconstrues what is said to him/her, unaware, withdrawn, unresponsive, echolalic, preoccupied, estranged, doesn't grasp essence or goal, autistic

Dependent, sought/required much support/reassurance/guidance/encouragement from the examiner, desperate for assistance, self-doubting, ill at ease

Indifferent, bland, detached, distant, uninvolved, uncaring, no interest in doing anything but playing out his/her time, haphazard, insensitive, tense, bored, showed the presence of an interfering emotion, over-cautious, related obliquely

Anxiety appropriate/proportionate to the interview situation, initially responded only to questions but later became more spontaneous, began interview with an elevated level of anxiety which decreased as the evaluation progressed, needed assistance to get started

Understands the social graces/norms/expectations/conventions/demand characteristics of the examination situation, comfortable, confident, relaxed, interested, curious, eager, intense, carefully monitored the testing situation, oriented, aware, alert, cooperative, no abnormalities, attends, responds, reciprocates, continues, participates, initiates, communicates effectively, clear and efficient, high quality of interaction, with depth

12 • Relating to the Exam.

For a Child:

BEHAVIOR WHEN WITH PARENT (custodial parent, grandparent, caregiver, major attachment figure, foster parent, etc.):

Played easily in the waiting room, put away the toys used
Level of play, with playthings appropriate for what age?
Control used by parent: degree, kind/methods/means, timing, over issues of ____
Relationship, supportive, agreed to?
Parents agreement/disagreement/conflict on discipline

SEPARATION FROM PARENT:

Degree and type of anxiety[1], coping mechanisms used on separation
The parent(s) management of separation was ...

S/he was reluctant to separate from her/his parent/accompany the examiner to/into the interview room came willingly into the examination/testing room/office with the examiner, accompanies the examiner easily/readily, separates easily/poorly/reluctantly from the examiner

Showed symptoms of **separation anxiety:** worry over possible harm to parent/parent will desert them/disaster will keep child away from parent, school refusal to stay with parent, refusal to sleep without parent, "clinging" or "shadowing" behaviors, nightmares about separation, physical complaints when separated, tantrums/pleading to not separate, excessive homesickness easily redirected or distracted from parent, needs much reassurance, responded well to reassurance, resists returning to parent, comfortable with adults, masters own anxiety

Reaction upon rejoining parent was ...

PARENTAL INTERACTION WITH EXAMINER:

Attitude/type of relating: arrogant, impatient, threatening, suspicious, cooperative, trusting, controlling/ manipulative, seductive, dependent
Role taken and role assigned to examiner, changes during interview

FEELINGS AROUSED BY CHILD IN EXAMINER:

For an Adolescent:

Limited spontaneity which was not inappropriate/abnormal for his/her age.

---

[1] John Bowlby described three stages of separation: 1) Initial protest with crying, screaming and general activity; 2) Despair with dejection, stupor, withdrawl, and decreased activity, and; 3) Detachment with indifference and hostility.

12.2 Rapport/Relationship to Examiner:

COOPERATION/POSITIVE BEHAVIORS: (<->)

affable
pleasant
friendly
chummy
outgoing
socially
    graceful
solicitous
tactful
cordial
gracious
amiable
warm
familiar
genial
jokes around
breezy
playful
easy
"upbeat"

inoffensive
"laid back"
low key
"mellow"
placid

frank
forthright
candid

Cooperative
helpful
easy to interview
enjoyed
    interview

without hes-
    itation
responsive
answers readily
obliging
agreeable
amicable

civil
polite
courteous
well-mannered

Pleasant
appropriate
engageable
available
open

Dependent
institutionalized
    agreeableness
deferential
ingratiating
trying to please
eager to please
effusive
obsequious
pleading
over-solicitous

obedient
confidential

oily
fawning
flattering

conciliatory
defers
humble
over-polite
over-apologetic
eulogistic
apple-polishing
mealy-mouthed
plaintive
help-seeking
barters affection
wants to please

Indifferent
no effort
frustrated
docile
passive
sedated
submissive
lackadaisical
doesn't try
accommo-
    dating
minimal
cooper-
    ation
sheepish

noncommittal
compliant
blasé
nonchalant
neutral
careless

seductive
immature
practical
joker
clowns
exhibitionistic

spooky

curt
monosyllabic
legalistic
passive agg-
    ressive or
    dependent

snippy

sassy
flippant

"forgets"

RESISTANCE/NEGATIVE BEHAVIORS: (<->) See also section 14.2 Anger

Guarded	Surly	Defensive	Demanding	Hostile	Argumentative	Belligerent
reserved	sulky	subtle	imposing	irritating	territorial	insulting
reticent	petulant	hostility	insistent	instigating	possessive	defiant
recalcitrant	balky	uncooperative	indignant	obnoxious	antagonistic	obstreper-
resistive	touchy	"sick and	confrontative	tests limits	contentious	ous
reluctant	pouty	tired"	presumptuous		oppositional	scolding
	peevish	resentful				
inaccessible	sullen	non-compliant	frustrated		manipulative	
distant	brooding	refuses	complaining	has an	provocative	
remote	crabby	adamant	domineering	"attitude"	quibbles	
evasive	testy		rebellious	bristled when	questions	name-
wary	gruff		rude	questioned	hypercritical	calling
withdraws	snappish		nagging	Superior	irascible	vilifying
withholding				condescending	quarrel-	slandering
avoidant	grouchy			pities	some	menacing
not forth-	scowls		Stubborn	distant	challenging	venomous
coming	"snippy"		mulish	aloof		threatening
tight-lipped			intractable	disdainful	abusive	nasty
	Childish		unbending	egocentric	derisive	malicious
suspicious	immature		unyielding	entitled	scornful	caustic
cagey	uncertain		unadaptable	cocky	sarcastic	intimidating
sneaky			rigid	over-bearing	carping	
			obtuse	arrogant	berating	
over-controlled			inflexible	contemptuous		
businesslike			negativistic	supercilious	facetious	
stiff			abrasive	toyed with	mocking	
unfriendly			opinionated	examiner	taunting	
desultory			willful	"knows-it-all"	sneering	
habit-bound			contrary	smart-alecky	smug	
only perfunctory/				cantankerous	pushy	teasing
superficial				"hutzpah"	sarcastic	
cooperation				"brassy"	quips	
					derogatory	
					loathes	

For a child

"mouthy", "mouths off," "sasses," talks back
non-compliant, throws, hits
attempts to undermine staff's authority

OTHER STATEMENTS ABOUT RAPPORT: See also Chapter 13. Presentation of Self

Rapport was easily/intermittently/never established and maintained
Response to authority was cooperative/respectful/appropriate/productive/indifferent/hostile/
    challenging/unproductive/non-compliant, poor attitude toward authority.
Required/allowed another to answer none/some/all of the questions posed
Seemed to enjoy the attention received

I could easily understand his/her meanings
I found it hard to like/feel for this person

Was cooperative within limits; s/he refused some test items/tests/topics
Was fully cooperative with the examiner only after determining my credentials

Doesn't accept direction from people in authority
Repeatedly/irrelevantly/provocatively interrupted the interviewer
Talked over me/interrupted, made efforts to control the interview

Inappropriate fowardness toward female staff

He/she appeared to be feigning cheerfulness/good spirits.
The testing/questions/history taking/examination was particularly trying for him/her

EYE CONTACT: see section 11.4 Eye Contact

12.3 Qualities of Communication:

GOOD COMMUNICATIONS:

Asks permission/makes appointment for best opportunity to communicate
Shows understanding, offers feedback/reflections/re-phrasings, shows patience/doesn't foreclose/close off
    prematurely, tolerates other's emotions, non-accusatory style
Uses "I" messages, "Owns" feelings, risks, is honest, no facade, present, can ventilate,

PROBLEMATIC COMMUNICATION:

As speaker:
    Overly critical, overly logical, accusatory, overwhelms listener with quantity of words, changes topics,
        sarcastic,
    Automatic/play-acting/irrelevant emotionality, overblown emotions, overly dramatic,
    Withdrawing, "tuning out"
    Jumping to conclusions/"mind reading," second guessing other
    Righteousness, condescending   Nagging, reminding
    Overfocus on the past   Threatening
    Excessive repetitions, hogging the floor/refusing to relinquish the floor,
    Uses time to criticize, lobby the professional,

As listener:
    Insincere "agreement," misses the point too often/"thickheaded," silent/"doesn't know what to say,"
        has to be reminded of the rules too often, fails to recall what was said, becomes speaker by
        arguing/criticizing/reacting/etc.

12.4 Response to the Methods of Evaluation/Tests/Questions:

COMPREHENSION OF INSTRUCTIONS/QUESTIONS: (<->) See also section 12.6 for Motivation

Rarely understands instructions, requires much repetition/elaboration, needed to have instructions repeated often, gets confused, required restructuring of my questions in a manner to make them more concrete and simplistic, required elaboration of the standard instructions before comprehending the nature of the tasks

May sometimes need elaboration of instructions, attentive, understands, good comprehension, required excessive time and repetition to understand what was required of him/her

Quickly grasps problem, anticipates the response expected/desired

APPROACH/ATTACK/STRATEGY: (<->) See also Summary Statements, later

Random	Indifferent	Scattered	Organized	Rigid
impulsive	giggled	inconsistent	coordinated	compulsive
	flippant	careless	controlled	
distracted		disorganized	goal-oriented	ritualistic
agitated		sloppy	active	perseverative
		uncoordinated	diligent	
	Haphazard		catches on fast	perfectionistic
Distrusts own	acts without		well-ordered	
ability	instructions	Baffled	thinks through	manneristic
self-doubting	non-plussed		before acting	
second guesses	thinks aloud		notes details	tense
self	absent-minded		uses trial-and-	plodding
insecure	guesses at		error approach	unsure
	answers		orderly	
refuses to guess			methodical	
/take chances	Hurried		deliberate	
underestimates	fast		persistent	
own abilities	rapid		neat	
	speedy		contemplative	
	rushed		pensive	
			matter-of-fact	
			thoughtful	
			efficient	

OTHER STATEMENTS ABOUT APPROACH/STRATEGY/ATTACK:

Waited for full instructions
Listened attentively to the interviewer's questions
No problems with test directions or instructions
His/her understanding of the spoken word was good/directions/instructions did not have to be
    repeated or rephrased/simplified
Only repetition/slowed presentation, not simplification, of test directions was required
Was able to follow multi-step directions
Fully responded to all tasks' demands

Consistent and organized
Organized his/her ideas before responding to test questions
Stepped back and reviewed behavior when s/he failed; did not stick with an obviously ineffective approach.
Perseverated in that he /she had difficulty adjusting and responding appropriately to the next task's
    demands/instructions

Worked quickly with little deliberation
Marginal approach to the evaluation reflective of ...
    mildly/moderately/severely reduced intellectual capacity
    poorly developed cognitive strategies
    generalized undisciplined mental processing
    lack of self evaluation/little concern for the quality of his/her responses.
Impulsive responses with poor organization and planning skills, without forethought, minimal
    reflection/consideration before answering
S/he was not task oriented

Used random trial and error approach on most tasks and showed little comprehension, visualization
    or analysis of the overall tasks, little learning from his/her attempts
S/he is not flexible in problem approaches/lacks problem attack skills/perseverates manner of
    problem attack
Used avoidance techniques in examination such as dropping test materials, starting conversations
    between subtests, attending to sounds in the hallway, asking repeated questions regarding the
    test materials and procedures, wandering off-task

12.5 Effort/Attention/Concentration: (<->)

Apathetic	Sluggish	Distractible	Normal energy	Eager
dull	worked slowly	low attending skills	cooperative	animated
uninvolved	in slow motion	easily distracted	interested	fascinated
uninvested	slow reactions	from task	adequate	
passive	slowed	loses concentration	good effort	initiates
anergic		does not stick	spontaneous	inquisitive
	Reticent	with task	open	enthusiastic
listless	unspontaneous	had great difficulty	attentive	
bored	taciturn	following directions	alert	well-spoken
disinterested		non-persistent		
inattentive	Flat			verbal
bland	no originality			garrulous
exhausted	unchanging			eager to
tired	expressionless			ventilate
listless	uncreative			talkative
indifferent	paucity of			
shuns effort	worthwhile ideas			candid
resigned				in touch
				with own
				feelings
Inconsistent	Perplexed			
skimpy responses	baffled			dramatic
sporadic	bewildered			over-abundant
varies with task	confused			
	uninformed			

Adequate attention span, concentration, little distractibility, anxiety or frustration
The source of distractions were ... and he/she was successfully able to resist distraction by ....
Demonstrated no negative attitudes

12.6 Motivation/Persistence/Perseverance: (<->) Degree of involvement in tasks

Refuses test items/subtests, only brief responses, had to be prompted to elaborate, gives up on easy items, seeks to terminate interview, quits quickly, gives up easily, "defeatist," s/he terminated effort following minimal concentration, responded slowly/gave purposefully erroneous responses as a form of resistance, performed halfheartedly, showed minimal compliance

Variable level of interest/motivation, slowed/varying reaction time to questions, hesitant, needs frequent/constant reinforcement/encouragement/reassurance/praise/commendation for continued performance, sustained effort only for ___ time period, often discouraged, low frustration tolerance, prefers only easy tasks, little tolerance for ambiguity, initially refused to attempt tasks but upon re-presentation later was cooperative

Withdraws, shows irritation/anger, complains, refuses

No motivation to succeed with difficult tasks/perform well for the examiner, took breaks and recovered willingness to continue, began to lose interest in the evaluation tasks and in conversing with the examiner after ___ time

Average perseverance and effort demonstrated, only rarely discouraged or inattentive, completed all tasks fully and competently, work oriented, applied him/herself to the tasks presented, was cooperative and put forth best effort on each evaluation task administered, willingly/eagerly attempted each task presented, participated well and fully in the evaluation process, once he/she understood the tasks he demonstrated serious efforts to respond to their demands

Became quite involved in the tasks, changes tasks appropriately, eager to continue, challenged by difficult tasks, concentrates on one task for a long time, finishes every task, distracted only by extreme circumstances, sustains effort, persists, diligent, systematic, conscientious, wanted to do well, testing seemed to be challenging and interesting to him/her

When the test materials became necessarily too difficult s/he became frustrated and wanted to give up

12.7 Response to Failure/Criticism/Feedback on test items and Self-awareness/Self-monitoring/Self-criticism See also section 12.2 Rapport (<->)

Oblivious to failure, no response to either success or failure, unaware of/unconcerned about/failed to recognize errors, examiner's questions/suggestions/hints didn't improve performance, low self-monitoring/error correction skills, accepts own inferior performance, satisfied with inadequate work, minimal concern and care about doing well on evaluations, indifferent, hypocritical, inappropriately over-confident

Flustered, embarrassed, ashamed, chagrined, apologetic, self-reproaches, self-derogates, feelings are easily hurt, reluctant to expose his weaknesses, rationalizes failures, extremely critical of own work/hypercritical, disparages own performance, not satisfied with less than perfection, vulnerable to humiliation, loathe to say s/he doesn't know so clammed up instead

Normal responsiveness and coping with failure, tries his/her best, surprised at failure, accepts mistakes with regret, accepts need to go on despite failure/mistake/incorrect answers, confident, calm, understands easily, adapts, modulates, good balance of self-criticism and self-confidence, self-sufficient, learns from errors/experience, accepts own limitations so failure has little effect

Self-congratulatory, proud, takes pride in accomplishments, delighted with success, persists, works harder, self-monitors, sought errors in own work and self-corrected, gives up only on items clearly beyond ability, refuses to concede defeat, wasn't discouraged by errors, was easily motivated by "Try again"

Required/did well with/ignored no/usual/copious praise
Praise had stimulating effects on her performance

He/she was unaware of the low level at which he/she performed
Efforts at compensation through ___ (e.g. a pedantic style) create a negative impression of which
    s/he is apparently unaware
His/her perception of his/her status and abilities are somewhat inflated
S/he is not so skillful as he/she thinks

For a Child:

Clapped/squealed with satisfaction/excitement/delight
Seemed to enjoy the opportunity to talk openly with the professional

12.8 Other Statements about Approach/Attack/Strategy, Task Performance, Attention, Attitude, Motivation, Persistence and Response to Criticism: Perhaps see Section 8.8 Reliability.

PRODUCTIVE:

S/he related each presented test item to some direct experience in his/her own life.
Asked relevant/insightful/helpful questions

COUNTER/NON-PRODUCTIVE:

Took a great deal of time, longer/shorter than usual reaction time/latency of response to questions
Worked at an even pace throughout regardless of task at hand

Showed the long-term effects of defective innate ability, low expectations, an unstimulating environment, and poor/minimal formal training
His/her performance was depressed by poor application of skills he/she does already possess/by fatigue
Completed tasks is a mechanical fashion with little comprehension of what s/he was doing/the goal

Stresses details but misses main point/"can't see the forest for the trees"/doesn't "catch on"/"misses the boat"

Defective performance was present only on items which ... and not on items/areas of ...

Had difficulty answering questions but cooperated to the best of his/her ability
Tried to provide meaningful answers to specific questions but no additional information was forthcoming.
S/he was frank with his/her answers but could not give detailed information.

Tried to have the examiner confirm one of a number of offered responses as the correct one
Answered almost all questions with "I don't know"
Invariably responded with "I don't know" to questions but, on repetition of the question produced a good/correct/scoreable response

Initially hostile but did become gradually less hostile/more forthcoming/sociable as the interview progressed.
His/her sense of outrage seemed to bubble along just below the surface throughout most of the interview.

Cautious, circumspect, and politic about the type and nature of the information provided.

For a Child:

When asked questions in his/her mother's presence he often/always/rarely glanced at/turned to her hoping she would answer the question/seeking confirmation of his answer/deferring to her superior knowledge.
Very resistive behavior: (<->)
Uncontrollable, destructive, untestable, acting out, temper tantrums, disruptive of testing, unruly, distractible, difficult to evaluate, difficult to handle, stubborn
Counts on fingers
Covered his face with his hands
Looked about the room but was redirectable

13.0 Presentation of Self: by the client to the evaluator, as seen by the evaluator. These behaviors can also be seen as Interpersonal Skill and Impression Management

13.1 Presence/Style: (<->)

Withdrawn	Shy	Threatened	Self-assured	autonomous
isolating	timid	distrustful	friendly	direct
	bashful	fearful		
estranged			inviting	dominant
distant	passive		jocular	surgent
suspicious	composed	plaintive	warm	business-like
guarded	placid	vulnerable	outgoing	assertive
asocial		weak	jolly	
introverted	Reserved	delicate	extraverted	stubborn
solitary	retiring	would crumble	chipper	insistent
seclusive	humble	fragile	animated	
detached	subdued	distraught	engaging	
aloof	reticent	threat-sensitive	charming	eccentric
dejected	introverted	unspontaneous		bizarre
	restrained	anxious		dramatic
	mild mannered	low resilience		
	unassuming			

13.2 Self-image/Self-esteem:: Self concept, identity, body image, body ego, personal space, property, sex role, sexual identity, age identity and role, confidence, self esteem, autonomy, goals for self, poor ego boundaries
See also Section 17.9, Dependent Personality

CONFIDENCE: (<->)

Expresses an exaggerated opinion of him/herself, believes s/he is exceptionally capable despite evidence to the contrary, grandiose, self-exalting, boastful, vain, has hutzpah, cocky, pompous, conceited, confident, self-respecting, modest, < NORMAL> unassuming, humble, self-conscious, awkward, self-doubting, unrealistic, inadequate, pessimistic, self-deprecatory, self-abasing, describes self as "a loser/failure/misfit," unworthy, untalented

Presents self as a victim of his/her life.
Has no apparent interest in or motivation to improve his/her lot in life.

PRIDE:

Dignity, self-respect/esteem/regard/image, confidence, righteousness,

Vanity, ego, airs, arrogance, conceit, condescension, narcissism, paints the consequences of his/her actions in a very rosy color. See also 17.15, Narcissistic personality

13.3 Dependency/Surgency: See also Presence, above

(<->) Spineless, meek, "a follower," servile, dependent, clinging, whining/whiney, suppliant, tenuous, tentative, frightened, docile, defers/deferential, inoffensive, passive, yielding, acquiescent, amenable, "wishy-washy," lacking in self-sufficiency, socially immature, compliant, assenting, consenting, cooperative, < NORMAL > spunky, self-confident, dominant, forceful, masterful, high-handed, autocratic, dictatorial, blustery, pugnacious, over-bearing, pushy, self-centered, demanding,

SUMMARY STATEMENTS:

Seems to be suggestible to the whims and commands of her peers who victimize her/expose her to ridicule.
She appears to be friendless and vulnerable for the sake of social acceptance
She tempts peers to take her money/books/possessions so that an adult/another will intervene on her behalf.

13.4 Social Sophistication: (<->)

Unsophisticated, gullible, naive, wide-eyed, suggestible, "Pollyanna"-like, "Little Orphan Annie", uneducated, unschooled, backward, inept, culturally unsophisticated, medically/psychologically naive, socially inept, backward, limited ability to interact, simple, simplistic, immature, passive, giddy, flighty, naive attempts at manipulation, guileless, over-used "Yes, Ma'am/Sir" and "No, Ma'am/Sir"

Mannerly, polite, graceful, poised, tactful, "finesses"

Sophisticated, socially skilled, cultured, street-smart, seductive, articulate, able to lobby/defend his/her interests

Blunt, pointed, tactless, provocative, abrasive, offensive, vulgar, rude, offered outspoken criticisms

Opportunistic, manipulative, sociopathic, callous, predatory, "innocent"/blames others, denies, irresponsible

Manners: well-behaved, mannerly, knows etiquette's rules, rude, sloppy, polite, tactful, gracious

13.5 Warmth: See also 12.2 Rapport - Cooperation

(<->) Over-indulgent, doting, affectionate, affable, tender, gentle, sympathetic, friendly, gracious, kindly, outgoing, considerate, convivial, companionable, intimate, gentle, genteel, sweet, soft-hearted, saccharine, oily, phoney, cold, distant, remote

13.6 Other aspects of Character/Presentation of Self/Demeanor:

Is self-contained and in good charge of him/herself, reserved, collected, matter of fact, static, mechanical, stereotyped, rigid, expressionless, stoic toward his/her illness/limitations

Prim and proper, straight-laced, prudish, dour, austere, prissy, "stuffed shirt", self-righteous, puritanical, rigid
Admits to the compulsive virtues of neatness, orderliness, and planning ahead
Pious, sanctimonious, over-religious, Bible-centered life, Church-centered life-style

Childish, waif-like, immature, juvenile, backward, silly, childish attention seeking, his/her manner is suggestive of a much younger person, suggestive of a person much younger emotionally than physically, "Nerdy", socially unskilled/inept, preoccupied with irrelevancies. See also section 17.12 Inadequate personality

Dull, simple-minded, "air-head", vapid, insipid
Inattentive, stares, forgetful, wistful, preoccupied, mind elsewhere, "space cadet", "Spacey", "Zombie-like", "burned out"

Pleading, begging, coaxing, needy
Presented him/herself as frail and inadequate person of whom one should not expect much

Apologized: ignored failures/mistakes/harm, indirectly, simply, fully, appropriately, effusively
Embarrassed/ashamed/self-blaming/self-reproaching/guilty, "worthless"

Worrisome, a "worry wart" or excessive worrier, easily threatened, inept, feelings are easily hurt, manifested anxiety throughout the interview around every topic, defeatist attitude
Became apprehensive when talking of behavior s/he now realizes was inappropriate

Flamboyant, exaggerated, dramatic, melodramatic, theatrical, histrionic
His/her somatic complaints are unusual, even singular, and were described in affect laden terms

Vivacious, bubbly, volatile, labile, pert
Over-sexualized: saucy, coy, titillating, suggestive, flirtatious, girlish, boyish
See also section 17.15 Narcissistic personality

Arrogant, bragging, cocky, disdainful, tended to praise him/herself excessively, mildly antisocial manner, cavalier, limited empathy
Assumed/maintained an attitude of tolerant amusement.
His manner was swaggering in order to impress the interviewer with his youthfulness/energy/ toughness, has a chip on his shoulder
Client uses embellishments and attempts to appear as a) a "bad actor" or powerful and dangerous person e.g. uses vulgarity to shock, presents as a "tough cookie" or, as b) possessing a high potential, or many friends, etc.
See also section 17.4 Anti-social personality

A "character", individualistic, idiosyncratic, "marches to his/her own drummer", unusual ways of perceiving/behaving, eccentric, "oddball", does not fit in, outlandish, flamboyant, strange, odd, peculiar, bizarre, weird

Menacing, frightening, imposing, awesome, intimidating, manipulating, "spooky", vaguely but intensely frightening, enjoys sadistic humor/is prankish

Intellectualizes: provides psychological jargon/"psychobabble"/labels when asked for descriptions of behaviors/symptoms.

A "Victim": recites life as a series of mishaps, melodramatically enumerates life's misfortunes, made a saga of his/her life in the telling, offered a woeful tirade/Jeremiad of woes/baleful stories/ "Oliver Twist" like story, presented her/himself as a "Born Loser" or perpetual victim or outcast

Client puts up a good front to cover ...
Was reluctant to expand on/denies her/his complaints/problems/symptoms

Voluble: See also section 11.5 Speech Behavior
Offered little information but responded readily to direct questions
Was very verbal but not articulate
Where one word would suffice/answer the question asked s/he produced a paragraph
Attempts to be helpful by trying to tell a great deal and so creates pressured speech
S/he made sure to tell me what s/he thought I should hear and know and then it seemed that s/he felt satisfied

13.7 Other Statements:

OFF-TASK BEHAVIORS:

> Clock-watched
> Offered/desired inappropriate bodily contacts
> Focused on the Examiner's office/accent/clothing/manner/role/appearance rather than the content of his/her/my speech or point of the interview

OTHER STATEMENTS:

> There are no obvious physical or behavioral stigmata which would set him/her apart from other individuals of his/her age, social or cultural group
> S/he put forth good effort to collaborate in the evaluation
> S/he is aware of the social norms and is able to conform to them
> Knows/utilizes/obeys the rules of conversation and turn-taking
> His/her responses reflect wishful thinking rather than realistic plans
> S/he is dependent on institutional support and content to be hospitalized/taken care of

For a Child:

> Pseudo-mature, uncommonly independent
> Primitive, socially inappropriate, non-aggressive behavior
> Attitude and feelings toward:
>> Clinic visits: grasp of purpose, awareness of own difficulties, reaction to symptoms, feelings about returning to clinic
>> Self: behavior, appearance, body, sex, intellect, worries, fears, preoccupations
>> Others: parents, sibs, school, peers, authorities
> Playing observed:
>> Plays with same/younger/older age peers
>> Approach and interest in toys, materials, toys actually used
>> Mode of play: incorporative, extrusive, intrusive
>> Manner of play: constructive, disorganized, mutual, distractible, disruptive
> Tractable to discipline such as ...

Speech and Verbal Interactions: See Sections 11.5, Speech behaviors and 12.2, Rapport

Reliability: See Section 8.8, Reliability

14. Emotional/Affective Symptoms and Disorders

14

Affects

14.1 General aspects of Mood and Affects: See Section 7.4 Affects for questions

Mood is usually considered to be a self-report (but sometimes an inference) of pervasive and sustained emotional coloring of one's experience, a persistent emotional trend (like the climate). Affect is of shorter duration, such as what the clinician observes during the interview, and is more variable and reactive (like the weather). Note and document any differences between the two during the interview

Give quotes/self report/verbatim of mood/affect/emotion

BEHAVIOR reflecting emotional state: See each emotion, below.

Tears, flushing, movements (tremor, etc.), respiratory changes and irregularities, voice changes, facial expression and coloring, wording, somatic expression of affects through ...

GEOGRAPHY:

Elevated/flat/depressed

SOURCE:

Reactive, endogenous, exogenous, characterological, life-long

AMOUNT/RESPONSIVENESS/RANGE: (<->)

Flat	Blunted[1]	Constricted	Appropriate	Broad
affectless	restricted	contained	integrated	deep
bland	restricted in range	low intensity	euthymic	intense
unresponsive	inexpressive	shallow	responsive	generalized
vacant stare	expressionless	muted	normal range	pervasive
absent	dispassionate	subdued	supple	
unvarying	detached	"low key"		
unchanging	unattached	apathetic		
remote	uninvolved	uninflected		
passive appearing	uncomplaining			
	unspontaneous			

Adequate level of emotional energy
No difficulty in initiating, sustaining, and terminating emotional expression

APPROPRIATENESS/CONGRUENCE:

Appropriate/incongruous to situation and thought content, face reflects the emotions reported, all thoughts were colored by emotional state, indifferent to problems, floated over his/her real problems and limitations, *la belle indifference*, affect was variable but unpredictable from the topic of conversation

Modulations/shifts of anxiety were inconsistent and unrelated to the content or affective significance of what s/he was saying

Shows a range of emotions/feelings and they are appropriate to the ideational content and circumstances
Emotional reactions were relevant to the thought content and situation
His emotions seemed appropriate during the interview/examination.

DEGREE:

Mildly/moderately/severely/profoundly... (E.g. depressed)

DURATION/MOOD CHANGES: (<->)

Mercurial/quicksilver, volatile, affective incontinence, dramatic, excitable, transient, unstable, rapid mood fluctuation, labile, fluctuates, plastic, changeable, moodswings, flexible, < appropriate >, diurnal/seasonal mood cycles, short cycles (days), long cycles, shifts in tension, mobility of emotional state, consistent, showed little/normal/much variation in emotions, frozen, permanent

EPISODE OF AFFECT DISORDER:

Initial, single, sporadic, episodic, repetitive, recurrent, irregular recurrences, cyclothymic, cyclical, seasonal, annual, anniversary reactions, exacerbated, chronic, in remission

Recurrent episodes appear to be worsening as the depression is more severe, longer/shorter symptom-free periods, periods of improvement are to a lower level, and medication produces slower/less improvement

---

[1] Consider the possible effects of current medications. See section 33.4 Medications causeing Depression.

14.2 Anger: See also section 12.2 Rapport - Resistance for more behavioral aspects

GENERAL ASPECTS:

Sources of, intensity, direction, target, handling, coping methods, impulse control
Situational/state or personality/trait, anger out/in, guilt over anger

HOSTILITY/VERBAL HOSTILITY/INDIRECT ANGER: (<->):

Irritated	Temperamental	Hostile	Shouts
annoyed	whining	provoked	furious
disgruntled	restive	embittered	threatens
cranky	piqued	exasperated	enraged
miffed	"pissed off"	indignant	incensed
displeased	"burned up"	simmering	choleric
"snippy"	"bugged"	seething	bellicose
bothered	smoldering	infuriated	
	brooding		
grudging	sullen		
resentful	ill-tempered		
	bad-tempered		

VIOLENCE/AGGRESSIVE BEHAVIORS: See also section 16.19 Impulse control

14.3 Anxiety/Fear: See section 7.5 Anxiety for questions

AUTONOMIC NERVOUS SYSTEM/SOMATIC HYPERACTIVITY/OVER-AROUSAL:

Pallor or flushing	Shortness Of Breath	Dizziness	Clamminess
chest tightness	difficulty breathing	hot flashes	shaking
heart palpitations	chest pain	vertigo	sweaty palms
fast heartbeat/racing/ tachycardia	choking/smothering fast and deeper respiration	room spinning light-headedness faintness	cold sweats/chills excessive perspiration sweaty-forehead
diarrhea	air hunger	syncope	dry mouth
urgent urination	hyperventilation	"wobbly"	
stomach		"butterflies"	piloerection/
stomach churned	numbness	queasiness	"goose bumps"
nausea	tingling	all-over weakness	
dry heaves	Paraesthesias	unsteadiness	
"lump in throat"			

"Fight or flight" response/arousal: all of the above and: more acute hearing, spleen contraction, dilation of peripheral blood vessels, bronchioles widen, pupils dilate, more coagulates and lymphocytes in blood, adrenaline secreted, stomach acid production decreases, loss of bladder/anal sphincter control, decreased salivation, etc.

BEHAVIORAL FACETS OF ANXIETY

Motor Tension: trembling, muscle aches, tightness, twitching, feeling shaky, tremulous, body swaying, rigid posture, stiff neck/back/muscles, sits on edge of chair, inhibited movements, restlessness, easy fatigability, sneezing

"Nervous habits" (<->)

self-grooming	Can't sit still/relax	avoids eye contact	Panicked
scratching	leg/arm swinging		rushed out
fidgeting	rocking		vomited
repetitive movements	pacing		fainted
fretful	stretching		
muscle tension	self-hugging		
wringing hands	body swaying		Avoidance
clutching hands			behaviors
tapping	worried look		avoidant
scratching	nail biting		withdraws
yawning/sighing	flashes of smiles		
	tears/crying		
	wide-eyed		facial
agitated	brow grooves		expressions
	tense facies		of fear
moistens lips			"deadpan"
coughing	hands restrained/in pockets		
swallowing	rigid arms		
clears throat	shuffles feet		
heavy breathing	wobbly knees		

Speech/voice: inhibited, strained, quavery, tremor, stuttering, voice cracks, uncompleted/disconnected sentences.

Vigilance and Scanning:

Easily startled, jumpy, oversensitive to stimuli, over-reactive

Lessened concentration, erratic, minds goes blank, unable to proceed, unable to function, immobilized, freezes

Difficulty falling asleep or staying asleep, mind racing

Affective facets of Anxiety: (<->)

Terrified	Fearful	"Nervous"	Calm	Imperturbable
horrified	apprehensive	uneasy	phlegmatic	stolid
rigid	frightened	harried	steady	
panic attacks	alarmed	irritable	unemotional	
panicky	distraught	vulnerable	stable	
frozen		fragile	composed	
petrified		tense	nonchalant	
paralyzed		edgy	"cool"	
	"on edge"	unable to relax	confident	
	frazzled	"uptight"	*sang froid*	
	flighty	jittery		

Cognitive facets of Anxiety: (<->)

Worries: "a worrier," "a worry wart," thoughts of impending doom, exaggeration of the objective danger, desire to escape, anticipates dreadful occurrences/doom/catastrophe, "my world is caving in/getting out of hand"/feels threatened by people or events commonly seen as of little or no concern, upset by fantasies/imagined scenarios/criticisms/attacks/hurts, dread, fear of dying/being attacked/losing consciousness/going crazy/being rejected or abandoned, apprehensive, worrisome, rumination

Baffled, confused, jumbled thoughts, blurred thoughts, perplexed, bemused, lessened concentration, unable to recall/indecisive, forgetful, preoccupied, many errors, reduced creativity

Ill at ease, uneasy, overwhelmed/can't manage/can't get control, can't control thoughts

Depersonalization, derealization, preoccupied with bodily sensations. See section 16.13 Depersonalization and Derealization for descriptors

Diminished initiative, productivity, creativity

INTERPERSONAL FACETS OF ANXIETY: See also Chapter 13. Presentation of self

Thin-skinned, easily threatened/aroused to anxiousness, insecure, vulnerable, oversensitive, self-conscious, timid, timorous, uncertain what to say or how to act
Dependent, clinging
Avoids eye contact
Withdrawal, reduced involvement
Blames others, hypercritical, self-deprecation

ANXIETY: *(subjective):* See section 14.8 Panic

High internal tension, feels inept, nervous, can't handle stress/pressure/demands, vulnerable, low self-confidence/efficacy, insecure, "fluttery", "quavery", "feels like I'll explode/my heart will burst through my chest"

ANXIETY: *(inferred):*

No depth of feeling when recounting events, erratic, guardedness, rigidity, confuses self, self-induced pressures, jumps from one subject/topic to another, low frustration tolerance, low stress tolerance, low tolerance for ambiguity, impulsive/acts out

OTHER STATEMENTS:

Shifts in anxiety level during interview not/related to subjects of discussion
Having a cascade of symptoms
Accident proneness, susceptibility to minor illnesses

For a child:

Fears of animals, ghosts, demons, "the bogey man", darkness, getting lost, parental illness/disability/death/loss, punishment, being embarrassed/humiliated

14.4 Cyclothymia: Modified from Akiskal, *et al.* (1979). Also consider section 14.11 Bipolar II diagnosis.

Biphasic course, alternating manic and depressive patterns, between:

Pessimism, brooding	Optimism, care-free attitudes
Unexplained tearfulness	Excessive punning, joking
Lethargy, decreased speaking	Eutonia, talkativeness
Hypersomnia	Decreased need for sleep
Introversion, self-absorption	Uninhibited people-seeking
Mental confusion, apathy	Sharpened and creative thinking
Shaky self-esteem	Low self confidence and grandiose overconfidence

Marked unevenness in quantity of productivity (e. g. unusual working hours)

14.5 Depression: See section 7.10 Depression for questions

Affective facets of Depression:

ANHEDONIA: See also section 11.4 Behavioral Observations, Facial expression, and 14.1 Affects, Amount/Responsiveness, above

Absence of pleasure, apathy, boredom, loss of pleasure in living, "nothing tastes good anymore", joylessness, lack of satisfaction in previously valued activities/hobbies, loss of interests, no desire/energy to do anything, no fun in his/her life

Indifference, "couldn't care less", lowered/no desires, nothing good to look forward to in life, indifference to praise/reward, emotional impoverishment, drabness, colorless, coldness, emptiness

DYSPHORIA: (<->)

Wretched	Melancholy	sadness	moody
inconsolable	despondent	blue	petulant
anguished	gloomy	"down in the	whining
suicidal	dejected	dumps"	plaintive
miserable	sorrowful	beaten down	
desperate	forlorn	glum	
pathetic	bitter	tearful	
worn out	dysphoric	doleful	
drained	morose	dour	
exhausted	funereal	cheerless	
in pain	despairing	somber	
suffering	disconsolate	downcast	
	grave	gloomy outlook	
	profoundly sad	"down"	
	woeful	"wiped out"	
	profoundly unhappy	troubled	
	morbid	dispirited	
	somber	"bummed out"	
	downhearted		

Thoughts of suicide: see sections 7.27 Suicide questions and 16.35 Suicide ideation descriptors

Behavioral facets of Depression: Vegetative signs/physical malfunctioning:

SLEEP PATTERNS: See also section 16.32 Sleep disturbances

EATING:

Appetite/hunger increase or decrease, anorexia, fewer/more frequent meals, fasting, selective hungers, "comfort foods," binges, weight increase or decrease

PSYCHOMOTOR RETARDATION/ACCELERATION: See also section 11.4 Movement

Absence of/lessened spontaneous verbal/motor/emotional expressiveness, long reaction time to questions (indicate number of seconds), thoughts stop/slowed/laborious/impoverished/racing

LIBIDO: (sexual interest, not activity) See section 14.9 Sexuality

BOWEL/BLADDER HABIT CHANGES:

Diarrhea/constipation, increased frequency of urination, over-concern with elimination, chronic use or abuse of laxatives, sensations of abdominal distention or incomplete evacuation

OVER-USE OF:

Prescription and over-the-counter medications (analgesics, laxatives, sleeping aids, vitamins), alcohol, caffeine

APPEARANCE: See also Chapter 11.2 Behavior Observations - Appearance

Facies: Sad/fixed/expressionless/unsmiling facies, downcast face, distracted look, blank stare, furrowed brow
Close to tears/tearful/teary, tears well up, weepy/weeps, cries, blubbers, sobs,
Smiled without warmth, 'smiling depression,'

Dissipated, worn, drained, "a shell of a person", haphazard self-care, self neglect

Wrings hands, rubs forehead, shuffling gait
Little inflection, flat/expressionless/monotonous voice
Audible sighs

ENERGY:

Anergic, lowered energy, slowed down, listless, "needs to be pushed to get things done", "everything is an effort", easy fatigue, tired, feels "run down", mopes, muddles through, weakened, lethargic, de-energized, torpid, lassitude, "can't shake off the blues," energy is just adequate for life's tasks, inability to cope with routine responsibilities, weary, drained, exhausted

OTHER:
All appetites are muted
Diurnal variation, depression's symptoms are worse in morning and lessen as day wears on
Persistent physical symptoms which do not respond to treatment (especially headaches, digestive disorders, and chronic pain)

Cognitive facets of depression:

CARING/ENERGY INVESTMENT:

Hopeless	Pessimistic	cold	Bored
helpless	suspicious	unconcerned	indifferent
cynical	disappointed	stoic	unspontaneous
unchangeable	disillusioned	phlegmatic	apathetic
nihilistic	skeptical	ennui	
defeated		weary	
futile	discouraged	humorless	
negative	demoralized	malaise	
bleak	disenchanted	weltschmertz	
feeling lost	defeatist		
dreary	loss of ambition		
futurelessness	goalessness		
	resigned		
repetition/urging			
needed			

MENTAL DULLNESS: (<->)

inadequate	ruminative	confused	lost
unable to cope	slowed	decreased concentration	empty
	indecisive	perplexed	unclear
	excessive worrying	worsened memory	vague
	worrisome		meaningless
	mulls over	frustrated	

S/he needed time to mobilize/gather his/her thoughts, matter-of-fact

SELF-CRITICALNESS/BROODING: (<->) See section 14.6 Guilt and Shame

vulnerable	embarrassed	ashamed	humiliated	cowed
self-doubting	sorry	self-reproaching	suppressed rage	over-awed
threat sensitive	chagrined	"a failure"	self-hating	overwhelmed
criticism-sensitive	self-blaming	"inferior"	self-abusing	
rejection-sensitive	self-depreciating	fault-finding	"worthless"	
self-pitying	regretful	self-critical	low self-esteem	
"poor me"		"useless"	self-condemning	
	ineffectual	"a loser"	ironical	
self-distrusting	unproductive	"a freak"	sarcastic	
intimidated	"inadequate"	"wasted my life"		
	inept	"a misfit"		
		ruined life		
		"life is over"		

BECK'S DYSFUNCTIONAL COGNITIONS:
    All-or-Nothing thinking
    Dichotomous Thinking, Oversimplifying: black/white of good/bad, right/wrong
    Arbitrary Inference: overgeneralizing/basing a conclusion on too little data or one incident
    Labeling and Mislabeling
    Mental Filter
    Disqualifying the Positive
    Jumping to conclusions (without any or too little evidence)
    Mind Reading (assuming you know the other's thoughts, usually negative)
    Fortune Teller error:
    Selective Abstraction: attending to only the negative aspects of a situation
    Magnification or Minimization/Loss of proportion: exaggerating of minimizing the meaning of an
        event
    Emotional Reasoning: Because I feel afraid, there must be danger
    "Should" statements
    Overprediction that the future will be repetitions of the past
    Assumption of excessive/personal responsibility/Personalization
    Self reference/consciousness

These are from others including Ellis
    Catastrophizing
    Telescoping

OTHER STATEMENTS FOR COGNITIVE ASPECTS:

Demonstrated Beck's negative view of the self, world and future, cyclic negative thought processes,
    dysfunctional cognitions

Attributions are negative, stable, global, internal
Dwelt on past failures, lost opportunities, what could never be, roads not taken, etc.

"feels like I'm here physically but not mentally/really present"
Distrusts own mind/thinking processes, feelings/guts
No plans for him/herself, no future, nothing to look forward to in life, only an empty repetition of
    meaningless actions
Alexthymia

Social facets of Depression:

INTERPERSONAL: (<->)

Reclusive	Avoids people	distrustful	irritating	strained
inaccessible	distances	resentful	irritated	relationships
asocial	self-absorbed	argument-	bitter	dependent
barricades self away	withdraws	ative	demanding	passive
isolates	low social interest	suspicious	crabby	unassertive
hermit-like	subdued	feels scorned	easily irritated	wary
secludes	painfully shy	feels abandoned	easily annoyed	
	separates from life/others			

Less talkative

SUPPORT-SEEKING: See also section 13.3 Dependent/Surgent

Complains of life's unfairness, righteous, gossips, envious, gripes, futily indignant, sympathy seeking, whiney, self-pitying, manipulative, emotionally hungry, seeks support only when in crisis, finds others always inadequately supportive or sympathetic

Other facets of Depression:

S/he is depressed because forced into dependency by disability/losses/injury
Depression is worse during winter (consider Seasonal Affective Disorder)
Dexamethasone suppression test results supported ...
Self-defeating, self-victimizing. See section 17.24 Self-defeating Personality Disorder

Masked Depression: Modified from Lopez-Ibor (1990)

PSYCHOSOMATIC SYMPTOMS:

Gastrointestinal: nausea, vomiting, gastralgia, meteorism, aerophagia, hiccough, constipation, diarrhea, ulcerative colitis, anorexia, bulemia
Respiratory: apnea, vasomotor rhinitis, asthma
Genitourinary: nervous bladder, impotency, premature ejaculation, hypersexuality, "frigidity," amenorrhea,
Cardiovascular: tachycardia, palpitations, extra systoles, precordial pain, cardiac phobia
Metabolic: obesity, thinness
Skin: eczema, neurodermatitis, alopecia

PSYCHOLOGICAL DISORDERS:

Self-destructive behaviors, sexual deviations, twilight states, alcoholism, addictions, gambling, phobias, obsessions, dysmorphophobia, kleptomania/theft, hypochondria, delusions, accident proneness

For a Child: (5-15 years)

Irritable mood, long lasting/frequent
Apathy, lack of interest in playing, isolation, agitation, despair, hypersensibility, insecurity, boredom, temper tantrums, fugues, feelings of inferiority, nihilistic thoughts, suicidal impulses, obsessive thoughts
School problems: learning difficulties, school phobia, dyslexia, concentration difficulties,
Vegetative symptoms: sleep disorders, terrors, appetite, weeping, asthenia, abdominal pains, alopecia aureata, tics, eczema, allergies, anorexia, bulemia, asthma
Other: Substance abuse, offenses, accident proneness, neurasthenia, dysmorphophobia feelings of emptiness, guilt, depersonalization,

ASSESSMENT SCALES for depression include: the Hamilton Rating Scale for Depression (Hamilton, 1960), the Beck Depression Inventory (1961), the Zung Self-Rating Depression Scale (Zung, 1965), and the Depression Adjective Checklist (Lubin, 1965).

Embarrassment: see 14.6 Guilt/Shame, below

Suicide: See section 13.19 Suicide

14.6 Guilt/Shame:

Self-condemning, self-reproaching, apologetic, penitent, begging forgiveness, repentant, pleading, sorry, at fault, ashamed, chagrined, contrite, remorseful, concerned, burdened, responsible,
Punitive superego, transgresses superego boundaries, unacceptable impulses, fears annihilation

Embarrassment, humiliation, mortification, guilt proneness, disgraced, reproached, depreciated, devalued, humbled, wishes to disappear/become invisible, avoids disclosure of flaws, hide inadequacies

Inferiority, fears rejection/abandonment, fails to attain goal, measure up

Cold, hardened, unreformed, cynical, unrepentant, conscienceless, shameless, unscrupulous, parasitic, incorrigible, predatory

ASSESSMENT: The Mosher Guilt Scales (1968) assesses sex guilt, morality-conscience guilt, and hostility guilt

The following distinctions are modified from Potter-Effron (1988).

CENTRAL TRAIT	SHAME	GUILT
Failure	Of being, falling short of goals, of whole self	Of doing, of moral self
Primary Feelings	Inadequate, deficient, worthless, exposed, disgust, disgrace	Bad, wicked, evil, remorseful
Precipitating Event	Unexpected, possibly trivial event	Actual or contemplated violation values
Involvement of Self	Total self image is involved: "How could I have done that?"	Partial self image involvement: "How could I have done that?"
Central Fear	Of abandonment, not belonging	Of punishment
Origins	Positive identification with parents	Need to control aggressive impulses
Primary Defenses	Desire to hide (withdrawal), denial, rage, perfectionism, gradiosity, shamelessness	Obsessive thinking, paranoid, intellectualization, seeking excessive punishment
Positive Functions	Awareness of limits of human condition, discovery of separate self, sense of modesty, identification with community, mastery, autonomy	Sublimation, moral behavior, initiative, reparation

14.7 Mania: See section 7.17 Mania for questions, and section 14.4 for Cyclothymia

AFFECTIVE FACETS OF MANIA: (<->)

Cheerful	High	Hypomanic	Exuberant	Manic	Ecstatic
light-hearted	gay	buoyant	elated	laughing	exalted
positive	laughing	silly	ebullient	binges	rapturous
bright	buoyant	giddy	false joy		euphoric
vivid	jovial	excessively	cheerful		false elation
intense	elevated	boisterous			
	effervescent			irritability	panics
				anger	hopeless

Labile	unstable	rapid fluctuation	accelerating course

BEHAVIORAL FACETS OF MANIA:

(<->) Fast/rapid speaking, rapid-fire speech, hyperverbal, overtalkative, overabundant, loud, verbose, garrulous, tirades, singing, rhyming, punning

(<->) Periods of hyperactivity/over-activity, paces, restless, speeded up, accelerated, quickened, fast, going fast, racing, frenzied, manic, anger, assaultive

Overconfident, exaggerated view of own abilities, starts many activities but does not finish or follow through with most

Insomnia, decreased need for sleep, no acknowledgment of fatigue

Incautious, poor social judgement, fearless, engaging in reckless activities (e.g. dangerous driving, foolish business investments or buying sprees, impulsive spending, sexual indiscretions or acting out) or greatly increased need for sexual activities, increased sexual drive/interests, hypersexual, disinhibited activities, increased smoking, telephoning

COGNITIVE FACETS OF MANIA: (<->)

Expansive	pressured speech	Flight of ideas	loosened associations	delusions
exaggeration	over-productive	illogical	disjointed	incoherent
grandiosity		racing thoughts	disorganized	bizarre
		thought	disoriented	
	idiosyncratic	bombardment	disconnected	
little or no insight	associations	word plays	thoughts	hallucinatory
				experiences
limited concentration				disorientation
brief attention span		sexual/religious	abrupt topic	ideas of reference
distractible		preoccupations	changes	
hyperbole			frivolous	

SOCIAL/INTERPERSONAL FACETS OF MANIA:

(<->) Impatient, intolerant, insulting, uncooperative, resistive, negativistic, critical, provocative, suspicious, angry, irritable, over-sensitive, touchy, easy/inappropriate anger, nasty, loud, abusive, crude, foul language, swears, curses, blasphemes, vulgar, bathroom language, obscene

Suspicious, guarded, distrustful, believes other collude against him/her, asserts that s/he was tricked into ..., denies validity or reality of all criticisms

Gregarious, likeable, dramatic, entertaining, pleasant, seductive, vivacious, cracks jokes, prankish insincere, naive, infantile, silly, *witzelsucht*

Entitled, self-important, grandiose, cocksure, emphatic, self-confident, "hutzpah"

Dominating, controlling, boastful, challenging, surgent, conflicts with authority figures

DELUSIONS: See section 16.11 Delusions

Fantasies of romantic involvement, grandiose business plans
False mania based on delusions

OTHER ASPECTS OF MANIA:

Euphoria: consider general paresis

14.8 Panic: See 14.3 Anxiety

Fear of fear, rapid escalation of anxiety, loss of control over anxiety, intense fear/discomfort, Unexpected/unpredicted/"out of the blue"
Fears of loss of control/die/go crazy/embarrass self/do something uncontrolled
Anxiety symptoms: see section 14.3 Anxiety, ANS symptoms

14.9 Sexuality: See section 7.22 for Sexual History Questions and 9.4 for Sexual Adjustment

ATTITUDES AND BEHAVIOR:

(<->) Disgusted, apathetic, inhibited, ashamed, puritanical, prudish, prim, restrained, passive, hesitant, permissive, romantic, amorous, erotic, sensual, assertive, passionate, seductive, over-active, soliciting, compulsive, demanding, lustful, lewd, wanton, aggressive, assaultive

Increased or decreased: desire, arousal, activity/relations, satisfaction, hypo/hypersexuality, reluctance to initiate, slow to respond, previously inhibited interests

Abstinent, celibate

Shame: See section 14.5 Guilt

14.10 Other Emotions:

SENSE OF HUMOR (<->):

Cosmic, wry, deadpan, dry, ironic, cynical, sarcastic, sophisticated, gentle, mirthful, playful, joking, jesting, jovial, impish, funny, entertaining, tells stories/jokes, teasing, flip, wise cracks, mocks, silly, slap-stick, witty, puns, off-color or offensive jokes, inappropriate remarks excused as "just kidding", tendentious, hostile, offensive, absent/non-existent sense of humor, humorless, "stuffed shirt", takes self too seriously, inappropriate laughter

Mirth response is brief/flashes/grim little smile, spontaneous, excellent/normal/adequate/diminished/ absent/sarcastic/ironical
He/she is capable of responding but not initiating humor

GRIEF:

Distress, sorrow, gloom, anguish, despair, heartache, pain, woe, suffering, affliction, troubles
Preoccupied with loss/loved one/consequences/memories, easily tearful, slowed thinking and responding with long latencies of response, stares into space
Feels helpless, vulnerable, useless, lowered self-esteem
Denial, anger, bargaining, acceptance, transcendence

Unresolved/morbid/pathological grief:

Denial of death, absence of grief, pathological identification, hypochondriasis, chronic depression, psychogenic pain, chronic grieving, avoidance of cues to deceased, isolation, re-attachment

Decreased immune system functioning,, increased use of drugs and alcohol, depression, over/misuse of medical care for grief.

A good starting point is Callahan, *et al.* (1992).

AMBIVALENCE:

Mixed feelings, conflicted, at cross purposes, "left hand doesn't know what right hand is doing", alternates, "want and don't want it at same time"
Indecisive, can't decide/make up mind, stuck

14.11 Proposed forms of Bipolar Disorders:

Form	Title	DSM-III-R
Bipolar I	Mania and depression	Bipolar disorder
Bipolar II	Hypomania and depression	Bipolar, NOS
Bipolar III	Cyclothymic personality	Cyclothymic disorder
Bipolar IV	Hypomania or mania precipitated by antidepressant drugs	Organic mood disorder
Bipolar V	Familial history of bipolar depression	Major depression
Bipolar VI	Mania without depression	Bipolar disorder

14.12 Other Statements about Affects:

Her/his affect was brighter than one would expect from someone in her/his position in life.
S/he is experiencing mental turmoil/upset/distress.

15. Standard Statements for a Mental Status Report

As there is no consensus on the inter-relationship of these components of cognition they are presented here in the order of roughly increasing complexity of their performance.

15

M S Stmts

Reliability/Trustworthiness: See Section 8.8, Reliability

15.1 No Pathological Findings:

Examination is normal/benign, In No Acute Distress, in No Apparent Distress, Within Normal Limits, average, unremarkable, intact, nothing unusual,
No limitations in any of the domains assessed by this/these instruments/examinations.

No evidence/signs of a thought disorder, major affective, cognitive or behavioral disorder were elicited.
No abnormalities of thought, affect, or behavior, no gross abnormalities, nothing bizarre, no cognitive slippage. I did not find any unusual kinds of logic or strange associations.
No/obvious indications of psychosis or organicity, no hallucinations in any field
S/he experiences thoughts in a spontaneous and normal manner, lucid and coherent, no disordered mentation, mentation is intact
No indication of disordered mentation in the form of incoherent or incomprehensible speech

He/she is in full/partial/marginal/shaky remission.
I failed to elicit any symptomatic behaviors/indicants of previously described symptoms or disorders.
Based on current observations there is no decompensation, deterioration, or exacerbation of past conditions.

No drug no alcohol abuse/legal/psychiatric history of diagnosis or treatment

Based on behavior observed during the interview, I believe ....
In my professional judgement ....

15.2 Levels of Consciousness: (<->) See also section 15.3 Glasgow Coma Scale, below.

Coma, comatose, coma vigil, unarousable, unresponsive, obtunded

Stuporous, delirious, responsive only to persistent or noxious stimulation, post-ictal, twilight/dreamy state, drifts off, fluctuates, arousable/rousable, semi-coma

Lethargy, reduced wakefulness, somnolent, only briefly responsive with a return to unconsciousness

Clouded consciousness, drowsy, falls asleep, responding requires heightened effort, lessened ability to perform tasks, frequent hesitations, starting/startles, disoriented, groggy, "drugged", under the influence of medications which ..., in a daze

Alert, responds to questions, attentive, makes eye-contact, interacts, asks questions, converses, alert, lucid, intact, was spontaneously verbal

Glasgow Coma Scale: Teasdale and Jenvet, (1974) for more precise numerical rating. See also section 6.2 Ranchos Los Amigos Scale

15.3 Orientation: See section 6.4 for Orientation questions

Incorrectly identifies self by name, mistakes/confuses present location, correct time, objects, others, Mistakes/confuses dates/persons/places
Is off the mark by __ years/months/days

While s/he did appear to be technically/oriented in the most simple sense/on simplistic measures ...
His/her appreciation and awareness of self was quite poor
Oriented to ___ but not to ___

NORMAL ORIENTATION: S/he was fully oriented times three/to time, place and person, times four/to things.

15.4 Attention: See section 6.5 for Attention questions

Unaware, unable to attend, inattentive, ignores questions, attention could not be gained nor held, attention limited by extraneous sounds/concurrent activities/fantasies/affects/memories, unengaged, daydreams, autistic reverie, muses, "wool-gathering"

Distractible, attention wandered, attentive only to irrelevancies, responses are irrelevant, unable to reject interfering stimuli from environment/viscera/affects, guided by internal not external stimuli, easily overloaded by stimulation, needed much repetition, cannot repeat familiar lists/phrases, attends only for brief intervals, can't absorb details needed for responsible judgements beyond the routine

Low attending skills, cannot follow a three stage command/written directions, cannot attend to coping/adaptive/purposeful tasks, cannot spell words forward and backward, preoccupied, selective attention/inattention, shows lapses of attention, redirectable

NORMAL ATTENTION: focuses/selects the relevant among the irrelevant aspects of a situation, maintains the focus, resists distraction, sufficient for question responding/interview/ psychotherapy/effective life management, shows freedom from distractibility, capable of prolonged attention but occasionally distracted, vigilant

15.5 Concentration/Task Persistence: See section 6.6 for Concentration questions

Unable to maintain concentration for more than several minutes/duration of the examination, defective when compared with peers, preoccupations with self or other interfere with, by report able to maintain for several hours, had difficulty with tasks requiring vigilance

It appeared that performance anxiety/fear of failure/fear of being found wanting/inadequate greatly interfered with his/her mental functioning, anxiety/preoccupations lessened/interfered with his/her concentration/immediate/recent memory

On SERIAL SEVENS: (<->)
  Was able to subtract 7 from 100 (#) times/down to 2 accurately.
  Did serial sevens down to (#) in (# seconds) with (#) errors when I stopped her/him.
  Was able to do serial 7s (#) times before making an error
  Self-corrected errors in the sequence.
  Serial sevens were performed with (#) errors but subsequent subtractions were accurate based on the prior numbers.
  Was un/able to subtract serial sevens accurately/could sustain concentration only to the first plateau/on (#) trials even with sincere effort.
  Demonstrated adequate numerical reasoning but incorrect computations because of interfering anxiety

  Shows decrements/lessening/limitations of mental efficiency

For a child: See sections 12.4 Response to the Methods of Evaluation

Daydreams, has strong/weak subjects, doesn't complete assignments in class/homework, materials are disorganized/messy, forgets teacher's instructions, has to be reminded to sit still/pay attention

Rancho Los Amigos Cognitive Scale can be used to assess the level of function in carrying out purposeful behavior. See section 6.2

15.6 Dementia: See also sections 15.7 Memory, 15.10 Reasoning, and 15.14 Judgement

PHASES OF DECLINE IN ALZHEIMER'S: Adapted from Reisberg (1983, 1985)

Stage	Cognitive Deficits	Personality Changes
1. Forgetfulness	Complaints of memory deficit such as forgetting names that were formerly well known or misplacing familiar objects but without deficits in work or social situations.	Appropriate concern with mild forgetfulness
2. Early confusional	Increased cognitive decline and signs of confusion: getting lost going to a familiar place; family and coworker notice forgetting of words/names; poor reading comprehension; inability to concentrate.	Denial of memory problems but anxiety accompanies symptoms of forgetfulness and confusion
3. Late confusional	Decreased knowledge of current events; forgetting of one's personal history; decreased ability to handle finances or to travel	Very obvious use of denial about memory problems. Flattening of affect and withdrawal from more challenging situations
4. Early dementia	Moderately severe decline and intensified confusion: inability to recall major current aspects of one's life such as address, phone number or the names of close family members/children; inability to recall major personal facts like name of one's high school; some time disorientation (e. g. for date); may need assistance with choosing proper clothing	
5. Middle dementia	Severe cognitive decline and confusion: occasionally forgets name of spouse; largely unaware of all recent events and experiences and many past life events; unaware of surroundings; does not know season of year; can distinguish familiar from unfamiliar persons.	Totally dependent on others for survival. Severe personality and emotional changes such as delusions, obsessions, and highly anxious. Fails to follow through on intentions due to forgetfulness
6. Late dementia	Very severe decline and confusion: loss of all verbal abilities; incontinent, need for assistance in eating and toileting; loss of basic psychomotor skills, e. g. inability to walk	Unresponsive to all but the simplest communications. Total loss of social skills and personality

15.7 Memory: See section 6.9 for Memory questions

INDICATIONS OF DEFECT: (<->)

> Forgetful, "spotty memory", "absent-minded", confused, uncertain/expresses doubts, befuddled, muddled, foggy, dreamy presentation, "spaced out", detached, Ganser's syndrome, confabulates, falsifies, perseverates, contaminations, diffusions
> Poor historian: confuses time frames/sequences, non-sequential, overfocussed on externals/ situational issues, vague, hesitant, overlong, guesses/estimates/approximates, disjointed, gaps, skips over, skimpy/superficial history

CAPABILITY:

> Can only <u>recognize</u>, sluggish <u>recall</u>, recalls only with much prompting/cueing, <u>reproduces</u> with much difficulty/inaccuracy

AMNESIA:

> Anteriograde (loss of experiences or materials learned since pathology/trauma), retrograde (loss of premorbid learning), <u>T</u>otal <u>G</u>lobal <u>A</u>mnesia, ictus amnèsique, fugue, amnestic/amnesic disorder, Korsakoff's syndrome, Wernicke's syndrome

PARAMNESIA:

> *Fausse reconnaissance,* retrospective falsification, confabulation, pre-knowledge of events/other's speech, *déjà vu, dejà entendu, déjà pensé, jamais vu,* hypermnesia, anomia, agnosia, propagnosia

IMPACT OF MEMORY DEFECT ON PATIENT: (<->)

> No/poor/effective/maximal use of compensatory mechanisms/coping skills, constricts life-style, ignores, denies

STATEMENTS ABOUT MEMORY PERFORMANCE:

Normal Memory:
> All components of memory are all grossly intact
> S/he is able to recount personal history normally.
> His/her remote, recent and immediate memories appear to be intact as far as I can determine without independent verification of the historical facts.

As Historian:
> Un/able to give an account of his/her activities/life events in a chronological order
> Memory, as reflected in his/her ability to provide an intact, substantial, sequential, detailed, and logical history/narrative was defective/quite poor/poor/adequate/normal/exceptional/unusual because.
> Memory for events in relationship to time was vague/murky/chaotic
> Could not recall the time frames of school/work/family development/treatments
> Client does not offer a rich description of important events from memory

Defective memory:
Un/able to recall three objects/words after five/ten minutes of different/unrelated activities
Faulty, limited recall, memory is limited/deficient/defective/a problem in all time frames
Memory is organically intact but anxiety/depression interfere
Defective/normal/exceptional in processes of registration, retention and, recall
Defective/normal/exceptional in immediate/short-term retention/recent/recent past/remote memory.
Shows the pattern of memory deficits typical of those with/with a history of (diagnosis) _____
_____ memory is not affected/normal but _____ memory is defective/exceptional
Remote and recent memories appear to be intact but there is an emptiness and lack of color in his/her descriptions of critical events

OTHER ASPECTS OF MEMORY:

Characteristics of malignant and benign senescent forgetfulness: From La Rue (1982)

Malignant	*Benign*
Shortened retention time	Failures to recall are limited to relatively unimportant parts of an experience (e.g. a name or date)
Inability to recall event of the recent past, including not only unimportant facts but the experience itself	Details forgotten on one occasion may be recalled at another time
Accompanied by disorientation to place and time and, gradually, to person	"Forgotten" data belong to remote as opposed to recent past
	Subjects are aware of shortcomings and may apologize or compensate

TECHNICAL TERMS FOR MEMORY:

Active/working/short-term memory
Acquisition, encoding, re-coding, chunking, rehearsal, transfer, storage, retrieval,
Forgetting: decay, displacement, interference, retroactive and proactive inhibition, consolidation block theory, retrieval failure theory, explicit memory defect
Effects of: primacy, recency, vividness, frequency
Methods of loci, mnemonics, elaborative rehearsal, tip-of-the-tongue phenomenon,
Types: episodic, generic, semantic, eidetic
Tests: explicit, implicit, spatiotemporal markers, priming, new learning, recall, recognition, sense of familiarity

---

15.8 Information: See section 6.10 for Fund of Information questions

Impoverished/deficient fund of information/general knowledge, unaware of current/practical/general information, doesn't know the facts regarding his/her culture
His/her fund of factual knowledge is low/extensive/spotty
He/she is unaware of many basic factual, measurement, historical, and geographical concepts

Limited education was apparent/demonstrated in low levels of the information typically acquired in grade school.
Considering his/her cultural background, level of formal and self-education her/his information was...

15.9 Stream of Thought: Speech as a Reflection of Cognition. See also section 11.5 Speech Behavior and 15.10 Reasoning

AMOUNT/PRODUCTIVITY: (<->)

Impoverished	laconic	Normal	rapid	Flight of ideas
moves slowly		spontaneous	overabundant	
restricted	hesitant	average	"logorrhea"	
decreased	slowed	abundant	copious	
unelaborated				
under-productive				
paucity				

NORMAL PRODUCTIVITY:

Showed an average amount of thoughts and they were neither speeded nor slowed/moved at a normal pace
Seems normal from the perspective of productivity, relevance, and coherence

COHERENCE: (<->)

Word salad, incomprehensible, incoherent, chaotic, repetitive, perseverative

Neologisms, condensations, clang associations, loosened associations, thought/associational disturbance/disorder, cognitive slippage, blocked, over-inclusive, 'silly' conclusions

Tangential, drifting, circumstantial, derailment, rambling, discursive, digressive/digresses, circuitous, circular, "rattles on", irrelevant, distracted, no stepwise progressions, no logical sequences, lacking internal logic, connects associations by small and unusual similarities, needed to be refocussed/redirected

Goal-directed, clear cause-and-effect thinking, logical, coheres with questions asked, pertinent, sequential, relevant, coherent, to-the-point, rational, linear

CONTINUITY: (<->)

Incoherent	Loose	Idiosyncratic	disconnected	Clear
incomprehensible	circumstantial	unusual	topic changes	realistic
clang associations	irrelevancies	associations	difficult to	rational
neologisms	tangential	personal	follow	lucid
word salad	vague	meanings	fragmented	consistent
confabulations	derailed	poorly defined	perplexing	coherent
verbigerations	rambling	conjectural	flighty	relevant
perseverative	garbled	preoccupied	confusing	integrated
chaotic	confused	unclear	disjointed	goal directed
jabbers	sidetracked		mushy thinking	intricate
babbles	evasive			logical
prattles	distracted		Byzantine	pertinent
autoecholalia	digressive		baffling	easy to
	circumlocutions		incorrect	follow
	paraphrases		conclusions	intact
	word substitutions		indefinite	sequential
	non-sequential			not pre-
	jumbled			occupied
	illogical			articulate
	circular			
	imprecise			
	elliptical			
	circuitous			

NORMAL THOUGHT CONTINUITY:

Her/his replies answered questions appropriately.
S/he presented her/his thoughts in an appropriately paced, understandable and relevant fashion.
His/her thoughts were clear, coherent, well organized, goal-directed and relevant to the subject at hand.
S/he reached the goal of his/her thought processes without introducing any irrelevant material.
His/her train of thought was goal-directed, relevant, and logical.
His/her stream of thought was coherent, focussed, and without digressions, irrelevancies, disturbances of logic or bizarreness.
There was no tangentiality, circumstantiality, or distractibility.

CONTENT: See also section 16.11 Delusions

personalized	trivial	obscene	over-detailed	self-critical
idiosyncratic	platitudes	profane	preoccupations	self-doubting
eccentric	empty	scatological	obsessions	ambivalences
odd	oversimple	sexual	over-valued ideas	
selective		earthy	magical thinking	injustices
carefully chosen		vulgarities		plaintive
sentimental	life situation	pornographic		accusatory
flowery	stressors	impolite	running away	regrets
philosophical	illnesses	blasphemous	escape	tragedies
bizarre themes	disabilities	sexual	violence	frustrations
magical think-	family/relatives		self-destruction	
ing		monothematic	suicidal impulses	

NORMAL THOUGHT CONTENT:

No obsessions or phobias, ideas of reference, hallucinations, delusions, faulty perceptions, perceptual disturbance, misinterpretations of consensual reality, or psychotic distortions. Not preoccupied with obsessions, phobias, or suicide.

PREOCCUPATIONS: See also sections 16.11 Delusions, 16.22 Obsessions, and Content, above

S/he is immersed in issues/themes of:

Mental health	Religion	Sexuality
obsessions	over-piety	
compulsions	excessive prayer	
fears/phobias	blasphemous ideas	Philosophy
symptoms	denigrating activities	
	irreligious practices/acts	
Death and dying	fears/delusions about clergy/theology	
suicide		
homicide	Relationships	Persecution (See 16.24 Paranoia)
dying	self-centeredness	
morbid thoughts	guilt, sinfulness	
losses	shame/embarrassment	His/her plight

Somatic/hypochondriacal concerns
current physical illness, mortal illnesses, popular diseases
S/he is understandably and appropriately preoccupied with her/his health
His/her thoughts about ___ (e.g. health problems) dominate his/her thinking but are not exclusive or preoccupying.

DISSOCIATION: (<->)

Day-dreaming, fanciful, trance, hysterical attack/episode, amnesia, fugue, somnambulism, automatic writing, out of body experience, extra-terrestrial travel, previous lives lived

OTHER STATEMENTS ABOUT STREAM OF THOUGHT:

Fails to answer questions	Loss of goal	Inter-penetration of themes
Over-inclusive	Loss of segmental set	Decreased speed of processing
Spontaneous but unproductive		

SUMMARY STATEMENTS ABOUT STREAM OF THOUGHT:

Speech was relevant and appropriate and without evidence of unusual ideation
No impairment reflective of disordered mentation
There was a normal flow of ideas/continuity
His/her associations were well organized
Shows good grammatical complexity
His/her logic was easy to follow although the responses were superficial

Does little analytic or discriminatory thinking
Converses in response to questions rather than speaking spontaneously, self sufficient in providing
    responses but volunteered little additional information, would not enlarge/expand on topics of
    interest, little/no elaboration of responses to my questions

Word retrieval deficits/reports "forgetting"/has difficulty finding words/groped for words, sudden
    stopping in mid-sentence/speech
Great difficulty gathering thoughts rather than in finding words
Substituted related words approximating the definitive/appropriate term
Paraphrastic errors, dysnomias, unusual word and sentence formations, errors of syntax,
        constructional dyspraxia, malapropisms
Alexia, alexethymia

When interrupted became confused and rambled

15.10 Reasoning/Abstract Thinking/Concept Formation: See section 6.16 to 6.19 for questions about similarities, absurdities, proverbs and concepts

Level OF INTERPRETATION: (<->)

Greatly defective, failed to grasp nature of question, overly-concrete, it was not possible to find proverbs simple enough for him/her to interpret, no evidence of abstract thinking or even extended thought processes

Distorted by thought disorder showing personification, bizarreification delusions

Concrete (noted only surface features or appearance aspects of stimuli), offers only very specific examples, paraphrases, reasons in a concrete manner, stimulus-bound associations, "I've heard that one before" (without elaboration)

Simplistic, difficulty with concept formation/judgment, similarities/differences, similarities/ comparative analogies, absurdities, abstraction, proverbs

Couldn't use appropriate/expected levels of abstraction in dealing with test materials, mixes up categories in hierarchies, poor abstract thinking and concept-handling ability, degree of generalization was over-broad/narrow, some difficulty with reasoning at an easy/moderately difficult/difficult level, offered unusual/idiosyncratic/antisocial interpretations

Functional levels of interpretation, responds only in terms of the uses for the stimulus item

Offered popular interpretations

Abstracted common properties of the stimuli (noted relation-ships between stimuli/shared structural features) used principles, reasoned abstractly, offers similar proverbs/spontaneous re-phrasings, comprehensive level of reasoning

Overly abstract, attended only to selected/irrelevant aspects of stimuli, artistic, overly philosophical/obscure/arcane references, highly theoretical, Byzantine

NORMAL ABSTRACTION:

He/she was able to form concepts well.
Handled ideas well and without concreteness
He/she was able to identify similarities, differences, and absurdities
Was able to analyze the meaning of simple proverbs, all at appropriate levels of abstraction
S/he could give me the deep meanings of the proverbs I offered.
S/he was able to respond with an abstract relationship between pairs of terms/items I presented to her/him.
Had common sense, functional understanding of everyday objects

LOGICAL INFERENCE:

Faulty inductive/deductive inference/reasoning, reaches conclusions based on false/faulty premises, errors of logic and judgement, incorrect conclusions, unable to relevantly support answers given
Autistic, dereistic, idiosyncratic, *non-sequiturs, pars pro toto,* trance logic, paleologic

15.11 Arithmetic: See also sections 6.15 for questions and 28.4 Math Ability descriptors

OVERALL: (<->)

Anumerate, lacks practical/everyday/survival/basic mathematical skills, dyscalculia
His/her skills are approximately equivalent to those mastered in school grade __(#)

FINANCIAL: See section 25.8 Financial skills

15.12 Question Handling: See also section 12.1 Relating to the Context of the Examination

Did not understand give and take of question and answer format/did not grasp nature of questions, gave inappropriate responses, not relevant, nor logical, nor goal directed

15.13 Social Maturity: See also 15.14 Social Judgement

When/as compared with others of same age/culture/education s/he demonstrated ....

IRRESPONSIBILITY: See also section 17.4 Antisocial personality

Denies/lies about responsibilities, steals/destroys other's property, cheats, blames innocents, shows no guilt, offers no explanations, fakes guilt, offers only empty," phoney" apologies, not remorseful, falsely begs/pleads, "crocodile tears," refuses to pay debts/for property destroyed

On the job s/he resists/doesn't cooperate with/ignores/defies rules/directions/deadlines, starts many tasks but does not complete any, manipulates coworkers into doing his/her work, "cons", needs close/continuous supervision, Absent WithOut Leave/slips away, tardy/takes too many/over-long rest periods/breaks/leaves early, intoxicated at work

SELF-CENTEREDNESS: See also section 17.15 Narcissistic personality

Manipulates, unrealistic/lacks/only immediate goals, selfish, uncaring, resents limits, self indulgent, impulsive, arousal seeking, acts out

FINANCIAL: See section 25.8 Financial Skills

SOCIAL: See also Chapter 26. Social functioning

Resistant to authorities (parents, supervisor, police, human service professionals), chooses/imitates inappropriate or pathological models, touches others/without consent/self inappropriately

Has only limited contact with others so little opportunity to behave inappropriately
Teases, threatens vaguely/to leave/revenge/destruction of property/violence, threatens when confronted with own irresponsible behaviors, intimidates

SUMMARY STATEMENTS:

S/he is as mature as his/ her age peers, is only pseudo-mature, has been 'parentified' by his/her family, is over-mature
Never/rarely/often/usually plays/socializes with/relates to persons of his/her own age group.
Prefers to relate to things/paper/numbers/ideas/people.

15.14 Social/Moral Judgement and Knowledge: See also sections 6.19 for Social Judgement questions, and 15.13 Social Maturity and 15.19 Decision Making for other descriptors

DEFECTIVE UNDERSTANDING/ LACKS "COMMON SENSE" :

Has substantial defects in his/her capacity to appreciate common/consensual reality
His/her thoughts are rational but not realistic
Has impaired ability to make reasonable and realistic life decisions
Will make major decisions without sufficient information/impulsively/depending on hearsay/ because he/she doesn't want to refuse a friend, impulsive, immature, infantile, awkward, Irresponsible
Would make decisional errors under even the mildest stress
Seems guided by false beliefs
Heedless, reckless, feckless, careless

NORMAL JUDGEMENT/HAS "COMMON SENSE"

Has common sense understandings, commonsensical
Subscribes to the usual explanations of people's motivations
Sought treatment for medical/psychological problems

Learns from experience/feedback/other's mistakes/vicariously/ or from correction/instruction
" Street-smart"

S/he is a thoughtful person who understands the likely outcome of his/her behavior and thinks ahead.
Responsible, understood/anticipates the likely consequences of his/her behavior/actions
Understands and can plan ahead effectively
Able to identify and control behaviors which would be harmful to her/him and contrary to acceptable rules/beyond the limits of the society/social group/community,

PROPRIETY/IMPROPRIETY:

Distinguishes socially acceptable behaviors from those not and acts on this understanding
Social judgement is intact to the extent of not displaying outlandish or bizarre behaviors
inappropriate to social interactions

Acted contrary to acceptable behavior
Judgement is intact in terms of understanding (e.g. the demand characteristics of social settings) but not in terms of behaviors
Did not comprehend the expected/usual consequences of his/her behaviors nor the impact/ impression made upon others
Inadequately cognizant/aware of the basic social conventions

VICTIMIZATION:

Engaged in actions harmful to self
Has been taken advantage of repeatedly
Not discriminating in choice of companions
Makes blatantly defective and self-damaging choices

PRACTICAL REASONING:

is defective requiring close support/monitoring to avoid loss/damage/exploitation, would be easily
mislead and swindled/misused/taken advantage of
Was sufficient for independent living/assisting his/her supportive person

OTHER STATEMENTS:

Has difficulty with performing the tasks supportive of/related to carrying out the decisions made
Given the defective quality of her/his thinking/understanding judgement has to be impaired
Has a lifelong history of ineffective coping
Evaluation of subject's judgement as based on a comparison with premorbid state or expected
ability based on intellect/age/education/social experience is ...
Executive functions: decision making, social perception, flexibility of thinking, judgement, generates
alternatives/solutions/position

For a child:
Excessive imagination, confuses wishes/fears/impulses with objective/consensual reality

15.15 Test Judgement:

Had reasonable responses to hypothetical judgement questions,
Responded appropriately to imaginary situations requiring social judgement/knowledge of the
norms/usual rules/customs and expectations of society.
Performance on the judgement questions asked/tests used was poor/adequate/good/normal/
expected/excellent which suggests that in the external/social/'real' world s/he would ...

15.16 Reality testing: See also 15.14 Social Judgement

Intact, functional, not distorted by psychodynamics, defenses or psychopathology, perceives the social world
as do most people, understands cause-effect links as do other people, shares common attributions of
causality

Functional/adequate/good/extensive fund of knowledge, awareness of the external world.

<hr>

15.17 Insight: (<->) See section 6.22 for Insight questions

NIL OR LITTLE:

No insight, blindly uncritical of own behavior, denies presence of psychological problems/ illness/symptoms, aware of problem but blames others/circumstances/physical factors/something unknown or mysterious for problems, rebuts psychological or motivational interpretations of his behavior, fights the system and does little or nothing to help her/himself, fatalistic resignation

Superficial, shallow, platitudinous, difficulty in acknowledging the presence of psychological problems, self-deceiving, unable to focus on issues, lacks objectivity

Denies, despite the evidence, that his/her current symptoms are important or that s/he needs help, or that he/she needs to change his/her attitude/behavior/feelings in some specific way, staff evaluations/findings were minimized, denied, obfuscated, and evaded in discussions with patient

Does not know what to make of his/her situation

SOME:

Unable to make use of correct insights, only flashes of insight
Doesn't understand self too well
Although he seemed to recognize some of his symptomatology he does not seem to have any insight into its mechanisms or processes.
Continues trying to make sense of his/her psychotic thinking
She has some insight into his behavior but apparently is not able to respond appropriately or perceive satisfactory solutions to his life situation.

FULL:

Believes he/she is ill, recognizes need for treatment, came to treatment voluntarily, labels own illness, takes medicines, attends therapy sessions, works in therapy, acknowledges psychological/ physical/historical limitations present

Accepts that his/her symptoms/problematic behaviors/failures in adaptation are at least in part due to his/her irrational thought/feelings/internal states, can identify the emotional/cognitive antecedents and consequents of symptomatic behaviors, recognizes relation of symptomatic behavior to (e.g. alcohol abuse) to emotional states, or to impact on life's duration/quality/ satisfaction

Open to new ideas/perspectives on him/herself and other important people, self-aware, psychologically minded, accepts explanations offered by care-givers

Understands outcomes of his behavior and is influenced by this awareness, is able to identify/distinguish/comprehend behaviors which would be contrary to social values/socially non-acceptable or personally counterproductive

Can apply understanding to change actions/direction of his/her life, understands causes/ dynamics/treatments/implications of his/her illness

For Disability Examination:

Applicant's perception of relationship between injury/illness and psychological conditions.

15.18 Motivation for Change: See also section 21. Prognosis

Motivation is limited by low frustration tolerance, dependency, ambivalence, low initiative
Motivation is needed for change/therapy/habilitation/rehabilitation/self-improvement

Affect: See section 14. Emotional/Affective Symptoms

15.19 Decision Making: See also section 15.14 Social/Moral Judgement (<->)

Easily confused, easily overwhelmed in choice situations, lacks understanding of options, fails to evaluate choices

Indecisive, flounders, dithers, procrastinates, ponders endlessly, avoids decision situations, reverses decisions, wishy-washy, vacillates, ambivalent

Unable to carry out choices verbalized, deficient in carrying out instructions/in finishing tasks started, can make only simple/work related decisions

Decisive, effective, follows through, tolerates frustration/ambiguity/delay/errors/peers/ setbacks/changes/ambivalence

---

15.20 Learning: Evidence for a deficit in learning

Does not learn new information/material with repeated exposures

Easily grasps concepts and methods on first trial, generalizes from earlier situations, uses theoretical models, alters own behaviors in light of experience/changed situation/requests from others

Curious, attentive

15.21 Other/Summary Statements for Mental Status:

Impaired mental control functions
Unable to shift cognitive sets, rigid, inflexible, inability to shift set/learn/plan ahead
Defective sequencing ability

Presence of a dementing process
Considering client's age and education....
Has only fleeting contact with "reality," internally entertained

Cognitive functioning seems limited rather than faulty
Showed a good balance of self-esteem/confidence and self-criticism
Precocious, very learnèd, brilliant

Problem solving ability is lacking/defective/distorted/limited by intelligence/disorder

For a Child
> Soft neurological signs (incoordination, poor balance, poor speech, delayed development, etc.), "Funny Looking Kid",

N.B.
1. Do not use "**senility**" to mean dementia because aging doesn't cause dementia, aging is not a disease, at no age is dementia a normal state, and in many cases dementia is reversible.

2. Be alert for AIDS Dementia Complex in high risk patients. Onset is insidious and estimated to occur in up to 60% of People With AIDS. Greenwood (1991) is a very good review and see section 16.2 ADC.

16. Standard Statements for ABNORMAL Signs, Symptoms and Syndromes of Disorder

This list of signs and symptoms EXCLUDES ALL THOSE REFERRING TO COGNITIVE MENTAL FUNCTIONING. For those, see Chapter 15. for Mental Status descriptors

Note: Remember to report positive as well as negative findings.

The categories of statements are presented here *in alphabetical order* as no hierarchy is agreed upon.

16 Sympts

16.1 Abuse: See also sections 16.7 for Battered Woman Syndrome, 16.29 for Child sexual abuse, 16.19 for Impulse Disorder

CHARACTERISTICS OF ABUSING FAMILIES: Based on Nietzel and Himelein, 1986

Parent's histories: experienced abuse/neglect, lack of parental affection, large families, married as teens

Current family status: socially isolated/lack of social support, marital discord/conflict, impulsivity of parents, parental illiteracy, parental retardation, stressful situation (poverty, poor housing, etc.),

Parental child-rearing: rarely praise children, strict demands, ignorance of development/unrealistic expectations, low level of supervision of children, early toilet training, dislike of caretaking, parental disagreement over child-rearing practices

Adult Children Of Alcoholics: See section 17.24 Codependent personality

Affects: See Chapter 14. Affects

Aggression: See section 16.19 Impulse Control

16.2 AIDS Dementia Complex: Can appear in up to 60% of People With AIDS and some who are only HIV+. Adapted from Greenwood, 1991.

COGNITIVE CHANGES:

Loss of memory, inability to concentrate, loses train of thought in midsentence, mild confusion, absentmindedness, mental slowness, agitation, inability to speak, loss of self care functions, unaware of degree of illness/losses, forgets to practice safer sex, seizures, indifference to surroundings, hypersomnolence, coma,
Verbal deficits across intellectual, memory and language tests, mutism,

MOTOR DYSFUNCTIONS:

Leg weaknesses, unsteady gait, poor coordination, handwriting difficulties, tremor, paraplegia, incontinence

OTHER CHANGES:

Headache, lethargy, reduced sexual drive, apathy, indifference, suicide risk
Withdrawal, especially in previously gregarious personalities
Cerebral atrophy, edema and areas of demyelination

The Center for Disease Control operates the National AIDS Clearinghouse for information materials: 1-800-458-5231.

16.3 Alcoholics, Types of :

I. Alcoholic, problem drinker, heavy drinker, uncontrolled drinker, alcohol addict, compulsive drinker

II. TYPES A AND B:

	Type A	Type B
Onset	Later, after 25	Earlier, before 25
Childhood and family risk factors	Fewer	More
Alcohol related social and physical consequences	Fewer	More
Psychopathological dysfunction	Less	More
Sociopathy	No	Yes
Developmental disorders	No	Yes
Distress in work and family	Less	More
Serverity of dependence	Less	More
Abuse of other substances	No	Yes
Inclined to experiment	No	Yes
Co-occurring psychiatric disorders	No	Yes
Controlled	More	Less
Tense	Less	More
Age	Older	Younger
Occupational status	Higher	Lower
Effective treatment methods	Interactional	Coping skills training

III. Type I and Type I

	Type I[1]	Type II
Frequency	More common	Less common
Gender of children of alcoholics	Both sexes	Primarily male
History of criminality in biological father	No	Yes
	Strong gene-environment effect	Weak Post-natal effect
Onset of abusive drinking	Later	Earlier
	Loss of control over drinking	
Spontaneous alcohol seeking/inability to abstain[2]	Infrequent	Frequent
Fighting and arrests when drinking	Infrequent	Frequent
Physiological dependence/loss of control	Frequent	Infrequent
Guilt and fear about alcohol dependence	Frequent	Infrequent
Novelty seeking	Low	High
Harm avoidance	High	Low
Reward dependence	High	Low

---

[1] This distinction is offered by Cloninger in Dinwiddie, S. H. and Cloninger, C. R. (1991).
[2] These are from Cloninger, 1987.

16.4 Alcohol Intoxication Symptoms:

Elevated pulse, blood pressure
Sweating, tremor, fever, tinnitus
Agitation, irritability, psychomotor activity, rage, violence, prolonged sleep
Ataxia, opthalmoplegia, nystagmus, peripheral neuropathy, cerebellar signs
Disorientation, "quiet global confusion", delirium, sensorium intact
Impairment of short term memory, confabulation, amnesia for rage episode
Perceptual distortions (visual and tactile), hallucinations (usually auditory, of command or derogatory type, often haptic)
Delusions, paranoid usually, and transient.
Seizure

AOD (Alcohol and Other Drugs): See section 7.25 for Substance Abuse questions, and sections 16.33, 16.34 for descriptors

16.5 Attention Deficit Hyperactivity Disorder: See sections 6.5 and 6.6 for questions.
A primary difficulty maintaining a focus of attention against distraction and which results in the disorganization of behavior as seen in inattention, impulsivity or hyperactivity. Can be seen as concentration disorder.

Assessment of ADDH for accuracy should use one of these scales with norms: the Connors Parent and Teacher Rating Scale, Conner's Abbreviated Teacher Rating Scale (10 items) (Conners, 1983), the Freedom from Distractibility factor of the WISC-R, Tests of Variables of Attention (TOVA), Gordon Diagnostic System (Gordon, 1986), ADD-H Comprehensive Teacher's Rating Scale (ACTeRS), or the Child Behavior Checklist (Achenbach and Edelbrock, 1983)

BEHAVIOR:

Restless, fidgets, wriggles, twists, squirms, "antsy," much 'out of seat'/off task behavior, does not sit through an interview or meal, always "on the go", prefers to run rather than walk, climbs on furniture, hops/skips/jumps rather than walking, fiddles with objects, taps/hits and makes noises, moves unnecessarily, disrupts shopping and family visits, acts 'wild' in crowded settings, baby-sitters complain about his/her behavior

Shifts from one incomplete task to another, does not finish what he/she starts, rushes/jumps from one topic of conversation to another,

Non-compliant, does not comply with instructions, does not sit when told to, breaks school/game's rules, unable to follow a routine (and these are not due to oppositional patterns or failure to understand the instructions so child should not be called defiant, resistant, "sassy"/"talks back", argumentative, or oppositional)

Does not play quietly, talks excessively, does everything in the noisiest way, makes odd noises,

Needs constant/continual/one-to-one supervision/monitoring/teaching, needs closeness and eye-contact to understand instructions, fails to attend to details in schoolwork or other activities

Adapts to changes in situation/routine/personnel poorly

Poor fine motor skills, is disorganized with possessions, clumsy, low concern for accuracy, neatness or quality of work, disregards instructions

Prefers action-oriented activities, avoids conversation

Impulsive, blurts out answers, reacts without considering, acts before thinking, limited self-regulatory functions

Senseless, repetitive, eccentric behaviors, darts, destroys toys and property
Ignores consequences of own behaviors and so engages in physically dangerous activities

COGNITIVE:

Easily distracted, self-distracting, lessened ability to sustain attention/concentration on school task/work/play, low attending skills, often stares into space and reports daydreaming
Needs/asks for repetitions of instructions, gets confused, doesn't "listen" although s/he hears normally, inattentive to significant details, misses 'announcements', needs excessive individual supervision,

Academic difficulties with: counting, time-telling, recognizing letters, adds/substitutes/reverses letters/words/sounds, copies letters and words poorly, word finding, stops in middle of a sentence or thought, confuses/reverses word order in sentences, mistakes similar sounding words

Low short-term memory skills, fails to remember sequences, loses place when reading

Disorganized work habits: difficulty organizing school work, does not study/prepare, organize, protect own work, do problem's steps in sequence, does not complete assignments on time, starts work before receiving instructions, loses the equipment needed, has great difficulty organizing goal-directed activities, poor at gathering materials and sequencing activities toward a goal, fails to finish tasks, is destructive of materials, loses things necessary for an activity such as toys, pencils, keys, assignments, books.

Refractory to usual instructional approaches
Seems unresponsive to punishment or rewards,

AFFECT:

Unpredictable and unrelated mood changes, often depressed/blue/sad, pessimistic, gloomy
Has low self-esteem/image, feels worthless
His/her feelings are easily hurt/offended, cries easily or frequently,
Easily angered/upset, gets overexcited
Irritable, easily frustrated, low frustration tolerance

SOCIAL:

Interrupts/intrudes/"butts in," talks out in class, talks out of turn, shouts/blurts out answers or comments, makes disruptive noises, does not wait his/her turn in group situations, no patience, impulsive, excitable, explosive

Fights with sibs/peers/teachers, violent, aggressive, destructive, plays "tough guy", often involved in physically dangerous activities without considering possible risks/dangerous consequences, hits/punches/strikes/kicks/bites, cries/withdraws, verbal conflict/insults/harasses/teases/coerces/intimidates/manipulates/"bosses"/provokes, disrupts other children's activities, betrays friends, peers avoid/reject him/her, has great difficulty keeping friends

Temper outbursts, unpredictable behavior,
Has difficulty only at specific times, behavior/mood deteriorates during course of the day,
Would tolerate only a minimum of questions about mood/behavior. If pressed would ...

SUB-TYPES OF ADDH: From Horacek, 1992

Poor perseverance - normal performance until time of onset of severe subjective boredom, loss of interest, fatigue, irritability, even sleep.
Frequent omission errors - frequent 1-2 second gaps in attention, unawareness of mistakes
Impulsivity - high vigilance so no errors of omission but fail to inhibit responses to non-target stimulus, the "oops" error, aware of error after the fact.
Variability of attention - high variability in response time, stimuli are noted 'in the nick of time', difficulty processing sequential information.
Hyperactivity - the distracting effects appears immediately on testing and persists, may do better or normally if allowed great activity level which may be self-arousing.
Distractibility - normal performance in an environment low in or free from distractions but do very poorly in real-world settings.
Overfocussed - "Absent-minded professor" who may be bright, divergent thinking, creative, "right-brained." May overcome attentional deficits with high motivation and cognitive strategies like reasoning and memory. May do well in difficult subjects but poorly in less stimulating classes requiring concrete information and memorization.
Mixed - a combination of some of the above and may also show emotional over-reactivity, learning disorders, anxiety disorders, obsessive/compulsive or motoric traits.

DEVELOPMENTAL PATTERN OF PEOPLE WITH ADHD:

Infancy: very frequent crying, sleep difficulties, restless sleep, overactivity, difficult to soothe
Preschool: inattentiveness, overactivity, temperamental/emotional, misconduct/aggression, rejection by peers
Elementary school: overactivity, impulsivity, inattention, fidgeting, poor school achievement, low self-esteem, slightly below average IQs, much subtest scatter/variability, clumsiness, disorganization
High school: restlessness, poor grades, failure to complete degree, rebelliousness, difficulty studying, lying, defiant, alcohol use
Post High school: restlessness, poor concentration, impulsivity, motor vehicle accidents, alcohol abuse, antisocial personality patterns, low self-esteem, emotional/behavioral problems

16.6 Autistic Disorder:

Marked lack of awareness of the existence of feelings in others
Does not seek comforting from others or seeks it in strange ways when distressed/upset/frightened
Does not imitate or does it strangely, mechanically
Lacks social give and take/reciprocity
Lacks social play, plays alone, uses others in mechanical way
No friendships, lacks understanding of social rules,

16.7 Battered Woman Syndrome: This is a subtype of PTSD so it has the core elements of arousal, avoidance, and intrusive memories. See Walker (1984, 1991). See also sections 7.1, 7.2, 7.3 for abuse questions and 16.1 for descriptors

Denial or minimization of the details of the abuse
Fear of being labeled crazy/exaggerating/making it up if seek help
Caught up in a cycle of violence
Low self-esteem, especially efficacy
Coping skills: putting the man's needs first even at great cost to herself, remaining in a psychologically and physically harmful situation, passive and dependent behavior.

Client needs assessment of the lethality/danger, various means of protection, and an escape plan.

SPOUSE ABUSE:

Non-violent: calm talking, sulking, withdrawing/isolating/ignoring/shunning, yelled/swore, insulted, called names, threatened abandonment of children/money/obligations
Intimidation: prevented movement/restrained freedom/space, interrupted activities
Treats of violence: hit/threw/drove dangerously/with weapons/toward children/pets/spouse/relatives
Violence: threw items, pushed, painful restraint, wrestling, bit, hit, used weapon
Assault: slapped, kicked, punched, choked, raped
Attempted murder: severe beating, out of control, use of weapon

Bulemia: See sections 7.11 for Eating Disorders questions and 16.14 Eating disorders descriptors

16.8 Chronic Fatigue Syndrome: Also called Chronic Post-Viral Fatigue Syndrome, Chronic Epstein-Barr Virus Syndrome. See Krupp, 1991 for an overview.

Persistent, interfering, debilitating, fatigue, 50% or more decrease from premorbid activity level
Easily and persistently fatigue after little exercise, abrupt onset of fatigue
Not relieved by rest
Mild/low grade fever, tender/palpable lymph nodes, inflammation of mucous membranes, sore throat, cough, chronic headaches, joint pain/muscle pain, diffuse pains
Weakness

Irritability, confusion, poor concentration, depression, photophobia, sleep disturbances

Chronic Pain Syndrome: See 16.23 Pain Disorder

16.9 Compulsions: See also sections 7.7 Compulsions questions and 16.22 Compulsions descriptors and also 7.17 and 16.22 Obsessions

Greist (1986) suggests this classification for rituals:
Cleaning of real or imagined contamination.
Repeating a ritual behavior a certain number of times.
Completing a sequence of actions correctly.
Checking and rechecking, especially locks
Being *meticulous* about the proper location of objects.
Hoarding or sorting or stacking of non-useful objects
Avoiding of contamination by rituals to make unnecessary the need to clean.

S engages in *rituals* for meals, sleep, dressing, house cleaning, washing, defecation, school/work tasks, or other mental tasks, etc.
S feels compelled to repeatedly *check* the house, kitchen, windows and doors, dangerous objects, children, etc.
S feels compelled to *repeatedly* touch or rub, hoard/collect, count, order, arrange and rearrange objects.

Goodman, W. K. (1989) has a full listing of obsessions and compulsions called the Y-BOCS.

Client denied problems with common compulsions

16.10 Conduct Disorder -
Socialized, Aggressive:
Socialized, Nonaggressive:
Undersocialized, Aggressive:
Undersocialized, Nonaggressive:

Stubbornly resists other's ways of doing things
Will cheat in order to win, Will lie to be seen as the winner
Believes others are against him/he is being treated unfairly
Makes an effort on a task or toward others only if it serves his/her interests
Selfishly accepts without any desire to return favors

Aggressive, violent, dangerous, assaults, fights with anyone, threatens
Lies/cheats/breaks any rules/steals/denies truth/blames others
Swears offensively, vulgarisms

Consider:

Number of close friends, duration of friendships, reaches out to others, feels guilt or remorse, blames others, informs on others, shows concern for others
Violence toward persons or property: vandalism, fire-setting, burglary, rape, mugging, assault, theft, purse snatching, armed robbery, extortion/blackmail
Running away, truancy, substance abuse

Cyclothymia: See section 14.4 Cyclothymia

16.11 Delusions: See also sections 7.8 Delusions for questions and 16.28 Schizophrenia for descriptors
Non-reality based beliefs, essentially unshakeable, defended despite evidence, and unique to the individual
or not supported by culture or subculture.

DEGREE:

(<->) Faint suspiciousness, distrust, pervasive distortions, magical thinking, personalized meanings,
overvalued ideas, ideas of reference, allusions to trickery and deceit, believes in ... but this in not
of delusional force, convinced of truth of, formed delusions/deluded, pseudologica fantastica,
lives in a fantasy world

The delusions
are fixed/trusted/doubted/rejected/denied.
are extensive/circumscribed/isolated/encapsulated
Degree of organization: fragmented, poorly organized/well organized/systematized
and extensive system of beliefs
are shared with others/family members (*folie à deux* or *à trois,* DSM-III-R is Shared Paranoid
Disorder).
rarely/often/continually expressed
elicited easily/with difficulty/only with exceptionally trusted others

CONTENTS of the delusion are of:

Grandiosity	Persecution[1]	Religion	nihilistic	suicide	Somatic
megalomania	reference	poverty		homicide	disease
omniscience	following	Erotomanic	fears	approaching	hypochondriacal
omnipotence	influence	wishes		death	infection[2]
extraordinary		sexual identity			distorted body
abilities	misidentif-	alleged lover		self-deprecation	image
self-importance	ication			self-accusation	foul odors[3]
special relat-	special	obsessions		guilt	disfigured[4]
ionship with	identity	preoccupations		derogation	
famous per-	alien control	monomaniacal focus		shame	voodoo
son or deity				sin	occult
		blamelessness			
	Jealousy	innocence		zooanthropic	
	infidelity				

Other contents:

Having neglected an urgent responsibility, caused harm to befall another person, inadvertently
contaminated others,
Being followed, people making fun of her/him, trying to control him/her, people know his thoughts
Being on a special mission for government/religion/politics
Intensely focussed on religious themes
Communication with the dead, mind reading, mental telepathy, fore-knowledge, Extra-Sensory
Perception, psychokinesis

---

[1] See also section 16.24 Paranoia.
[2] E.g. Parasitosis
[3] Bromosis.
[4] Dysmorphophobia. Distinguish from disatisfaction with appearance.

Ideas of reference: personal/special/unusual messages from television or radio, other's behaviors

The *effects* of the delusions on the subject's life situation seems to be crippling/large/limiting/minor/ circumscribed.

The *origin* of the delusions seems to have been in ___ .

Differing *types* of delusion in different disorders:
in mania	grandiose
in depression	guilt, somatic
in OBS	secondary to a perceptual disturbance
in paranoia	of jealousy and persecution
in schizophrenia	of being controlled, sometime persecution, bizarre/impossible

SECOND-RANK DELUSIONS: These are delusions based on or about other psychological phenomena such as hallucinations, other delusions, or on affects such as mania and are not pathonomic of schizophrenia. E.g. emotional blunting, confusion, disorders of mood.

16.12 Denial: From Breznitz, 1988. Denial can be adaptive and maladaptive.

Types:	*Example*
1. Denial of provided information	"No on ever told me about it."
2. Denial of information about a threat	"No one ever told me there was anything to worry about."
3. Denial of personal relevance	"That doesn't apply to me."
4. Denial of urgency	"No rush."
5. Denial of vulnerability	"It can't/won't happen to me."
6. Denial of emotion	"I'm not scared."
7. Denial of the emotion's relevance	"Yes, I'm scared but there is no reason to feel that way."

16.13 Depersonalization and Derealization: Loss of the continuity of consciousness, identity and motor behaviors. See section 7.9 for questions

Reports observing oneself from a distance/corner of the room, as if outside one's body, body appears altered, feels mechanical/robot-like

Self-estrangement, extreme feelings of unreality/detachment from self/environment/surroundings, floating in the sky, "dreaming"/living a dream, as if the world were not real, sometimes not part of the world

Experienced her thoughts as not her own, as if his body and mind were not linked

Depression: See sections 7.4 for questions, 14.5 Depression for descriptors, and 16.35 Suicide

Depression, masked. See section 14.5 Masked Depression

16.14: Eating Disorders: See Section 7.11 for Eating Disorder questions

ANOREXIA, ANOREXIA NERVOSA:

Physical presentation:

Cachexia/cachectic, emaciated, amenorrhea, bradycardia, hypothermia, edema

Cognitive:

"Food phobia," morbid fear of gaining weight/becoming fat, distorted, implacable attitude toward
    food, avoidance of "fattening" foods, over-valued ideas of dread of fatness
Satisfaction with bodily appearance, distorted body image so believes s/he is always too fat,
Denial of exhaustion/hunger/illness
"Positive" view of family, enmeshment with a parent, mothers as anxious/over-protective/indulgent/
    self-martyring/martyrizing, denial of family conflict
Perfectionism, self-disciplined, pride of weight management, self-inflicted starvation,
Obsessional, preoccupation with food, obsession with thinness
Emotional overcontrol
Fear of pubertal changes

Behavior:

Laxative/diuretic misuse/abuse, fasting, starvation, over-exercising

Social:
Shy, compliant, dependent,
Sexual immaturity and inexperience
Less antisocial behavior than bulemic
Mistrusting of professionals

BULIMIA:

Eating more than normal in a two hour period with sense of lack of control as manifested by eating
    larger than normal amounts: rapidly, to uncomfortable fullness, without feeling hungry, or
    throughout the day without planned mealtimes

Rapid consumption of high-calorie food in short time period, ends the binge with abdominal
    pain/sleep/self-induced vomiting

Labels:

Bulimarexia (not a widely accepted term), bulimia nervosa, gorging, binge eating, self-induced
    vomiting/emesis, binge-purge cycling/syndrome, gorge-purge syndrome, dietary chaos
    syndrome, gastric dilation

Physical Presentation:

Insomnia, constipation, lanugo, premature aging, hair loss, dental problems (erosion due to acid vomitus), amenorrhea, dehydration, weight fluctuations, cardiovascular disorders, electrolyte imbalances
Near normal weights, irregular menstrual periods, intense hunger,

Cognitive:

Distorted body image, irrational body image, overconcern with body appearance/shape/weight, dissatisfaction with bodily appearance, fear of obesity, this fear does not decrease as weight drops,
Inability to think clearly, dichotomous thinking, over-personalization, low self esteem, perfectionism, rationalization of eating/symptoms
Effects on self-esteem (weight central to self evaluation, felt powerlessness re weight, lifelong dieting, self-loathing, disgust over body size) and body weight (usually obese, great bodyweight fluctuations - ≥ 20 lbs. ≥ 5 times),
Awareness that eating pattern is abnormal, preoccupation with food, craving/urges/hungers,

Behavioral:

Hyperactivity, over-exercising, frequent weighing, overuse of laxatives/diuretics/cathartic/thyroid preparations/appetite suppressants, shoplifting, junk food consumption, binge eating, vomiting, sneaking binges, severely restrictive diets/fasting, attendance at weight control clinics.
Suicide attempts

Social:

Eating alone due to embarrassment over amount eaten.
High achievement, academic success
Oversensitivity to criticism, fragility, vulnerability
More antisocial behavior than anorectics
Perceives intense family conflict,
More trusting than anorectics of those who want to help
Impulsive
More sexually experienced than anorectics, dramatic

Affective:

Feeling disgusted with oneself/self-deprecation, depressed, guilty and other marked distress over binge eating.
Depression, masked anger
Specific affective precipitants of binge

Other:

These may or may not matter:
Food composition (various foods or only some such as sweets, salty, snacks, etc.).
Dissociative qualities ("numb", "spaced out").
Higher than usual levels of various psychopathologies and medical conditions.
If symptoms are more intense consider diagnosis of Bulemia Nervosa; if less intense consider diagnosis of Eating Disorder NOS.

OBESITY: See also section 11.2 Behavioral observations, weight

Factitious, obsessional concerns, overweight, obese, chronic, stable, compulsive dieting, escalating weight over time/diets

PICA:

Explosive Disorder: See section 16.19 Impulse control

Extra-Pyramidal Symptoms: See section 16.31 Side effects of medications

16.15 Fetal Alcohol Syndrome:

Small weight and height, smaller than average head size
Deformities of hear, genitals, kidneys, nervous system
Face: small eye slits, droopy eyelids, flattened nasal bridge, short nose, malformed ears, long upper lip, short jaw, narrow forehead
Mental retardation is variable, deterioration with age
Incoordination, impulsiveness, poor speech and hearing

16.16 Hallucinations: Sense deception, perceptions without sensations. See sections 7.13 Hallucinations for questions and 16.28 Schizophrenia

SENSORY MODALITY: EXAMPLES

Visual:	Unformed/lights/flashes, formed/people/animals/things, Lilliputian: See section 16.18 Illusions
Tactile (haptic):	Electricity, sexual sensations, tickling
Kinesthetic:	Creeping, crawling, biting, gnawing, twisting, churning, pains
Auditory:	Noises or voices (see below)
Olfactory:	Disgusting/repulsive/objectionable odors, of death or disease
Gustatory:	Poisons, acid, foul tastes
Visceral/somatic:	Phantom Limb, "hollow insides", "rotting insides"
Vestibular:	Sensations of flying, falling, lightness
Synesthesia:	Blending sense impressions, e.g. smells red

CONTENTS OF AUDITORY HALLUCINATIONS::

Noises: whistling, ringing
Voices: whose?, male or female, age
Disconnected words, muffled voices, his/her own thoughts, remarks addressed to him/her,
Daymares, flashbacks
Idiosyncratic themes

Informative, friendly, benign, comforting, helpful, socially focused,
Arguing, dialoguing/conversing among themselves, commenting on thoughts/behavior/motives,
    grandiose
Condemning, malevolent, accusatory, persecutory, harassing, hateful, spiteful, threatening
Controlling, seductive, compelling, premonitory, hortatory/imperative/commanding
Conquering: menacing, commanding, berating, consuming, terrorizing, constant, relentless, isolating

Presence of another person, extracampine, autoscopy, *doppelgänger*, replacement of another/self

ATTITUDE TOWARD HALLUCINATIONS:

(<->) Ego-alien, frightened, terrified, resisted/struggled against, engages in conversations/dialogue
    with imaginary interlocutor, comforting, ego-syntonic, accepted

(<->) Convinced of their reality, vivid fantasy, "altered state", impossibility, "only a fantasy",
    doubting its reality/own perceptions, making various efforts to control/cope with it, "bizarre",
    "rare"

CIRCUMSTANCES OF OCCURRENCE:

Hypnogogic, hypnopompic, with delirium, in withdrawal, flashbacks, spontaneously, unbidden
Extent of cultural/situational anxiety/external stimuli on the hallucinatory experience
Undiscoverable relationship to circumstances

INTERPERSONAL ASPECTS:

Hallucinations are denied by the patient but s/he seems to be responding to internal stimuli
They involve small/moderate/great distortion of consensual reality
Suspected, dialogical, undoubted, denied, seemed to be attending to unseen stimuli

COMPARISON OF ORGANICALLY AND PSYCHOGENICALLY BASED HALLUCINATIONS: Based on Biele (1974)

Organically-based	Psychologically-based
Sharply demarcated Vivid and well formed Polychromic and/or polysonic Hypermobility, i.e. bugs creep Accompanied by terror, apprehension Perseverative quality Patient *acts* as though he/she really sees/ hears/feels	Fleeting and transient Vague, shadowy, misty Usually in shades of gray Patient has an *ideas* that s/he sees, feels, etc. but does not act consistently. May be associated with patient's psychodynamics

16.17 Homicide Risk Factors: See also section 16.19 Impulse control, Violence

COGNITIONS:

Intense wish to kill, specified or named victim, command hallucinations, ambivalent wish to kill, non-specific hostility

RISK FACTORS:

A history of ...
   violent, destructive or antisocial behaviors
   violent acts in unrelated settings, arrest or assault repeatedly in the same setting, carrying of weapons, chronic problems with the authorities, criminal record
   Attempts to kill by stabbing, strangling, or shooting, physical abuse causing harm, slapping, pushing, punching, unpredicted destruction of objects

Other risk factors:
   Young male, little education, psychotic patient with delusions, substance abuse history, character disorder diagnosis
   No home family, friends or institutional support or involvement, has home but no one can observe the patient, family not interested in patient

Homosexual Identity, Development of: See section 30.8

16.18 Illusions: See also section 7.14 Illusion questions

Sense deceptions, deceptive sensations, visual/auditory/tactile distortions, speeded up or slowed
    passage of time
Macropsia, micropsia, Lilliputian, gigantism

Intermittent Explosive Disorder: See section 16.19 Impulse disorder

16.19 Impulse Control Disorders:
Violence/Aggression: See sections 7.15 for questions, 14.2 Anger, 16.17 Homicidal risk, 16.35 Suicide

TYPES OF IMPULSE DISORDERS:

Kleptomania, pathological gambling, pyromania/firesetting, sexual impulsivity (sexual addiction:
    See section 16.30), intermittent explosive, trichotillomania/self-damaging/self-mutilating
    behaviors, "nymphomania," "satyriasis," "sexual addicts"

TYPES OF IMPULSES:

Hostile, aggressive, violent, destructive, amorous, sexual

DEGREE OF CONTROL: (<->)

Overcontrolled	Patient	Volatile	Impulsive	Violent
armored	tolerant	loses temper	may attack	explosive
inhibited	controlled	short fuse	"blows his/her top"	aggressive
denied	thoughtful	low frustration	impetuous	combative
over-cautious	deliberate	tolerance	hot headed	assaultive
rigid		quicksilver	flares up	
		quick tempered	lashes out	
		"flies off the handle"	belligerent	
		stormy	abrupt	
cool-headed	"riled up"		precipitous	
restrained	easily offended		unpredictable	
self-possessed	excitable		incontinent	
staid	irritable		reckless	
	easily irritated		outbursts	
			leaves situation	
			hasty	
			rash	

FEARS HE/SHE MAY:

Embarrass him/herself, lose control, "wet pants"/lose bladder control, faint
Harm self or others, homicidal ideation, threats, behavior
Not be able to resist impulses to commit delinquent or illegal acts

REASON'S INFLUENCE:

Acts without weighing alternatives, likely to act without consideration of alternatives/with little hesitation, unreflective, acts without examination, unmediated, "acts on spur of the moment", easily agitated, off-handed/ill-considered actions, self-centered actions, seeks immediate gratification of urges, heedless, willful, limited intellectual control over expression of impulses, poor planning

VIOLENCE AGAINST:

Objects/property/self/family/strangers/women/animals/authority figures/weaker persons, any available target, outside the home

ANTISOCIAL BEHAVIOR: See also section 17.4 Antisocial Personality

Obstructiveness, cheating, lying, stealing, crimes, arrests, fighting, forceful aggression, irresponsibility

CORRELATES OF SERIOUS AGGRESSION:

Tortures animals
Hidden aggressive acts
Fighting with weaker opponents
Pride in history of aggression
Stealing
Lying

Profitless damaging of property, especially one's own
Apparently purposeless aggressive actions
Careless of risk of self harm when acting aggressively
"Out of control" when aggressive
Plans aggressive actions

OTHER VARIABLES TO BE EVALUATED FOR ASSESSMENT OF VIOLENCE: From Beck (1990)

History of violence before mental health diagnosis/treatment.
Mental status: judgement, arousal, psychosis, impaired consciousness
Impulsiveness: history of driving violations, spending money, sexual/social relationships, risk-taking behavior, work history
Use of intoxicants, history of drug/alcohol abuse
Availability of weapons, of victims
Childhood exposure to violence, history of abuse/neglect, chaotic family, violent subculture
Instability: frequent moves, unemployment
Ability to vent frustration/anger non-violently: verbal skills, intellect, coping mechanisms, support system
Need or external controls as internal ones are lacking/defective/easily overcome

Re violent behaviors:
    Location, time, frequency, others present or alone, method, relationship with object of violence, lethality of method,
    Motives/benefits/perceptions, threats, precipitants
Other behavior: postural tension (on chair's edge, gripping edge), voice (loud, strident, louder), motor activity (restlessness, pacing, leaving), startle response (easily, full).

FACTORS ASSOCIATED WITH VIOLENCE RECIDIVISM: Adapted from Monahan, 1981.

Criminal history: Recidivism increases with each prior criminal act. Risk of recidivism exceeds 50% with more than five prior offenses.
Age: youth is highly associated with crime. Greater risk if a juvenile at first offense.
Gender: Males are much more violent.
Race: Blacks at higher risk than other races.
SocioEconomic Status: lower status and job instability.
Drug and Alcohol abuse history.
Non-stable, non-supportive family environment.
"Bad company" peers and associates
Greater availability of victims: either a broad range of victims or repeated assaults on a narrow class of victims who remain available (e. g. girlfriends).
Access to weapons.
Access to alcohol.

Insight: See section 15.17 Insight descriptors

16.20 Late Luteal Phase Depressive Disorder: These are the signs of Pre-Menstrual Syndrome and LLDD is more severe and may be seen as pathological by the DSM-IV. From Steege, *et al.* (1988) and Severino and Moline (1989). Disabling symptoms in the week before menses:

VEGETATIVE:

Appetite/eating changes, anorexia, craves specific foods,
Sleep changes/hypersomnia/hyposomnia/insomnia, lethargy and fatigue, stay in bed, naps

AFFECTIVE:

Mood swings, feeling overwhelmed/stressed, sadness, anxiety, persistent anger/irritability, lability, suicidal ideation, crying,
Decreased interest in activities
Tension, "on edge," restlessness
Affectionate
Excitement, well-being, burst of energy/activity

PAINS:

Cramps, headache, mastalgia, joint/muscle pain, general aches and pain, muscle stiffness, backache,

AUTONOMIC NERVOUS SYSTEM:

Nausea/vomiting, palpitations, sweating/cold sweats, "hot flashes/flushes," dizziness, fuzzy vision, numbness/tingling, heart pounding, chest pain, ringing in ears, feeling of suffocation

FLUID BALANCE:

Weight gain, "bloating," oliguria, edema, breast tenderness/swelling,

COGNITIVE:

Lessened concentration/distractibility, forgetfulness, confusion, lowered judgement, indecision, decreased efficiency, lowered school or work performance, accidents, motor incoordination
Impulsive
Orderliness

INTERPERSONAL:

Paranoia, oversensitivity to rejection, isolation, avoidance, loneliness

DERMATOLOGIC:

Acne, greasy/dry hair

16.21 Malingering: See section 17.11 Hypochondriacal personality

According to Rodgers (1990), contrary to DSM-III-R this condition is not rare, not easy to detect, not a global response style, is not significantly correlated with psychopathy or criminality, or with the presence of other valid psychiatric symptoms, and is not easily detected on psychological testing.

Better criteria for malingering of mental disorders include:
1. Highly atypical symptom presentation (rare, blatant, absurd, indiscriminate). Rogers (1984) offers these: recounts symptoms of extreme severity, endorses a large number of symptoms, describes symptoms which are inconsistent with clinical formulations and diagnostic impressions, endorses highly specified symptoms, exhibits a "heightened" recall of psychological problems
2. Non-corroboration of this presentation by interviews with collaterals, on psychological or clinical medical tests
3. Exclusion of patients with diagnoses of borderline personality or factitious motivations.

Adams (1991) lists the following as markers of possible malingering:
4. Patient being directly referred by their attorney.
5. Marked discrepancy between claimed disability and objective findings.
6. Lack of cooperation with either evaluation of recommendations.

CRITERIA FOR DIFFERENTIAL DIAGNOSIS of symptoms suggesting physical illness: Based on Hyler and Spitzer (1978).

Diagnosis	Can a known physical mechanism explain the symptom?	Are the symptoms linked to psychological causes?	Is the symptom under voluntary control?	Is there an obvious goal?
Conversion	Never	Always	Never	Sometimes
Malingering	Sometimes	Sometimes	Always	Always
Psycho-somatic disorders	Always	Always	Never	Sometimes
Factitious disorders	Sometimes	Always	Always	Never (other than medical attention)
Undiagnosed physical illness	Sometimes	Sometimes	Never	Never

Terms for similar conditions: malingering, simulation, exaggeration, magnification of pain and disability, over-evaluation, functional overlay, conversion hysteria.

Mania: See section 14.7 Mania

Mood: General aspects of mood and descriptive terms for Anxiety, Depression, Anger and other emotions can be found in Chapter 14.

Multiple Personality: See section 17.14 Multiple Personality Disorder

16.22 Obsessions: See sections 7.17 Obsessions for questions, 17.18 Obsessive Personality
Goodman, W. K. (1989) has a full listing of obsessions and compulsions called the Y-BOCS.

RUMINATIONS/REPETITIVE:

Thoughts, colors, sounds, music, names, titles, numbers, phrases, memories, unpleasant images, impulses (hurt, blurt, harm, steal, cause disaster), not/saying certain things, over losing things, over needing to remember, etc.

Monomania, monothematic thought trains, repetitive themes, egomania, megalomania, overvalued ideas (e.g. dysmorphophobia)

Contamination/Cleaning: touching or being touched, bodily excretions, clothing, dirt/trash/contaminants, animals, resulting illness of self or other

Sexual: erotomania, children/incest, homosexuality in heterosexuals, aggressive sexuality, "perversities"

Religious: sacrilege, blasphemy, morality, right and wrong

Somatic: illness or disease, body parts

16.23 Pain Disorder/Chronic Pain Syndrome: See section 7.19 Pain for questions

PAIN BEHAVIORS:

Groans, flinches, winces, grimaces, grits teeth
Slow and careful movements and body placements, assumes/maintains odd positions, need to shift
    position/stand/walk/stretch frequently
Takes multiple/ineffective medications,
Increased resting ("down"/horizontal) time and decreased active ("up/vertical") time,
    appears fatigued, decreased sleep effectiveness
Decreased or absent sexual activity/duration/frequency/interest
Interference with appetite
Lessened concentration

MOOD:

Restricted range and intensity of expression
Irritability, "cranky", anger, hostility, threatening, resentful of unfair way treated by helpgivers/
    insurance carriers, overly or disrespectful, critical
Depressed, demoralized, pessimistic, expressions of hopelessness, hopeless of change/
    improvement/ return to work, intermittent depressions as reaction to pain's exacerbation

THOUGHT CONTENT:

Preoccupied with losses/accommodations/somatic conditions/treatments/pains/symptoms/health
    status and its implications, focus on small signs of progress, may create illusory correlations of
    pain/limitations/depression/symptoms with progress/change/bodily processes
Ruminations of "Why me?", causation, revenge, financial concerns, death wish
Feels "like a cripple", worthlessness because 'worth less', helpless, optimistically reports
    "learning to live with it/the pain"
Desperate for the situation to change but doubting the effectiveness of any intervention.
Has a sense of entitlement, focuses on the unfairness of the situation
Inward focus on physical self which is not hypochondriacal but a reaction to chronic pain
Suicidal ideation in the form of passive death wishes
Feels/believes himself harassed/unappreciated by his current or former employer(s), or Workman's
    Compensation Boards/insurance companies/Social Security Disability
Reports being "sick and tired" of pursuing insurance claims, being medically evaluated, filling out
    forms, "jumping through hoops", to only obtain what is rightly his/hers.

SOCIAL:

Decreased social activities/withdrawal/isolation, decreased or absent recreation
Adopts role of "patient": dependency, passivity, helplessness, avoidance/ displacement of
    responsibility, medical/biological model of pain and recovery, seeks a "miracle cure" vs.
    accepts limitations and "tries it another way," etc.
Wants to be believed more than being relieved, concerned that his/her symptoms be accepted as
    authentic

Notes: For some clarity of the evaluation of the psychogenicity of pain see Thomas Hackett's (1978) MADISON scale. He believes that pain is more likely to be psychological if the client shows: Multiplicity of varieties and places, Authenticity or need to be believed, Denial of emotional problems or of the effects of emotions on pain, Interpersonal relationships affect on the pain, Singularity/uniqueness of the pain problem/this patient, "Only you" can help me, and Nothing helps or Nothing changes the pain.

For more detailed documentation of the pain use the McGill-Melzak Pain Questionnaire in Turk and Melzack (1992) or in Melzak and Wall (1982), Feurstein and Skjei (1979), and Hase (1992).

16.24 Paranoia: See also sections 7.20 for questions, 16.11 Delusions, 17.19 Paranoid Personality

(<->) Persecutory ideas, demonstrations of suspiciousness, distrust, belief that everything is not as it should be, paranoid trends, paranoid cognitive style (See Shapiro, 1965), reports paranoid ideation, feels scrutinized, systematized delusions, reinforced delusions,

Paranoid mode of thinking: 1) suspiciousness; 2) protective thinking (selective attention to confirm suspicions and blaming of others for own failures); 3) hostility; 4) paranoid illumination: everything falls into place; 5) delusions of influence, persecution, and grandiosity
Delineates Cameron's "Pseudo-community" of those united in a plot against the subject

Pervasive suspiciousness about everyone/everyone's actions, inappropriate suspiciousness, expects people to seek retribution, views people as vindictive, sees self as victim of others/enemies/vendetta, partially supported delusions, likely story of persecution, evidence of persecution, on guard, hyperalert, vigilant, wary, spied on, plotted against, attempts made to harm, attacks, attacks foiled

Believes him/herself to be exceedingly virtuous, denies that he/she distrusts others, persistently naive about other's motives, believes him/herself to be especially sensitive, overvalues own subjective knowledge

Not paranoid, denies any special powers or missions, feels that he/she is quite well treated by individuals and the community

---

16.25 Phobias: See section 7.21 Phobias for questions
Persistent, recognized-as-unrealistic fears, high levels of circumscribed anxiety, and avoidance of the anxiety-arousing situations/animals/social settings/persons.

TYPES:

Traumatically learned phobia, simple phobia, animal phobias, school phobia, social phobia, agoraphobia, acrophobia, algophobia, claustrophobia, xenophobia, zoophobia.

About 375 named phobias are listed in an appendix to Gould Medical Dictionary (Blakiston, 1972)

16.26 Post-Traumatic Stress Disorder/Syndrome

Components and symptom clusters
1. A previous **stressor** commonly considered to present a severe threat or experience
2. "Flashbacks" or other ways of **re-experiencing**/re-living of the traumatic situation
3. Emotional **numbing**, deadening, lack of emotional responsiveness to usual experiences or
    patterns of **avoidance** efforts symptoms
4. Symptoms of increased arousal/Secondary symptoms:

easy Startling	Vigilance	Sleep disturbance
"Survivor guilt"	decreased Concentration and Memory functioning	

   Avoidance of stimuli which are similar to or elements of the original traumatic situation because
       these cause experiences of recall
   Worsening of symptoms when in situations like the original.

Fear of intimacy	General alienation	Impulsive behaviors
Intolerance of authority		

PTSD for Viet Nam Service:
1. Stressors/Traumatic events could include: receiving incoming fire, receiving sniper fire, having a unit
    on patrol ambushed, having a unit engage in a fire fight, patrolling rivers, etc.
5. Where does the client stand in the recovery process?
    a. Changes over the years, precipitating events for seeking help.
    b. Control loss leading to violence, to intrusive memories
    c. Integrity problems: feelings of betrayal by the government, how the war was fought,
        responsibility for acts of omission or commission
    d. Ambiguity:
    e. Personal responsibility and guilt
6. Posture of Client: current and past adjustment, attitudes toward treatment and constraints on
    treatment.

Symptoms by decreasing frequency in WW II Vets with Combat Fatigue (Archibald and Tuddenham,
    1965): depression, restlessness, irritability, poor sexual adjustment, poor economic adjustment, excessive
    jumpiness/startle response, easily fatigued, waking during night, difficulty concentrating, sweaty
    hands/feet, severe headache, difficulty falling asleep, memory difficulties, momentary blackouts,
    dizziness, excessive smoking, abdominal discomfort, heart palpitations, combat dreams, pervasive
    disgust, shortness of breath, sighing and yawning, diarrhea, difficulty swallowing

Preoccupations: See sections 15.9 Stream of Thought, 16.22 Obsessions, and 16.11 Delusions, for
    content

16.27 Rape Trauma Syndrome: See Burgess and Holmstrom (1974). Reactions to life threat.

ACUTE PHASE:

Impact: shock/disbelief, Controlled style or expression of high emotion such as crying, anger, anxiety, restlessness, tenseness.
Somatic: Physical trauma such as bruising, muscle tension (headaches, fatigue), sleep disturbances (insomnia, crying out), startle reactions, gastrointestinal (stomach pains, appetite, nausea), genitourinary (discharge, itching, burning, pain, rectal bleeding and pain)
Affective: fear or violence and death, humiliation, embarrassment, anger, revenge, self-blame

LONG-TERM/REORGANIZATION:

Changing residence/phone number, taking trips, visiting family for support
Nightmares:
Traumatophobia: (fear of cues for recall of rape) being indoors/outdoors, alone/crowds, people behind them, sexual behaviors

Silent Rape Reaction: previous undisclosed rape [like delayed PTSD]

16.28 Schizophrenia: See also these sections: 16.16 Hallucinations, 16.11 Delusions, 15.9 Stream of Thought

THE 4 A'S: Eugen Bleuler's four A's of Schizophrenia: Disorders of Association, Affect, Ambivalence, and Autism. Schizo because of the split between thought and feelings.

SCHNEIDERIAN OR FIRST-RANK SYMPTOMS OF SCHIZOPHRENIA:

Primary delusional perception: a common perception takes on special significance and is elaborated in a delusional way.
Passive reception of a somatic sensation imposed from an outside agency
Thought transmission/broadcasting/insertion/withdrawal/interference
Clouding
'Made' (externally directed) impulses (delusions of somatic passivity)
'Made' (externally directed) volitional acts
'Made' (externally directed) feelings or sensations
Voices arguing with the subject in the third person, calling his or her name
Voices making a continuous commentary on the subject's actions
Voices speaking the subject's thoughts aloud (écho de pensées)

SECOND-RANK DELUSIONS: See 16.11 Delusions

THE PROCESS-REACTIVE DICHOTOMY OR GOOD-POOR PREMORBID ADJUSTMENT is one indicator of the course of the disorder.

	Reactive	Process
Premorbid: functioning	Normal Good sexual adjustment, more married, stable marriages Good work and social adjustment Good life situation to return to	Maladjustment Lack of social relationships and interests. Interpersonal incompetence. Poor social, vocational, sexual functioning. Instability
Family history:	Little psychopathology in relatives	
Onset:	Clear, understandable precipitant Later in life	Gradual Earlier in life
Symptoms:	More severe, florid Panic and confusion	Apathetic Gradual loss of thoughts/emotion/activities
Course:	6 months or less from onset to florid symptom picture Acute	Longer hospitalizations Chronic
Secondary diagnosis:	Schizo-affective, depression	
Presumed cause:	Biogenic	Psychogenic

DIAGNOSTIC SUBTYPES of schizophrenia have been proposed based on the kinds of symptoms presented

	Type I - Positive Subtype	Type II - Negative SUBTYPE
Diagnosis:	Paranoid, Undifferentiated, Disorganized, Catatonic, Residual	Simple
Symptoms:	Positive: Behavioral excesses Hallucinations, delusions Thought disorder, incoherence Bizarre or disorganized behavior	Negative: Behavioral deficits Poverty of speech, thought processes Blocking, great latency Flattened affect, anhedonia, Asociality, withdrawal Avolition, apathy Attentional impairment Psychomotor retardation, monotone
Brain abnormalities:	Overactivity of dopamine in limbic system Normal CT scans	Underactivity of dopamine in frontal cortex Enlarged ventricles.
Intellectual impairment:	Minimal Worse short-term verbal memory Overattention	Significant Worse processing visual information Underattention
Premorbid functioning:	Better	Worse
Onset:	Acute	Insidious
Gender:	More women	More men
Course:	Episodic, exacerbations and remissions	Chronic

Response to treatment:	Favorable response to neuroleptics	Poor response to neuroleptics
Prognosis:	More likely to return to previous level of functioning	Less likely to return to functioning
Social funct- ioning:	Normal social functioning between remissions and exacerbations	Poor social functioning in social, vocational, educational, relationship areas

3. Paranoid and Non-paranoid based on the presence or absence of delusions of persecution or grandeur. Paranoids are likely to remain more intellectually intact, have a higher level of maturity, better pre-morbid functioning, later first hospitalizations

4. Other no longer accepted categories: Schizo-affective schizophrenia, pseudoneurotic and pseudopsychopathic schizophrenia

N. B. These distinctions may well be continua on which patients can be placed at different times rather than mutually exclusive categories or even types.

16.29 Sexual Abuse: Signs of child sexual abuse: See section 7.1, 7.2, 7.3 for Abuse questions

PHYSICAL:

Genital or anal area pain/swelling/itching/bleeding, bruises, torn/stained/bloody underwear, frequent urinary tract infections, painful urination, vaginal or penile discharge, symptoms of Sexually Transmitted Diseases, pregnancy

BEHAVIORAL:

Unexplained changes in eating habits, sleeping habits (nightmares and insomnia), difficulties in sitting or walking, excessive masturbation, indiscriminate hugging/kissing/seductive behaviors with children and adults

AFFECTIVE:

Excessive and especially sudden fearfulness about particular persons or places

SOCIAL:

Clinging, withdrawal, regression, poor peer relations
At school: refusal to attend, absences, drop in grades, refusal to attend or participate in physical education, arriving early or leaving late

COGNITIVE:

Premature knowledge of sexual behaviors, changes in fantasy play to themes of sexuality or harm

You know that suspected child abuse must be reported. The Child Help USA Hotline is 1-800/ 4 A CHILD. Your state or local number is

16.30 Sexual Impulsivity/"Addiction"/"Compulsion" From Barth and Kinder (1987)

Preoccupation with sex, transfixed
Feel driven to seek out sexual encounters
Feel regret, depression, suicidal ideation afterwards
Have sexual encounters even with the risk of disease, arrest
Childhood history of restrictiveness (leading to acting out) or neglect/abuse (leading to seeking gratification as escape)

Schneiderian symptoms: See section 16.11 Delusions

16.31 Side Effects of Medications:
The most easily available source of information is the *PDR Guide to Drug Interactions, Side Effects and Indications* in its latest edition. The following list is adapted from Bernstein, (1989)

BEHAVIORAL:

Fatigue	Psychomotor retardation	Drowsiness	Insomnia
Lethargy	Sleepiness	Nightmares	Oversleeping
Weakness			Excessive sedation

COGNITIVE

Confusion	Delirium	Internal tension

NEUROMUSCULAR:

Akinesias	Tardive dyskinesia	Akathesias	Dystonias
Reduced seizure threshold			

PARKINSONIAN:

Reduced arm accessory movements, cogwheel rigidity — Resting tremors
Mask-like facies, woodenness — Excessive salivation
Rigidity — Restlessness
Shuffling gait — Bradykinesia
Involuntary muscle movements: lip smacking, tongue rolling, tongue thrusting, jaw clenching, drooling, tics, tremors, dyskinesias, oculo-gyric crises, torsion spasms

OTHER BODILY REACTIONS:

Blurred vision	Cardiac rhythm changes	Itching	Dryness of mouth
Other visual problems	Postural hypotension	Eczema	Decreased sweating
Blood changes	Uticaria	Difficulty voiding/Urinary retention	

Photosensitivity
Impaired temperature regulation (risk of heatstroke)

Irregular menstruation	Difficulty with erection/"impotence"	Delayed ejaculation
Constipation	Pallor/flushing	Weight gain
Decreased sexual drive		
Breast enlargement	Liver problems	

Agranulocytosis

NEUROLEPTIC MALIGNANT SYNDROME: From Pearlman, 1986
  Rare, sometimes fatal. Severe parkinsonian rigidity with high fever, ANS instability (flushing/pallor, unstable blood pressure, diaphoresis, tachycardia), altered consciousness, altered CPK and increased white blood cell count. Usually within 10-28 days (mostly) after depot Prolixin/fluphenazine or Haldol/haloperidol.

TARDIVE DYSKINESIA:
  Irregular, spastic, choreiform or slow, writhing, athetoid movements. Usually mouth (chewing, swallowing, licking, sucking, tongue movements, blinking, grimaces) and sometimes fingers.
  Usually occurs after 3-6 months but up to 6 years of treatment. While often irreversible many recover.

ACUTE DYSTONIC REACTION:
  Spasms of the neck, trunk, or of the muscles of the eyes usually occurring within the first few days of neuroleptic medication. Torticollis, retrocollis, hip rocking, oculo-gyric crisis, laryngealspasm

16.32 Sleep Disturbances: See Section 7.24 for Sleep questions

The sleep pattern must be associated with daytime fatigue or impaired functioning. Avoid the use of the term insomnia alone as it has multiple meanings and so is vague.

Difficulty <u>F</u>alling <u>A</u>sleep, Initial Insomnia, sleep Latency
Sleep <u>C</u>ontinuity <u>D</u>isturbance, interrupted/broken/fragmented sleep, Middle Insomnia
<u>E</u>arly <u>M</u>orning <u>A</u>wakening, Terminal Insomnia (frequent in depression)

The manual for diagnosis is the Diagnostic Classification of Sleep and Arousal Disorders from the Association of Sleep Disorders Centers.[1] It has these major headings:
  I. Dyssomnias
    A. <u>D</u>isorders of <u>I</u>nitiating and <u>M</u>aintaining <u>S</u>leep (DIMS)
    B. <u>D</u>is<u>o</u>rders of <u>E</u>xcessive <u>S</u>omnolence (DOES): sleep attacks, sleep drunkenness,
          narcolepsy, sleep apnea, etc.
    C. Disorders of the Sleep-Wake Schedule
  II. Parasomnias (Dysfunctions associated with sleep, sleep stages, or partial arousals)
        Nightmare, dream anxiety, night terror, sleepwalking disorders

OTHER SLEEP PATTERNS:

Night Terrors (pavor nocturnus in children, reported by other and not recalled by subject in
    morning, sudden screaming, thrashing, or calling out, sleep is not interrupted or if awakened
    s/he cannot recall scream or reason for scream)
Nightmares (frightening, often paranoid quality, recalled in morning and disruptive of sleep)
Vivid Dreams (all but real, well organized contents, of neutral mood, felt as very different from
    usual dreaming, concerning persons and events from dreamer's remote past)
Nocturnal vocalizations, nocturnal jerking/myoclonus/"restless leg syndrome"/itching/crawling
    symptoms, somnambulism (sleepwalking)
Lucid dreaming
Somniloquy, somnirexia,
Sleep apnea, obstructive/upper airway apnea, central apnea, mixed apnea
Narcolepsy, sleep paralysis, cataplexy,
Hypnogogic/hypnopompic hallucinations
Asomnia, hyposomnia, hypersomnia
Bruxism
Incontinence, bedwetting/enuresis, urgency

OTHER:

Poor sleep architecture
Sleep deprivation, sleep debt, chronic fatigue
Total sleep time is decreased/increased/unaffected/normal/not determinable, daytime naps
Reversal of day/night cycle, circadian disorder
"Lark" (morning alertness) or "Owl" (evening alertness with morning ineffectiveness)
Other etiological considerations: depression, chronic illness, pains, consumption of meals,
    stimulants, tobacco, alcohol, sleeping medications (both prescribed and over-the-counter),
    irregular bedtimes, sleep disruptions from small children or other sources, transmeridian travel,
    poor sleep hygiene, poor sleep environment, being away from home, strenuous exercise near
    bedtime, trying too hard to go to sleep, due to night work/rotating shifts/family demands

---

[1] Classification of sleep and arousal disroders. (1979) *Sleep, 2,*1, 137.

16.33 Substance Abuse and Use: See also Section 7.25 and 7.26 Substance Abuse Questions

Policy is becoming the use of the phrase "Alcohol and Other Drugs (AOD) for these.

SIGNS OF INTOXICATION:

Smell of alcohol on breath, slurred speech, lessened concentration, slowed movements and responses, loosened associations, flat or exaggerated affect expression, disoriented, dozed off, defective memory, discoordination, unusual pupil size

Elevated pulse, blood pressure
Sweating, tremor, fever, tinnitus
Agitation, irritability, psychomotor activity, rage, violence, prolonged sleep
Ataxia, opthalmoplegia, nystagmus, peripheral neuropathy, cerebellar signs
Disorientation, "quiet global confusion," delirium, sensorium intact
Impairment of short term memory, confabulation, amnesia for rage episode
Perceptual distortions (visual and tactile), hallucinations (usually auditory, of command or derogatory type, often haptic)
Delusions, paranoid usually, and transient.
Seizure

SYMPTOMS OF PROBLEM DRINKING:

Preoccupation with alcohol, drinking. Spends spare time buying, selling, taking or talking about drugs
Drinking pattern: impulsive, gulping drinks, in inappropriate circumstances, solitary, "Medicinal," secret, hidden bottle, loss of control, use drugs and alcohol together
Guilt over drinking
Periodic attempts at abstinence
Social avoidance/isolation
Missing appointments, work, etc. in order to drink
Daily use, morning tremor, morning drinking
Tolerance, withdrawal symptoms, use to control withdrawal symptoms
Use to intoxication/unconsciousness when drinking
Arrests: Driving While Intoxicated, Driving Under the Influence, public intoxication, fighting

MOTIVATION FOR USE:

To expand consciousness, feel more at ease, expand sensual experiences, improve sexual performance, reduce feelings of helplessness or worthlessness, to forget family or school pressures/problems

16.34 Substance Abuse/Alcohol - Responses to Treatment:

IDENTIFICATION AS AN ALCOHOLIC/ADDICT: (<->)

Does not agree to any intemperate use/drinking problem/bingeing/alcoholism, brags about sprees, admits to intemperate use of alcohol/drugs, "Not addicted", does not appreciate the need for treatment

Too easily/glibly admits his/her alcoholism, self-medicates with (substances), acknowledges the negative consequences of his/her use but fails to recognize using as self-defeating, verbally identifies as an addict but shows no changed behaviors such as improved social skills, resists/denies alternative problem solutions which would support freedom from addiction, is unconcerned/too little concerned with failure of previous treatments for substance abuse, hopeless of change, seeks only to avoid problems from addiction/use or to please other people and not to change own symptomatic behaviors, verbalizes motivation but seems insincere, "just going through the motions"

Identifies self as "an alcoholic", has made sobriety his/her first priority, demonstrates insightful identification as an addict/cross addict through change in identification/life-style/relationships/behaviors, was open and receptive/understood the concepts presented, shared honestly his/her complete chemical history, dealt with the issues from a dysfunctional childhood, knew s/he was powerless over addiction and could not recover without help and support from others, demonstrated progress of the disease and the impact on his/her life, grieved over his/her losses, expressed regret, anger/felt cheated, released a lot of emotion, cried, reports hope, demonstrates hope through new behaviors, prepared an aftercare plan including a daily plan, home group meetings, how to attend (#) of meetings per week for a total of (#) meetings/weeks/days

Able to offer support/be appropriately confrontative, kept sobriety as his/her top priority, willing and did do whatever was necessary, had a positive and optimistic attitude toward the future, fearful of facing the outside world, spiritual commitment as an asset in a continued struggle, understood and practiced Relapse Prevention techniques, resisting/avoiding high temptation situations, recognizes and has plans for preventing that Hungry, Angry, Lonely, Tired leads to drinking

SPOUSE:

Participated, highly codependent, willing to examine self, became involved in his/her own recovery, supportive, blaming, angry and resentful, untrusting, needing to be convinced, uncooperative, codependent

AA AND OTHER TREATMENTS:

History of previous chemical dependency treatments, duration, longest period of sobriety afterward
Client denies need for/denigrates/rejects/attends grudgingly/mechanically/regularly/daily/is proud of membership in AA, client knows name of/is a Sponsor
S/he attended rehabilitation programs with only short-term/time limited/progressively greater/excellent success at abstinence/control

OTHER STATEMENTS:

> Concerning her insight, she treats her alcoholism with indifference and resignation, and feels hopeless and defeated so that she continues to abuse alcohol as a life-style.
>
> He rationalized about his drinking in an illogical manner suggesting its value to him. For example, he uses it to sleep, control the 'shakes', loosen up, and reports that being drunk saved his life in an auto accident.
>
> This clinically frustrating patient has been approached, encouraged or lectured by most of the staff to little effect.
>
> S/he is addicted only to one of several drugs used
>
> Has been exposed to, learned about, understood, applied and changed because of disease concept of addiction/identity as an alcoholic/cross addiction/codependency/etc.

16.35 Suicide: See also sections 7.27 for questions about suicidal ideation, and 16.19 for Impulsiveness

DEGREE OF SUICIDAL IDEATION AND BEHAVIOR: (<->)

"Impossible", highly unlikely, improbable, against strongly held religious beliefs or philosophy of life, "never" considered, wishes to live, reasons for living exceed reasons for dying, no thoughts of giving up or harming self

> Passive death wishes or ideas, "subintentioned/subintended death" (Shneidman), "chronic suicide" (Menninger), "wish to die", would leave life/death to chance, wishes without plan, tired of living

> > Considered and abandoned, flimsy rationales for refusing suicide, unlikely, not currently considered, fleeting thoughts of suicide, passive suicide attempt, would avoid steps necessary to save or maintain life, suicidal "flashes," whims

> > > Thoughts/ideation, wishes to end life, expressed ambivalence, inclination, wonders if s/he will make it through this, raises questions of life after death, debating

> > > > Verbalizations, recollections of other's suicide, plans, discusses methods and means, stated intent, used as a threat, thoughts of self-mutilation, asks others to help kill him/her

> > > > > Behaviors, gesture, non/low lethality, non-dangerous method, acts of self-mutilation, symbolic/ineffective/harmless attempts, "parasuicide," command hallucinations with suicidal intent

> > > > > > Attempt(s), deliberateness, action planning, method/means selected/acquired, high lethality method, giving away possessions, arranging affairs, wrote note, told others of intent

> > > > > > > Persistent/continuous/continual efforts, unrelenting preoccupation

INCREASED RISK/POTENTIAL OF SUICIDE IS GENERALLY RELATED TO:

1. Psychiatric status:
Having a psychiatric disorder/diagnosis raises rate 8-10 times and having depression raises the rate 80-100 times (and sever depression raises it 500 times) all for males.
Among psychiatric patients the rates of suicide for males and female are about equal because the rate for females rises greatly.

2. Psychological symptoms:
Hopelessness, helplessness
Anhedonia
Sense of lessened worth, guilt over fault
Acceptance of unalterability of painful situation, finality, irresolvable, incurable, permanent
Somatic/vegetative aspects of depression (sleep)
Extreme anxiety or panics
Increased irritation
No sense of control over ideations, etc.
Consistent pattern of leaving life crises rather than facing them
Psychosis, especially command hallucinations
Remission of psychotic episode but continuing depression
Cycling of mood within an episode of depression

Psych. symptoms are acute, not chronic
Psychotic delusions
Sleep disturbances
Confusion and disorganization of thoughts
Loss of reactivity
Recent angry, enraged or violent behavior
Morbid preoccupation with death or suicide

3. Demographics:
Caucasian (3X more adult and 2X more adolescent succeeders than Blacks and other minorities)[1]
Male (3X more succeeders, 1/3 as many attempters than females)
Medical, dental and mental health professionals, lawyers, etc.
Young adult (15-24) or geriatric (twice average rate for those 75-84, four times for white males age 85)
Most succeeders are white, US-born men aged 45-60 Protestant
Divorced status, repeated, or in last 6 months   Never-married or widowed status

4. Feasible plan of action:
Availability of means/method/opportunity/resources (e.g. weapons)
Highly lethal method selected
Specific detailed plan
Has made preparations (means, privacy)   Written suicide note
Made final arrangements   Concealed/denied ideation to interviewer
Feels capable, competent, courageous of action   Anticipates action soon
Little imminence of rescue   Clearly determinable time of suicide attempt

5. Prior suicidal behaviors: (While most completers attempted before only 10-20% of attempters succeed)
Current ideation of longer duration, higher frequency, greater acceptance
Recent attempts   Intended to die in earlier attempts
Multiple attempts (50-60% of succeeders have one previous attempt), multiple threats, statements
High lethality method in past attempts
Attempts with little chance of discovery
Attempts on anniversaries of significant events
Attempters are 3 times more likely to be female, and younger with 50% being under 30 years.

---

[1] I am grateful to Robert W. Moffie, Ph.D for correction and clarification of this issue.

6. Social isolation

No friends nearby

Living alone or with other than family members

Few or no family members available

Highly dependent personality

Loved ones all rejecting, punitive or unsupportive

Loss of sense of continuity with past or present

No warm, close interdependent relationships

Partner is also suicidal

Family history/role models of death by suicide

Spouse who is self absorbed, competitive

Family instability, early rejection

No therapeutic alliance with therapist

7. Stressors:

Sudden onset of stress

Irrevocable losses: serious medical illness or disability, chronic illness, failing health

Failure to perform major life role behavior, unemployment, failing grades resulting in humiliations

Self evaluation is excessively based upon performance in standard gender roles

Recent loss of persons, positions, possessions without replacement

Anniversary of death or loss

8. Other risk-increasing variables:

Alcoholism: Currently intoxicated, or long history of alcohol abuse without current drinking

Considering homicide as well as suicide

Refusal or inability to cooperate with treatment

History of criminal behavior

Prior inpatient psychiatric treatment

Depression with low level of 5-HIAA, high level of cortisol, high ratio of adrenaline to
noradrenaline

Beginning of recovery from depression

Few or weak deterrents

Motivation based on revenge, attention getting

Giving away favorite possessions

Organic brain syndrome

Impulsive

Putting life's affairs in order

Life risking "accidents"

Suicide modeled or reported in the media, suicide of friends/co-workers/colleagues

For a child:

Stressors such as loss of a significant other, recent suicide of peer or family member, legal
difficulties, unwanted pregnancy, recent changes of school, depression, withdrawal, birth of a
sibling

Causes of suicide and rationales differ with developmental age.

COPING WITH THE AFTERMATH OF SUICIDE: From Lukas and Seiden (1990) which is recommended.

Continuing questions about the cause, our role, prevention.

Bargains made to cope:

1. The Long Good-bye: unending mourning and fixation.
2. Scapegoating: blaming a few others, displacing rage from the suicider.
3. Guilt as punishment: assumption of responsibility and self-blame.
4. Cutting off: strangling all feeling including pleasure.
5. Physical problems: somatizing and focussing on these.
6. Running: endless moves and changes
7. Suicide:

OTHER:

Anomic, Egoistic, Altruistic suicides (Durkheim); Indirect Self-Destructive Behavior (Faberow)

Death seeker, death initiator, death ignorer, death darer (Shneidman)

More formal assessment measures include scales of ideation (Beck, Kovacs, and Weisman, 1979;
Reynolds, 1987), intent (Beck, Schyler and Herman, 1974), hopelessness (Beck, 1987).

Thought's Continuity, Content and other aspects: See section 15.9 Stream of Thought

Violence: See section 16.17 Impulse disorder

17. Personality Patterns

For each syndrome, personality disorder, character or behavior pattern there are listed descriptive words and phrases organized into clusters. No validity claims are made for the clusters or their contents, only that these descriptors are commonly used in psychological reports and in research studies. Because the clusters and concepts overlap do review other similar types.

It is sometimes useful to convey a client's personal style by reference to characters in the public media but this is easy to overdo.

17

Psnlty

17.1 A and B personality types:

TYPE A
Time Urgency:

Impatient, hurries, under pressure, prompt and often early for appointments, watches clock, walk/talk/eat rapidly, does multiple activities simultaneously, lives in the future/always planning, feel that "there's never enough time"

Hates delays: irritable, restless with other's pace, high impatience at having to wait for someone, rage at having to wait in line, detests wasting time, drives over the speed limit, evades red lights, is "hard on equipment," always underestimates the time a job will take,

Hostility:

Competitive, "must win," reluctant to share power/control/delegate, takes on more and more work, pursue more challenging tasks, makes bets, finds competitive aspect of all activities, plays as hard as works, detests losing, plays to win even against children/friends, sets higher goals for self, challenging, concerned with getting and having rather than being, hard driving
Aggressive, ambitious, gets higher grades/income, measures everything in numbers/dollars, attributes success to own speed
Dominates conversations, emphasizes words in speech, finishes other's speeches, interrupts speakers, dislikes small talk
Continual emergency reaction

Self-destructive tendencies:

Over-working, gorging on high-fat foods, overuse of stimulants, low levels of exercise, high alcohol intake, smoking, no time for self care
Works during vacations, over-plan vacation's activities, works in bed, inability to relax/be unproductive, fails to notice beauty/scenery/"smell the flowers," overschedule themselves, overcommitted, guilt over relaxing, always works more than eight hours a day,
Sits on edge of chairs, make fists, clench jaws, taps fingers, jiggles legs, rapid blinks, never still,

Cognitive:

Constant struggle for control/avoiding helplessness, inhibited need for power
Perfectionistic, demand continuous self-improvement, demand excellence in every area, always seeking to improve efficiency, underestimate own achievements, more disappointment and self doubt

Affective:

Negative, cynical, critical, ruthless in self-reproach, self-examining

"Workaholic":

Recreation only with friends from work, better communication at work than at home, organized hobbies, work as substitute for intimate contacts, reading is all work related, work late more than peers do, when awakened thoughts go to work, live by deadlines and quotas, creates unnecessary deadlines
Type B
Relaxes readily, focuses on the quality of their life, paces themselves, easygoing, "One day at a time,"
Less ambitious, lower incomes/grades
Less irritable

17.3 **"Addictive" Personality:** There has been little research support for this category.

Dissatisfaction with life
Extreme dependence, resentment of authority, flagrant selfishness, insistence on immediate gratification

<u>A</u>dult <u>C</u>hildren (and/or grandchildren) <u>O</u>f <u>A</u>lcoholics/<u>A</u>ddicts (ACOAs). See section 17.7
Codependent Personality

17.3 Aggressive Personality: See also section 17.21 Sadistic personality

CARDINAL FEATURES:

Aggression, low self restraint

BEHAVIORS:

Reckless, unflinching, fearless, undeterred by pain/danger/punishment, vicious, brutal, pugnacious, temperamental

INTERPERSONAL:

Competitive, intimidating, dominating, surgent, obstinate, controlling, opinionated, authoritarian
Humiliating, abusive, derisive, cold-blooded, persecutes, malicious

COGNITIONS:

Opinionated, close-minded, prejudiced, bigoted, authoritarian

SELF-IMAGE:

Proud of independence, hardheaded, tough, domineering, power-oriented

---

17.4 Antisocial Personality: Also called Psychopathic and Sociopathic Personality. Those who engage in criminal behavior without 'psychological' motivation should be diagnosed as Adult Antisocial Behavior, coded V 71.01, and those whose criminal behavior is due to conformance with subcultural norms are diagnosed Dyssocial personality in ICD-10.

CARDINAL FEATURES:

Predatory attitude and behavior toward others, long-standing indifference to, and repetitive violation of others rights. Parasitic life-style, repetitive socially destructive behaviors.

SOCIAL:

Irresponsible:
Untrustworthy, evades responsibility, uses guilt inductions on others, unreliable, rejects obligations, superficial relationships, ruthless, argues about 'Who's in charge'
Irresponsible parenting, marital instability, frequent marriages
Wandered from place to place without a home for a long time, told a lot of lies, used an alias, trouble because failed to pay his/her bills

Multiple marriages/divorces, suddenly left/hit/unfaithful to his/her spouse, seriously hurt/neglected a child

Cavalier, acting wild, slept around with people he/she didn't know very well, earned money by pandering/procuring/pimping/having sex with another person

Unique and self-serving ideas of "right and wrong," lies easily, frequent lying other than to avoid negative consequences

Feels or believes him/herself to be harassed/misused/victimized, resents, distrusts, suspicious, justifies behavior with lies and manipulation

A chronic pattern of infringement on the rights of others, violates social codes by lies or deceits, chronic speeders and drunk drivers, reckless, all kinds of financial irresponsibility

Indifferent to the rights of others, breaks rules, rebellious

Revengeful, petty,

BEHAVIORS:

Impulsivity, impetuous, spur-of-the-moment, short-sighted, incautious, imprudent, lack of long term plans

History of drug/alcohol/telephone/etc., overuse and abuse, but this is not cause of antisocial behaviors

Behavior problems:

From an early age, criminal convictions, diagnoses as antisocial personality, poor probation/parole risk, many types of offenses

History of truancy, initiating physical fights, used weapons in more than one fight, tortured animals, physically cruel to other people

Deliberately destroyed other's property, fire setting, steals/vandalize/"messes up" property

Has forced someone into sexual activity with him/her, promiscuity

Illegal or immoral activities:

Lying, stealing, swindling, cheating, conning, commission or involvement in minor or serious illegal or delinquent acts, breaking the law,

Trouble with the police/juvenile or school authorities, truancy/plays a lot of hooky, been a discipline problem/expelled/suspended from school,

Conned/manipulated/cheated people out of their money/possessions, predatory, often victimizes the easiest/weakest members of society, "white collar" criminal, "bottled up" anger

Used a weapon in a fight, convicted of a felony, served time, arrested

COGNITIONS:

Low planning, lack of consideration of alternatives or consequences, projects blame, rationalizes, Machievellianism: ends justify any means

Does not profit from experience of punishment

Low insight

AFFECTS:

Lacking in remorse/guilt/regret, insensitive, lacks compassion, hardened, callous, cold-blooded, emotionally detached, low motivation to change, easily bored, low frustration tolerance, shallow affects

Irritability and aggressiveness, short tempered
Intolerance of delayed gratifications, irritable and easily provoked to violence

VOCATIONAL:

Unstable employment: fired, ran away, quit a job impulsively/without another to start, "didn't work because he/she just didn't want to", court martialed/demoted, missed a lot of work or were late a lot and so got into trouble

For a Child: (Consider Oppositional Disorder, Conduct Disorder)

Truancy, starting fights, vandalism, tortured or abused ("played tricks on") animals/pets, early and extensive drug and alcohol use, behavior difficulties, theft, incorrigibility, running away overnight, bad associates, impulsivity, recklessness and irresponsibility, slovenly appearance, lack of guilt, pathological lying

PSYCHOPATHY IN CRIMINAL POPULATIONS: Adapted from Hare (1980)

1. Glibness/superficial charm
2. Previous diagnosis as a psychopath
3. Egocentricity/grandiose sense of self worth
4. Proneness to boredom
5. Pathological lying and deception
6. Conning/lack of sincerity
7. Lack of remorse or guilt
8. Lack of affect and emotional depth
9. Callous/ lack of empathy
10. Failure to accept responsibility for own actions
11. Short-tempered, low frustration tolerance, poor behavioral controls
12. Drug/alcohol abuse not directly causative of the antisocial behaviors
13. Lack of realistic long-term plans
14. Promiscuous sexual relations
15. Frequent marriages
16. Early behavior problems
17. Juvenile delinquency
18. Parasitic life-style
19. Impulsivity
20. Irresponsible parenting behaviors
21. Many types of offenses
22. Poor probation/parole risk

CLECKEY'S CLASSIC CRITERIA: Modified from *The Mask of Sanity* (1976):

Considerable superficial charm, poise, calmness, verbal facility, pleasant and convincing exterior,
Lies/cheats/steals with poise
Unpredictable, unreliable, disregard for obligations, no sense of responsibility in work, sexual, family or financial relationships
Insincerity, untruthfulness, disregard for the truth, lies, deceptions, conning, uses ruses, prevaricates
Lack of remorse, guilt, shame, concern, or even anxiety
Inexplicable impulsiveness, poor planning, no inhibitions on behaviors, recklessness, almost unmotivated misdeeds, perverse quality to these behaviors, pranks, vulgarity (antisocial behaviors)
Failure to learn from experience, poor judgement
Failure to believe his/her behavior will be punished
Egocentricity, grandiose sense of self worth

Incapacity for attachment, lack of concern for others, empathy, loyalty, callousness,
Poverty of deep or lasting emotions, shallowness, lack of emotional depth
Lack of capacity for insight or seeing oneself as others do
Ingratitude, arrogance
Impersonal, trivial and poorly integrated sex life
Average or above intelligence
Absence of delusions or other signs of irrational thinking , anxiety or other neurotic symptoms, suicide
    attempts, or a life plan or ordered way of living

Anxious Personality: See 17.16 "Nervous" Personality

Attention Deficit Disorder with and without Hyperactivity: See section 16.5 ADDH

17.5 Avoidant Personality:

CARDINAL FEATURES:

Oversensitive and vacillating, watchful for any hint of disapproval, discomfort in all social situations

INTERPERSONAL:

Yearns for closeness/warmth/affection/acceptance, but fears rejection/disapproval in relationships
Withdrawing, guarded, private, lonely, shy and reticent, timid, compliant
Wary, distrustful, vigilant for offenses/threats/ridicule/abuse/humiliation, hypersensitive/keen sensitivity
    to potential for rejection or humiliation by others, expects not to be loved, needs constant
    reassurance/guarantee of uncritical affection
Fears "goofing up"/gaffs/social errors/gaucheries/*faux pas* and so "making a fool of themselves",
    fears crying/blushing/embarrassment

AFFECTS:

Anguished, intensely ambivalent, anxious, "bored"

SELF-IMAGE:

Devalues own accomplishments, angry and depressed at self for social difficulties, sees self as
    isolated and rejected, basically defective/flawed/odd, inadequate

OTHER:

Vicious cycle of low self-esteem, fear of rejection, shallow or awkward attempts at social relating,
    hypersensitivity to lack of enthusiasm/disapproval, concludes/confirms rejection, withdrawal, fear of
    relationships, loneliness, yearning, trying again, rejection, etc.
Extensive reliance on fantasizing for gratification of needs for contact and anger discharge

COGNITIONS:

Belief that others know of their anxiety and are constantly watching for their mistakes

Alden (1992) is a fine starting point for cognitive-interpersonal treatment.

17.6 Borderline Personality:

CARDINAL FEATURES:

Instability in all aspects of living, personality functioning, mood and social relating, lack of personality consistency/cohesiveness, "cuts loose"/abrupt shifts of affect/relationships/"mini-psychotic" episodes

INTERPERSONAL:

Close, demanding, dependent relationships
Intense and unstable relationships, inexplicable changes in attitude/feelings toward others, capricious, "ups and downs", vacillating reactions, dependency-independency cycles,
Intense dislike of isolation and loneliness so engages in a series of transient/ stormy/brief relationships, superficiality of relationships based on alternating idealization and deflation

AFFECTS:

Labile, mercurial, brittle, erratic, unpredictable, rapid and short lived mood swings
Barely hidden anger/under the surface, pessimism, argumentativeness, irritable, easily annoyed, sarcastic, intense and sudden rages or depressions, sudden dramatic and unexpected outbursts, spells of emptiness and boredom, dejection and apathy, numbness
Areas of seemingly unalterable and crushing negativity, worthlessness/badness/blame/fault assumption
Tenuous and shifting controls, rage over failure of others to provide soothing, rage at intimates

IDENTITY:

Fragmentation of self, splitting
Shaky, shifts of identity/gender identity/career choices/long term goals, frequent "Who am I?", questions, nebulous/multiple identities/personalities, instability of self-esteem, self-image, personal and sexual identity, uncertain values, loyalties
Lacks internalized soothing/holding function so relies on others
Threats to right to survive

BEHAVIORS:

Impulsiveness
Impulsivity/poor judgement
Manipulative suicide threats/gestures or attempts/overdosing
Running up huge bills/shoplifting/gambling sprees
Eating binges/sexual acting out
Addictive traits and patterns, drug misuse and abuse
Self destructive/mutilating/damaging behaviors, overdoses, reckless driving
Symptom list:

OTHER:

Mixed picture with elements of other Personality disorders present, often with affective disorder diagnoses.
Overdiagnosis/misdiagnosis of Borderline is more likely with: (Morey and Ochoa, 1989) less experienced, female, psychodynamically-oriented, non-psychologist clinicians; poorer, white/Caucasian, female patients

---

17.7 Codependent Personality: See also these diagnoses: 14.5 Depression, 14.3 Anxiety disorders (PTSD, Panic disorder, social phobias), and many other personality disorders, especially Borderline.

INTERPERSONAL:

Unassertive, does not pursue own rights, adapts rather than changing a bad situation
Submission to others for predictability/security, self-sacrificing
Oversensitive to other's difficulties

Puts up a front, hides "true self"

Withdraws, isolates, loneliness

Roles adopted:

Rescuer: protecting/covering for the addicted person by making excuses absences or social mistakes
Caretaker: minimizes negative consequences of addicted person's negligence
Joiner: rationalizing or participating/assisting in addicted person's chemical dependency
Hero: protecting the family's public image/draw attention away from the addiction with enormous/"superhuman"/self-sacrificing efforts
Complainer: blaming all the family's problems on the partner's addiction, no hope of change
Adjuster: avoiding discussion of the addiction in hopes it will disappear, hiding concern and confusion with apathy

For a Child: *Rescues parents by:*
Overachieving: to give the family something to be proud of
Entertaining: never taking anything seriously to relieve tension, "class clown"
Withdrawing: escaping to friends homes or alone
Rebelling: acting out anger, causing trouble to draw attention away from family problems

Family

Extreme family loyalty
Family rules: "Don't talk, don't trust, don't feel"
Distorted family image: happy, no problems, see only the good
Over-developed sense of responsibility and concern for others
Control is valued, lack of control is terrifying, order, stability, routine, regularity, peace, not chaos
Only superficial relationships, no intimate ones as equality/equivalence is required for justice

Caretaking:

Excessive caretaking/dependency especially when stressed, undeserved loyalty
Over-responsible/over-reliable (to compensate for the addict's irresponsibility), anticipate other's
    needs ("enabling"), need to control people and situations, rigidity,

Dependency: longing for love, approval, tolerate abuse, meeting other's needs before one's own

Denial: ignore/rationalize/minimize problem, denies increased substance abuse

Loss of daily structure: missing appointments, having meals at irregular times, not getting to bed or
    up on time
Fails to complete tasks, follow through, make plans, easily overwhelmed with tasks, reactive not
    proactive
Crisis orientation not long term, good in crisis situation/beginnings and endings but not in middles

SELF-IMAGE:

Low self-esteem: self blame for any problems/other's substance use, guilt-prone, shame and guilt,
    "I'm bad/no good", extreme/unproductive self criticism/flagellation, assumption of blame due
    to inconsistency of parental behaviors
Insecurity, low self-esteem, fear/belief in one's unloveability/insanity/badness/dirtiness, Powerlessness

Shame at addiction, secretive, Very reluctant to ask for help

Acts the way they believe is "normal," doesn't know what is normal behavior, emotional responses
Anxious over not feeling/acting sufficiently "normal", feel different from anyone else you know

Adopts extreme role models and standards which would be acceptable to a group with low self-esteem

AFFECTS:

Depression, negativity, uncontrollable mood swings, no fun in life, dulled feeling, alexethymia,
    anhedonia, or enjoy only when at someone else's expense
Seriousness, life as series of problems and crises to be solved, worry is normal
Frequent resentments and anger, "Got a raw deal from life"

Fears/anxieties, fear of anger: theirs and other's, because it will end the relationship, indecision, fears of
    being hurt, abandoned, rejected

COGNITIONS:

Obsessive thinking, overreliance on analytical thinking, perfectionism
Delusions/Irrational beliefs: *Amor omnia vincit* (or at least substance abuse),
Dishonest, lies, denial, unaware of dishonesty, "(His behavior) is not the 'real' person"
Low memory of childhood

BEHAVIORS:

Physical, sexual, psychological abuse and neglect
"Addictive" behaviors: eating disorders, substance abuse, obsessive-compulsive disorder
Compulsions and obsessions
Acting out to get attention or approval

OTHER:

Health problems: stress related disorders, lack of personal care
Became addicted to cope with frustrations and pain
Neglected attention in childhood, "stroke starved", leads to denial of own needs

For a Child:

Premature adulthood and responsibilities, struggle with adult problems as child, loss of childhood

Impact of addiction varies with developmental stage of child when living in addictive household
  Bonding stage -> world is not safe
  Exploratory/separation stage: engulfed or abandoned -> passivity, no right to say "No"
  Latency stage -> failure to learn rules, what is normal, problems solving skills. Live with lies, denial, and anxiety

CHARACTERISTICS OF CODEPENDENTS: Modified from Schaef (1986)

1. External referencing: distrusting own perceptions, lacking boundaries, believing one cannot survive without a relationship/addicted to relationships, fearing abandonment, believing in the perfect union,
2. Caretaking: become indispensable, become a martyr
3. Self-centeredness: personalizing all events, assuming responsibility for other's behaviors,
4. Over-controlling: increasing control efforts when chaos increases, attempting to control everything and everyone, controlling without caring for those controlled, believing that with more effort you can fix the addict/family
5. Feelings: unaware of feelings, distorting emotional experiences/accepting only acceptable feelings, fearfulness,
6. Dishonesty: managing all impressions made, omitting/ lying about the truth, rigidity
7. Gullibility: being a bad judge of character, unwillingness to confront, over-trusting, accepting what fits the way on wishes things were,

Cermak (1991), in a very thoughtful analysis of the problems, offers these criteria:

LAY SYMPTOMS OF CODEPENDENCE:
Changing who you are to please others.
Feeling responsible for meeting other people's needs at the expense of your own.
Low self-esteem
Driven by compulsions
Denial

DIAGNOSTIC CRITERIA:
a. Continued investment of self-esteem in the ability to influence/control feelings and behavior, both in oneself and in others, in the face of serious adverse consequences.
b. Assumption of responsibility for meeting other's needs, to the exclusion of acknowledging one's needs.
c. Anxiety and boundary distortions around intimacy and separation.
d. Enmeshment in relationships with personality-disordered, chemically dependent, and impulse-disordered individuals.
e. Exhibits at least three of the following:
    1. Excessive reliance on denial.
    2. Constriction of emotions (with or without dramatic outbursts).
    3. Depression
    4. Hypervigilance
    5. Compulsions
    6. Anxiety
    7. Substance abuse
    8. Recurrent victim of physical or sexual abuse
    9. Stress-related medical illnesses
    10. Has remained in a primary relationship with an active substance abuser for at least two years without seeking outside support.

Ackerman (1987) is a bibliography of 700 references in the clinical and empirical literature. In general there has been little empirical support for the validity for a pattern of characteristics in ACOAs (See, for example Logue, *et al.* 1992 and Sher, 1991).

17.8 Compulsive Personality: See also section 17.18 Obsessive Personality

CARDINAL FEATURE:

Repetitious behaviors or else irresistible anxiety

BEHAVIORS:

Highly regulated/organized life-style, a "checker", a "hand-washer"
    Rituals of magic or checking, hoarding

COGNITION: See Shapiro (1965)

Rumination prevents task completion, hyper-careful, doubting, indecisive, poor decision making and follow-through, poor time management

Excessively moralistic concerns, scrupulousness, intense self-evaluation/scrutiny, 'black or white' judgements

Perfectionistic approach, over-attention to detail and avoidance of error, neatness, meticulous, a "fanatic," need for immediate closure

Officious, concern with form over content/procedures/regulations more than the goal/letter of the law not the spirit/orderly task procedures rather than the outcome, sees the world in terms of schedule/rules/regulations

AFFECTS

His/her only pleasure is in elaborate planning, only mild/brief pleasure with the completion of projects, a "work" not "pleasure" orientation

Joyless, solemn, grim, controls most emotions, unrelaxed, occasional intense righteous indignation

Perceived lack of control of environment leads to intense depression, great need and effort to control tension and anxiety

Fears of contamination

SELF-IMAGE:

Industrious, reliable, efficient, loyal, prudent/careful

INTERPERSONAL:

Demanding on others for doing thing his/her way,
Is seen as somber, formal, cold
Respectful, conventional, follows the proprieties, polite, correct
Shows reaction formation in positive, socially acceptable presentation of self

17.9 Dependent Personality: See also section 17.24 Self-Defeating Personality and 17.7 Codependent Personality

Do not confuse this with, or assume sexual masochism

CARDINAL FEATURE:

Undue dependence upon others

INTERPERSONAL:

Passive, docile, compliant, conciliatory, placates, self-sacrificing, deferring, uncompetitive
Dependent, allows others to assume responsibility for self, reliance on others to solve problems or
    achieve goals, to decide on employment/friendships/child management/vacations/clothing/purchases,
    absence of independent decision making, avoids external demands and responsibilities, low self-
    reliance, low autonomy, exaggerated and unnecessary help-seeking behaviors
Submissive, dominated, secondary status, self-defeating, abused, unable to make demands on others,
    "Niceifier", childlike, immature
Vicious cycle of dependency, abuse, proof of helplessness and worthlessness, avoidance of taking
    self-respecting or independent actions, lessened self-esteem, greater dependency, subordinates
    own needs so as to maintain protective relationships/fulfill core role/identity
Over-devoted, super-loyal, attached, over-loving, "Love Slob, willing to tolerate more negatives in a
    relationship than the evaluator, over-hopeful of change, too trusting, sacrificing for "love"

BEHAVIORS:

General ineffectiveness in autonomy but not incompetence, but may demonstrate exceptional skill in
    some areas,
Lacking in skills/motivation for independent life
Abused: neglected, insulted, belittled, berated, "imprisoned", exploited, tolerates partners abusive
    affairs/beatings/drunkenness

MOOD:

Hidden depression and angers, whiney, tantrums, complains,
Separation leads to depression, terror of abandonment

SELF-IMAGE:

Self derogating, belittling, martyr-like, self-sacrificing, low self-confidence, "inferiority complex",
    " stupid", humble, self-effacing, self-deprecating, inadequate, inept, fragile
Hidden strengths, denies/undervalues own skills

COGNITIONS:

Believes in magical solutions to problems
Naive, gullible, unsuspicious, "Pollyanna"
Belief in salvation through love (*Amor omnia vincit*)
Guilt proneness, assumes blame

17.10 Histrionic Personality:
Current usage does not support "Hysteric", and they are not all females.

CARDINAL FEATURE:

Attention seeking through self-dramatization and exaggerated emotion

AFFECTS:

Exaggerated, labile/rapid/vivid/shallow affect, easily "overcome" with emotions, easily enthused/ disappointed/angered/excitable, theatrical/flamboyant/intensely expressed reactions, overly dramatic behaviors, creates dramatic effects, seems to be acting out a role, exaggerated and unconvincing emotionality

BEHAVIORS:

Overreacts to minor annoyances, inappropriate, affectations, affected, over-reactive, overdetermined
Repeated/impulsive/dramatic/manipulative suicide gestures/attempts
Creative and imaginative

COGNITIONS: See Shapiro (1965)

Forgetting, repression, unreflective, self-distracting, distractible
Lives in a non-factual world of experience, impressionistic perception and recollection/global/diffuse, lacking in sharpness, non-analytical
Impressionable, susceptible to the vivid/striking or forcefully presented
Magical solutions to problematical situations, hunches, "women's intuition", child-like, does not adapt to change well
Superficial and stereotyped insights

INTERPERSONAL:

Seductive, exhibitionistic, vain, manipulative, asserts "a women's right to change her mind", dominates conversation, trivializes topics, lengthy dramatic stories, self-dramatizing, facades, "life of the party"/center of attention, fickle, wants to please
Romantic outlook: fantasies of rescue, nostalgia, sentimentalism, idealization of partner; world of "villains and heroes", makes poor social relationship choices and decisions, poor judgements about partners/friends/spouses, stormy relationships, with little real or durable enjoyment
Initially seen by others as warm and affectionate, guileless, vivid. Later seen as selfish, narcissistic, shallow/superficial and insincere, ungenuine, inconsiderate, self-pitying, shows astonishment/ little understanding of the implications of her or his behavior/its consequences/effects on others/destructiveness
Oppressively demanding, taking without giving, egocentric, vain, petulant, easily bored, requires excessive external stimulation, attention-seeking, help seeking, manipulates for reassurances, excessive needs for attention/praise/approval/gratification
Helpless, dependent, suggestible, uncritical, unassertive, sees assertion as rude or nasty, seen as fragile
Impetuous, period of wild acting out, irresponsibility, chemical abuse, bar-hopping, bed-hopping/sexual promiscuity/casual sexuality, low/poor impulse control/judgement/insight, thoughtless judgements
Self-centered, is either hurt, deserted or betrayed in all relationships, brief and superficial contrition, sees self as sensitive and vulnerable, unsubstantial sense of self, absence of political or other convictions

STYLIZED/CARICATURED "FEMININITY" :

"Faints" at the sight of blood, swoons, "vapors", coy, seductive, flirtatious, sexually provocative, excessive time spent in romantic fantasies, blushes, easily embarrassed, giggles, naive, lacking in accurate sexual knowledge, seductive for help not sex, preoccupied with sex
Vain, selfish, immature, overdependent, shallow, self-dramatizing/sexy/flamboyant/dramatic clothing/ hairstyle/makeup, looks/dresses like a teenager/prostitute/"slut"/"tramp"

SELF-IMAGE:

Charming, gregarious, stimulating, playful
Sensitive to others/feelings
Selective incompetencies in areas of low importance, e.g. numbers, specifics

SOMATIC COMPLAINTS:

Vague, changeable, movable, "women's problems", complains of aging/appearance changes, feigns illness, swooning, always wrong weight, *La belle indifference* (infrequent)

17.11 Hypochondriacal Personality: See also 16.21 Malingering. These are from Tyrer, *et al.* (1990):

Preoccupation with maintenance of health through dietary restriction, 'healthy' medications, vitamins
Distorted perception of minor symptoms so that they are elevated to major and life-threatening diseases
Demand for medical consultations for investigation, treatment and reassurance, and when these are unproductive seeking alternative health care providers
Rigid and persistent beliefs about health and life-styles

"Familiar face", "Crock" (treated by a "Quack"), "Gourd", "Thick chart patient"
Dependent hostility - expecting both care and failure.
Complaints, hypersensitivity to medications, need (?) to suffer, joyless/unfulfilling lives, overresponsible

THE SPECTRUM OF SOMATIC PRESENTATION: The Real Patient and the Crock and the Crook. From Nadelson (1986)

Sickness assignment

	Medical A	Psychiatric B1	B2	Legal C1	C2
Specific Diagnostic Category	Infection, trauma, cancer metabolic disease	'Psychosomatic" or "Psych. factors affect. phys. cond."	Repetitive somat- izers, psychogen- ic pain, hypo- chondriasis, conversion disrdr.	Facticia- producers, Munchausen	Malingerers
Psychological Forces as Mechanism	"No" psychic factors	Unconscious production of symptoms and signs		Conscious of production of signs and symptoms	

Data do not suggest greater presentation in the elderly or females.

17.12 Inadequate Personality:

CARDINAL FEATURE:

Under-responsive in all life functions, immature, vulnerable, preoccupied

INTERPERSONAL:

Underproductive/ineffective in all areas: conversational initiatives, qualities of emotions, depth of
    relationships
Victimized or abused, taken advantage of, gullible
Passive and unaware

SELF-IMAGE:

Intense feelings of inadequacy and inferiority, self-conscious (often painfully so)

AFFECTS:

Anxious and insecure
Weepy sentimentalism, involvement in melodramatic situations, over-seriousness with authority
    figures

OTHER:

Undifferentiated
Primitive defenses, unable to use intelligence to address problems

17.13 Manipulative Personality: See also sections 17.4 Antisocial and 17.15 Narcissistic Personality

CARDINAL FEATURE:

Unprincipled and deceitful in dealing with others who have something s/he wants.

BEHAVIORS:

Externalizes all blame, takes no responsibility for unfavorable outcomes
Repeated, impulsive, dramatic, self-serving suicide gestures/attempts
Evasive/indirect responses to questions, dishonest, untruthful
Connives, cheats, deceptive, fraudulent, Machiavellian, unethical, unprincipled, unscrupulous, cavalier,
    showy acts of devotion
Disloyal, untrustworthy, unfaithful, unscrupulous

SELF-IMAGE:

Grandiose ideas about him/herself

SOCIAL:

Likeable, attractive, engaging, center of attention, socially capable/ effective/charming/graceful,
Tells tall tales, flip, glib, fast, witticisms, attempts to con, puns, word plays, overabundant ideas
Imposter, narcissistic

17.14 Multiple Personality Disorder: See also section 16.13 Dissociative disorder

Most studies have found extensive overlap with the symptoms of Borderline Personality disorder. Ross, *et al.,* (1990) has suggested that the crucial differentiator is some form of amnesia or blank spell in MPD. Good references are Ross (1989), and Putnam (1991)

SEPARATE SELVES:

One central self/primary/**Host** personality, belief that the primary personality cannot handle the
memories/pain, primary personality must be punished/should die
Host is depressed, anxious, compulsively good, "masochistic", moralistic, and seeks treatment

Alters: semiautonomous subpersonalities, many (3 to 100, mean = 15), strikingly different from
primary personality, some are good and some bad, some common "roles" are: Child, Protector,
Persecutor, Opposite/Other Sex alter, a perfect person, odd names/characterological titles

Mutual and unidirectional amnesias of the selves

Transitions are sudden, unexpected, precipitated by stress, or some regular pattern of social or
environmental cues, often accompanied by headaches, feelings of weakness, amnesia/blackouts,

HISTORY OF CHILDHOOD sexual and or physical abuse, neglect: believe self responsible for abuse suffered,
deserved abuse because of badness, anger, imperfection, belief that the abuse will/does continue
although impossible, MPD as coping with victimization

PRESENTING SYMPTOMS: in descending order of frequency:

Amnesia, depression, history of childhood sexual abuse, fugue, suicide attempts, auditory
hallucinations, history of drug abuse, history of childhood physical abuse, sexual dysfunction,
headaches, child personalities, history of alcohol abuse, history of any type of conversion disorder,
history of rape (from Coons and Milstein, 1986)
Problems with showing anger, frustration, defiance
Problems with trust, safety, betrayal, suspicion, will be disbelieved

SIGNS OF MULTIPLE PERSONALITY IN CHILDREN:

Confusion about location/time/person, responding to more than one name, marked and rapid shifts
in personality, forgetting recent events, losing track of time, intense denial of guilt when confronted,
hearing of voices
Extreme or odd variations in skills such as handwriting, in food preferences, in artistic abilities, in
responses to discipline
Self-injurious behaviors, somatic complaints or hysterical symptoms: sleepwalking, sudden blindness,
loss of sensation

17.15 Narcissistic Personality: See also section 17.13 Manipulative Personality

CARDINAL FEATURE:

Self-centeredness

ASSOCIATED FEATURES:

Exhibitionism, craves adoration

SELF-IMAGE:

Grandiose sense and fantasies of self-importance/uniqueness/entitlement, "special",
Easy loss of self esteem, "a fraud/fake", times of intense self-doubt, self-consciousness
Fantasies of continuous conquests/successes/power/admiration/beauty/love, brags of his/her talents
   and achievements, predicts great success for self, believes entitled to and deserving of a high salary,
   overvalues all of his/her own achievements

INTERPERSONAL RELATIONSHIPS:

Entitled, confident, self-assured, expects to be treated as a sterling success or gifted person or at least
   better than others, special and preeminent, hides behind a mask of intellectual or other superiority,
   exaggerated self-esteem easily reinforced by small evidences of accomplishment and easily
   damaged by tiny slights and oversights, compliment hunger, enduring feelings of mortification and
   worthlessness triggered by failure
Fragile self-esteem, loss of self esteem when disapproved, crushed/inflamed by life's wounds, responds
   to criticism with rage or despair or cool nonchalance, compulsive checking on other's regard, may
   ruminate for a long time over non-threatening social situations and interactions, extensive brooding
Relationships are seen entirely in terms of what others can offer, lack of objectivity, arrogant, socially
   insensitive, exploitative, resents any failure to immediately and totally gratify his/her needs,
   demanding of affection/ sympathy, flattery and favors, insatiably requires acclaim for momentary
   good feelings, flouts the social rules, alternates idealization of and arrogant contempt for friends,
   long history of erratic relationships, takes others for granted, drives people away, his/her
   understanding of social conventions is distorted by egocentrism
Striking lack of empathy, indifferent to rights of others, heedless, reckless, neglectful, indifferent,
   thoughtless, tactless, selfish, ungrateful, unappreciative, delinquent, sloppy,
Oppositional/argues with authorities/instructions/examiner/supervisor, little attention paid to work tasks,
   lies to protect ego/privileges/position, rationalizes, self-deceives, distorts facts, insistence on having
   his/her own way
Grandiose, cocky, intimidating, belligerent, resentful, pretentious, sarcastic, cavalier, boorish, bumptious,
   obnoxious, self-indulgent
Conversations so circumstantial that others lose interest

AFFECTS:

Nonchalance, imperturbable, insouciant, optimistic, all unless ego damage/threats
Chronic unfocussed depression
Absence of expressions of warmth

COGNITIONS:

Envy
Preoccupation with own performance's value, attention getting behaviors

17.16 "Nervous" Personality: See section 14.3 Anxiety

"High-strung", worrier, "worry-wart", anxiety-ridden, "bad nerves", excitable, easily upset, unstable, moody, skittish, temperamental

Picky, chronically dissatisfied, carping, fault finding

Avoids/dislikes crowds, socially anxious, shy, sensitive, thin-skinned, low self-esteem, hard on him/herself

Low stress/frustration tolerance, "cracks up", "falls apart"

17.17 Normal Personality:

Rather than rely on the absence of pathology here are several options for describing a healthy or highly functional personality. Criteria of Positive Mental Health.

A. Michael B. Frisch (1991) offers these 17 areas of life function as assessed by his Quality of Life Inventory:

Health	Realistic self-regard	Having a Philosophy-of-Life
Work	Recreation	Learning
Creativity	Social Service to others	Civic Action
Love Relationship	Friendships	Relationships with Children
Community	Relationships with Relatives	Having a Home

Having a stable and adequate Standard of Living

Neighborhood safety, aesthetics, naturalness, people

B. Freud: "Arbeiten und leben": to be able to work and love

C. From Marie Jahoda, (1958)
1. Awareness, acceptance, and correctness of self concept
2. Mastery of the environment and adequacy in meeting demands of life
3. Integration and unity of personality, whole-hearted pursuit of your goals
4. Autonomy and self-reliance
5. Perception of reality and social sensitivity
6. Continued growth toward self actualization

D. From Edward Shoben, (1957)
1. Aptitude for capitalizing on past experience
2. Self control
3. Ability to envisage ideals
4. Social reliability [predictability]
5. Capacity to act independently while still acknowledging the need for relationships [interdependence]

D. Harold A. Mosak suggests normality means:
1. Frequency: the common, the usual, normal.
2. As I think others act: Referential
3. As a therapist acts: Therapist as referent
4. Me: Taking oneself on faith
5. As I used to be: My premorbid condition
6. Conformity to social rules and norms, the normative: Being a good student [i.e. no trouble to the educational establishment], a good kid [quiet and undemanding],

7. Mediocrity/mediocre: nothing in excess, the mean
8. Square, boring, straight, "Dullsville"
9. Perfection
10. The absence of symptoms

17.18 Obsessive Personality: See also 17.8 Compulsive Personality, 16.9 Compulsions, and 16.22 Obsessions

CARDINAL FEATURE:

Over-ideational, worries, overconscientiousness

COGNITIONS: See Shapiro (1965)

Ruminates, doubting, balances pro and con, ponders, over-ideational, over-deliberateness, "thinks too much", distrusts own judgements, rejects new ideas or data, flounders, dithers, ponders endlessly
Indecisive, avoids decision situations, reverses decisions, wishy-washy, vacillates, fears making any mistake
Must never be irresponsible/careless/inappreciative/bad/imperfect/flawed[1], over responsibility, overconscientious,
Overdependence on intellect and logic, overconfidence in own will power, intolerant of affects
Procrastinates, dawdles, delays, avoids, denies, ineffectiveness, important tasks done last, mistakes immediate for important
Preoccupation with trivial details, over-concern with technical details, compelled attention to details, "can't see the forest for the trees", "rearranges the deck chairs on the *Titanic*", a fanatic, a stickler for details, gives unnecessary warnings and reminders

Preoccupation with the mechanics of efficiency such as list making/organizing/schedule making/ revising/following rules, fears of loss of control
Exquisite care of belongings/"preciousness", meticulous
Perfectionism, demandingness, rigidity, inflexibility, "never good enough", concern with doing things the one right way, judgmental, moralistic
Religious concerns: scrupulosity, seeking repeated reassurance from spiritual guides, repetition of religious rituals because of their possible invalidity, sense of sinfulness and guilt

Tense activity, effortful, burdened, driven, suffers under deadlines, pressured, racing thoughts
Mild rituals, ritualistic interests, repeated 'incantations', magical thinking (e.g. ones's specialness)
Controlled by "Tyranny of the Shoulds" (Karen Horney), "Musterbates" (Albert Ellis)

Attention is rigidly and narrowly focussed on own interests, on technical details. Novel stimuli are rejected as distractions

AFFECTS:

Isolation of affect, loss of spontaneity, stiff and formal in relating, incapable of genuine/intense pleasure in anything, ambivalences, mixed feelings, depression
Terrified of being embarrassed/humiliated, fears being found inadequate/wanting/making a mistake
Terror of the unknown, uncontrollable, unpredictable

---

[1] From Marcia L. Whisman, ACSW, St. Louis, MO.

INTERPERSONAL:

Proper, careful, dutiful, stilted, dogmatic, opinionated, inflexible
Uncomfortable on vacations or unstructured times
Demanding and controlling, but resists other's control

17.19 Paranoid Personality: See section 16.24 Paranoia

CARDINAL FEATURES:

Distrust and vigilance

INTERPERSONAL:

Distrusts, un/mistrustful of others, over-cautious, suspiciousness, unwarranted distrust, expects
mistreatment and treachery, distrusts motives of others, suspects manipulations, distrust previous
"allies"

Skeptical/cynical view of others, power themes in conversations, expects poor treatment from others,
questions loyalty of others, believes others are trying to put him at a disadvantage/are plotting
against/laugh at/comment on him/her, or call him homosexual him/her

Vigilant, sensitive to deception, betrayal, deprecation, put-downs, listens for insulting/questioning
references, hypersensitivity to criticism

Guarded, immune to correction, defensive, reinforced expectations lead to isolation/enhancing distrust
Hostile, belligerent, oppositional, confrontational, argumentative, stubborn, quick to take offense, easily
offended, desire to vanquish/humiliate/deprecate, makes disparaging remarks

Revenge fantasies, preoccupied with/desires to get even, carries grudges, schemes

Desires to remain independent, no close relationships, refusal to confide, aloof, distant, isolated,
withdrawn, retreats, secretive, terror of being controlled, continuous and extreme defense of
autonomy, dread of passive surrender, a loner unless in total control of other/group, jealous of
other's status

Made indirect references to/hinted at/ideas of reference, knowing looks, winks, oblique

Difficult, rigid, oppositional, deflects criticism onto others, recognizes no faults in self, denies
responsibility or blame, blames others for all negative outcomes and frustrations, externalizes blame,
never forgives or forgets, 'chip on shoulder'

Carping, hypercritical, fault finding

Arrogant, prideful, overbearing, boastful, sensational plans, grandiosity, inflated appraisal of own
worth/contacts/power/knowledge, takes a superior posture, disgusted by other's weakness

Attention is narrowly focussed, searching for confirmation, clues. Novel stimuli are interpreted for real
meanings

COGNITIONS: See Shapiro (1965)

Projects, distorts the significance of actions and facts, loss of a sense of proportion

Rigid and repetitive searching for confirmation of suspicions/ideas of reference/personalized meanings, attends only to conforming evidence/clues, belief in own convictions of underlying truth, magnifies minor social events into confirmations of the evil intentions of others and their lying, exaggerating distortions resulting in delusions, flimsy or unfounded reasons produce intense suspicion, sensitive to slights

Vigilant for signs of trickery/exploitation/abuse, hypervigilant, constant scanning for treachery, resentful, hypersensitive, hyperalert, hypersensitive, oversensitive to any changes/the unexpected/ anything out of the ordinary, fears of surprises

Creates a "pseudocommunity" (Cameron)

AFFECTS:

Shallow emotional responses, cold and humorless, absence of tender or sentimental feelings, unemotional, restricted, enigmatic and fixed smile/smug, humorless
Edgy, rarely relaxes, on guard, tense, anxious, worried, threatened, motor tension, touchy, irascible
Jealous, envious, jealousy of progress of others

SELF-IMAGE:

Bitter, overlooked, feels mistreated, taken advantage of, tricked, pushed around, abused, threatened, collects injustices, suspects being "framed/set up"
Grandiose, self-important
Rational, unemotional, careful, sees self as objective and unemotional

DELUSIONAL SYSTEM: See also section 16.11 Delusions

Belief in unusual or irrational ways of knowing e.g. reading the future, magical thinking, ESP
Delusions of power, status, knowledge or contact

OTHER:
Auditory hallucinations/voices which command, mock or threaten
Litigious

Passive Personality: See 17.9 Dependent Personality

17.20 Passive-Aggressive Personality:

CARDINAL FEATURE:

Intentional ineffectiveness and unacknowledged hostility

INTERPERSONAL:

Indirect control of others without taking responsibility for actions or anger, denies/refuses open statements of resistance/maintains own "good intentions", superficially submissive,
Indirectly expressed resistance to demands of others for performance, thwarts/frustrates authority/spouse/partners/relatives
Intentional but unconscious passivity to hide aggression., denial or confusion over own role in conflict, gives mixed signals -go away and come close - to those closest
Overcritical, "left-handed" compliments, subtle attacks, blames, insults, complains to others/"bitchs", critical of boss/all authorities/those with power/control over him/her, carping/fault-finding as defense against intimacy/commitment
Autocratic/tyrannical, demanding, manipulative, harassing, ambivalent, ruminates
Troubled/conflictual marriages

AFFECTS:

Denial of most emotions especially anger, hurt, resentment, hostile motives, cannot say a direct 'No'

VOCATIONAL/ACADEMIC:

Intentional inefficiency that covertly conveys hostility, veiled hostility, resents control/demands. Fails to meet deadlines
Qualifies obedience with: tardiness, dawdling, sloppiness, stubbornness, sabotage, "accidental" errors, procrastination, forgetfulness, incompleteness, withholding of critical information/responses/replies, leisurely work pace
Not lazy or dissatisfied with job but spotty employment record, no promotions despite ability

Psychopathic Personality: See section 17.4 Antisocial Personality

17.21 Sadistic Personality:

CARDINAL FEATURE:

Cruelty

FEATURES:

Demeaning, aggressive dominating behavior pattern, embarrasses/humiliates/demeans others
Brutal, enjoys making others suffer, has lied to make others suffer, intimidates/frightens/terrorizes others to gain own wants, restricts others autonomy, uses power in harsh manner for discipline or mistreatment, uses threats/violence/physical cruelty to dominate others, quickly escalates level of violence to re-establish dominance, fascinated by violence/injury/torture/weapons/martial arts, etc.

N. B. Consensual sadomasochistic activities have these characteristics (Modified from Weinberg, 1978): 1) agreement about which partner is dominant/submissive; 2) shared awareness that they are playacting; 3) informed, voluntary, explicit consent; 4) a sexual context; 5) shared awareness that this behavior is sadomasochistic.

17.22 Schizoid Personality:

CARDINAL FEATURE:

Social remoteness and emotional constriction.

SOCIAL:

Solitary, aloof, social isolation, no close friends, "loner," withdrawn, unobtrusive, an isolate, remote, indifferent to others, only attends to formal and external aspects of relationships
Solitary interests, daydreams, self-absorption, may seem "not with it", inaccessible

Limited social skills, unresponsive, unable to form attachments, "fades into the background", peripheral roles, rarely dates or only passively

Indifferent to other's praise/other's feelings/criticism, complacent, lacking in social understanding

Normal or below average work performance and achievement, unless work does not require social contact

COGNITIONS:

Impoverished/barren/sterile cognitions

Circuitous thinking, preoccupied with abstract and theoretical ideas, vague and obscure thought processes, unconventional cognitive approach

Intellectualizes, mechanical,

Excessive compulsive fantasizing, fantasies are sources of gratification and motivation, hostile flavor to fantasies

Vague and indecisive, absentminded

BEHAVIORS:

Lethargic, low vitality, lack of spontaneity, sluggish

AFFECTS:

Emotional coldness, limited capacity to relate emotionally, flat, impassive, blunted affect, emotional remoteness, absence of warm emotions toward others, no deep feelings for another, unfeeling, only weak/shallow emotions, weak erotic needs, cold, stark affects

17.23 Schizotypal Personality:

CARDINAL FEATURES:

Having the interpersonal difficulties of the schizoid plus eccentricities or oddness of thinking/behavior and/or perception

BEHAVIORS:

Idiosyncratic
Odd, curious, bizarre, undoing of "evil" thoughts or "misdeeds"
Odd speech with vague, fuzzy, odd expressions
Odd clothing or personal style

COGNITIONS:

Magical thinking: superstitiousness, clairvoyance, telepathy, precognition, recurrent illusions

Autistic, ruminative, metaphorical, poorly separates personal and objective/fantasy and common realities, dissociations, depersonalizations and derealizations

Sees life as empty and lacking in meaning
Sometimes paranoid ideation and style

AFFECTS:

Chronic discomfort, negative affects

INTERPERSONAL:

Suspicious, tense, wary, aloof, withdrawn, tentative relationships, gauche, eccentric, peripheral, clandestine
Dull, uninvolved, apathetic, unresponsive or obliquely reciprocating

17.24 Self-Defeating Personality: See also section 17.9 Dependent Personality.
N.B. Beware of gender bias in the application of this diagnosis.

CARDINAL FEATURES:

Chooses situations which would cause him/her to suffer mistreatment, failure or disappointment

AFFECTS:

Avoids pleasurable or success experiences, does not perform success-producing tasks despite possessing the ability,

INTERPERSONAL:

Excessive and unsolicited self-sacrifice/sacrifice induces guilt in others and then avoidance, provokes rejection by others and then feels hurt or humiliated, responds to success with depression/guilt/self-harming behaviors

Rejects or does not pursue relationships with seemingly caring or needed/helpful (e.g. a therapist) partners, undermines self, seeks hurt/humiliation, "snatches defeat from the jaws of victory", chooses unavailable partners, sees those who treat him/her well as boring or unattractive, selects relationships with abusive persons, sexually stimulated in relationships with exploitative or insensitive partners, "masochistic", incites anger/abuse/rejection

Sociopathic Personality: See section 17.4 Antisocial Personality

Type A and Type B personalities: See section 17.1 A and B Personalties

---

17.25 Interpersonal Diagnoses of Personality :

The DSM's categories are about individuals fairly well isolated from the social context in which their maladaptive behavior occurs. Mclemore and Benjamin (1979) argue that diagnoses ought to be rigorous descriptions of interpersonal and social behavior of interest.

A. One model (Benjamin, 1982) suggests incorporating the most relevant dimensions: autonomy/interdependence, friendliness/hostility, and dominance/submission.

B. Transactional analysis is another well worked out paradigm.

C. Schutz's FIRO-B. See Schutz (1958)

D. Leary (1957) also deserves more attention than it has received.

18. Diagnostic Statement/Impression

18.1 Diagnosis is Qualified as:

Initial, deferred, principal, additional/co-morbidity, rule out ..., admitting, tentative, working, final, discharge, in remission, quiescent

DSM-III-R offers specification as: Mild, Moderate, Severe, In Partial Remission, Residual State, or Full Remission

18.2 ICD-10 Chapter V: International Classification of Diseases, 10th Edition, Chapter V: Mental and Behavioral Disorders. 1992. Compiled by the World Health Organization of the United Nations, ICD-*10* codes have been completely revised. They are, gingerly and incompletely, indicated in the far right column, below, where they match. The mental health part, Chapter 5, of ICD-10 is available from the American Psychiatric Press, for (as of 1993) $45 (Order # DACA4422).

18.3 The Diagnostic and Statistical Manual

DSM III-R: This available from American Psychiatric Press, Inc., Order Department, 1400 K Street, N.W. Washington, D.C. 20005 or 1-800-368-5777 for (as of 1993) $43.95 (hardcover, Item # DACA2018) or $32.95 (paperback, Item # DACA2019) plus $5.00 shipping and handling. Call for information; their catalog is informative.

DSM-IV: The names and code numbers indicated below are not official as of the date of printing this book so they are indicated in brackets "[ ]."
DSM-IV is promised after 11/93. When final, you can write in the code numbers and cross out any proposed diagnoses which fail to appear in the final edition.

The Multiaxial system
Axis   I   Clinical syndromes and V codes - All Disorders (maladaptive patterns or clinical syndromes) except Personality Disorders and Specific Developmental Disorders
        II   Specific Developmental disorders (in children) and Personality disorders (long standing patterns, in adults). Personality disorders may be moved to axis I in DSM4.
                V71.09   No diagnosis on axis I or II
                799.90   Diagnosis deferred on axis I or II
        III   Physical disorders and conditions present which are believed to be relevant to the disorders listed on Axes I or II.
        IV   Severity of psychosocial stressors.
        V   Global assessment of functioning.

V-Codes: Consider the noting of these "conditions not attributable to a mental disorder that are a focus of attention or treatment."

These diagnoses categories are **listed in order of most frequent use** and **then in numerical order** within the category. This is an *almost* complete and *almost* final listing and is presented only for convenient reference by the knowledgeable clinician. If there is any uncertainty about the choice of diagnosis the appropriate manuals should be consulted.

DSM4	Name of Disorder	ICD-10

18.4 Anxiety disorders:

DSM4	Name of Disorder	ICD-10
300.00	Anxiety, Not Otherwise Specified [Same in DSM4]	F41.9
.02	Generalized anxiety disorder[Same in DSM4 and includes Overanxious Disorder of Childhood]	F41.1
.01	Panic, without agoraphobia (specify severity of panic attacks) [Same in DSM4]	F41.0
.21	Panic, with agoraphobia (specify severity of agoraphobic avoidance) [Same in DSM4] [Cued panic attacks] [Uncued panic attacks]	F40.01
.22	Agoraphobia, without history of panics	F40.00
.23	Social phobia [Same in DSM4]	F40.1
.29	Simple phobia/Specific phobia [Same in DSM4]	F40.2
.30	Obsessive Compulsive Disorder [Same in DSM4]	
	ICD-10 offers these: Mostly Obsessions = F42, Mostly Compulsions = F42.1, Mixed = 42.2, Unspecified = 42.9	
.81	[Post-traumatic stress disorder]	
.89	Post-raumatic stress disorder (specify if delayed onset)	F43.1
293.80	[Anxiety disorder due to a general medical condition] [Acute stress disorder] [Brief reactive dissociative disorder]	F43.

18.5 Affective disorders:

DSM4	Name of Disorder	ICD-10
296.2x	Major depression, single episode [Same in DSM4]	
.3x	Major depression, recurrent (specify if chronic, or if melancholic) [Same in DSM4]	
300.40	Dysthymia (old depr. neurosis), (specify primary/secondary, early /late onset) [Same in DSM4]	F34.1
311.00	Depressive disorder, NOS [Same in DSM4]	F34.9
	For the above specify if seasonal pattern (consider Seasonal Affective Disorder)	
V62.82	Uncomplicated bereavement [Same in DSM4]	
296.0x	[Bipolar I, single manic episode]	F30.9
.5x	Bipolar, depressed. ICD-10 offers these: With psychotic symptoms = F31.4, without = F31.5	

.4	[Bipolar I, most recent episode manic]	
.4x	Manic [Bipolar I, most recent episode hypomanic]	F31.
?	Mania (not bipolar) ICD-10 offers With F30.2 and Without F30.1 Psychotic Symptoms	F30.
.5	[Bipolar I, most recent episode depressed] (See Chapter 14. 11 Bipolar disorders)	
.6x	Mixed	F31.6
.7	NOS [Bipolar I, most recent episode unspecified]	F31.9
	[Single episode type]	
	[Recurrent type]	F33
	[Rapid cycling bipolar disorder]	
.80	[Bipolar disorder, NOS]	
.83	[Mood disorder due to a general medical condition]	
.89	[Bipolar II - Recurrentajor depressive episodes and hypomanic episodes]	
.90	Mood disorder, NOS	
301.13	Cyclothymia [Same in DSM4]	F34

Code current state on above diagnoses as x =: 1 = mild, 2 = moderate, 3 = severe, without psychotic features, 4 = with psychotic features (specify mood congruent/incongruent), 5 = in partial remission, 6 = in full remission, 0 = unspecified. [Same in DSM4]

	[Mixed anxiety-depressive disorder]	F41.2
	[Minor depressive disorder]	
	[Recurrent brief depressive disorder]	F38.10

18.6 Adjustment disorders:

309.00	with depressed mood [Same in DSM4] ICD-10 is F43.20 for Brief and F43.21 for Prolonged depressions	
.24	with anxious mood [Same in DSM4]	
.83	with withdrawal	
.28	with mixed emotional features [Same in DSM4]	F43.22
.23	with work or academic inhibition	
.30	with disturbance of conduct [Same in DSM4]	
.40	with mixed disturbance of emotions [and Conduct] ICD-10 is F43.24, and conduct F43.25	
.82	with physical complaints	
.90	Adjustment disorder, NOS [Same in DSM4]	F43.9

18.7 Personality disorders: Code on Axis II

301.00	Paranoid [Same in DSM4]	F60.0
.20	Schizoid [Same in DSM4]	F60.1
.22	Schizotypal [Same in DSM4]	F21.
.40	Obsessive compulsive [Same in DSM4]	Anakastic is F60.5
.50	Histrionic [Same in DSM4]	F60.4
.60	Dependent [Same in DSM4]	F60.7
.70	Antisocial [Same in DSM4]	
V71.01	Adult antisocial behavior [Same in DSM4]	Dyssocial is F60.2
.81	Narcissistic [Same in DSM4]	
.82	Avoidant [Same in DSM4]	F60.6
.83	Borderline [Same in DSM4] ICD-10 Unstable, Impulsive is F60.30	F60.31
.84	Passive aggressive	
.90	Personality disorder, NOS [Same in DSM4]	F60.9

18.8 Impulse control disorders:

312.39	Impulse control disorder, NOS [Same in DSM4]	F60.9
.39	Trichotillomania [Same in DSM4]	F63.3
.31	Pathological gambling [Same in DSM4]	F63.0
.32	Kleptomania [Same in DSM4]	F63.2
.33	Pyromania [Same in DSM4]	F63.1
.34	Intermittent explosive disorder [Same in DSM4]	
V71.01	Adult antisocial behavior	

18.9 Childhood disorders:

317.00	Mild mental retardation [Same in DSM4]	F70.
318.	Moderate [Same in DSM4]	F71.
.10	Severe [Same in DSM4]	F72.
.20	Profound [Same in DSM4]	F73
319.	Unspecified [Same in DSM4]	F79
	Borderline is coded as V40.00 on axis II [Same in DSM4]	

299.	Autisic disorder [Same in DSM4]	F84
.10	[Childhood disintegrative disorder]	F84.3
.80	[Rett's disorder] [Pervasive developmental disorder]	F84.2
	[Asperger's syndrome]	F84.5

315.00	Developmental [Reading disorder] In ICD-10 Spelling is F81.1	F81
.10	Developmental arithmetic disorder [Mathematics disorder]	F81.2
.31	Developmental [Expressive language disorder] [Mixed receptive/Expressive language disorder]	
	ICD-10 is Expressive (F80.1) or Receptive (F80.2) Language disorder	
.39	Developmental articulation disorder [Phonological disorder] [Communication disodrer, NOS]	
307.0	Stuttering	F98.5
	Cluttering	F98.6
315 .40	[Developmental coordination disorder]	
.80	Developmental expressive writing disorder [315.2 - Disorder of written expression]	
.90	Specific developmental disorder, NOS [315.9 Learning disorder, NOS]	
V62.30	Academic problem [Same in DSM4]	F81.9

314.	Undifferentiated AD-D [A-D/HD, predominantly inattentive type]	F90.0
314.01	ADHD/Inattentive type, Hyperactive type, Impulsive type [predominantly hyperactive-impulsive type,	
	combined type]	F90.1
.9	[A-D/HD, NOS]	

313.81	Oppositional defiant [Same in DSM4]	F91.3
312.00	[Conduct disorder], solitary aggressive type	
.20	Conduct disorder, group type	
.90	Conduct disorder, undifferentiated type [Disruptive behavior disorder]	
V71.02	Child or adolescent antisocial behavior [Same in DSM4]	

309.21	Separation anxiety disorder [Same in DSM4]	F93
313.89	Reactive attachment disorder of infancy or early childhood	F94.1
313.00	Overanxious disorder. [300.02 in DSM4] ICD-10 is F93.1 for phobic and F93.2 Social anxiety	

313.21	Avoidant disorder of childhood or adolescence	
.23	Elective mutism [Selective mutism]	F94
.82	Identity disorder [Problem] [Same in DSM4]	

307.20	Tic disorder, NOS [Same in DSM4]	F95.9
.21	Transient tic disorder [Same in DSM4]	F95.0
.22	Chronic motor of tic disorder	F95.1
.23	Tourette's [Same in DSM4]	F95.2
.30	Stereotypy, Habit disorder [Stereotypic movement disorder]	F98.4

319.00	[Disorder of infancy, childhood, or adolescence, NOS]	F98.9

18.10 Eating and Elimination disorders:

307.10	Anorcxia ncrvosa [Same in DSM4] /Anorexia nervosa, non-bulemic type (only	
	dieting/fasting/exercise	F50.0
.50	Eating disorder, NOS	F50.9
.51	Bulemia nervosa [Same in DSM4] (bingeing and purging, laxatives) [Anorexia nervosa,	
	bulemic type]	F50.2
	[Binge eating disorder] (bingeing only, without vomiting or laxatives)	F50.4
.52	Pica [Same in DSM4]	F98.3

.53	[Rumination disorder]	
.59	Feeding disorder of infancy or early childhood]	F98.2
.60	Functional enuresis, primary or secondary type, nocturnal only, diurnal only, both [Enuresis]	F98.0
.70	Functional encopresis, primary or secondary type [Encopresis]	F98.1

18.11 Organic conditions: [DSM4 versions of these are not decided as of date of publication]

290.00	Senile dementia, NOS.	F03
.30	Senile onset, primary degenerative <u>D</u>ementia of the <u>A</u>lzheimer <u>T</u>ype	F00.1
.20	with delirium, with delusions	F05.1
.21	with depression	
	(and code 331.00 Alzheimer's's disease on Axis III for all of these above)	
291.20	Dementia associated with alcoholism	F10
294.80	Organic mental disorder, NOS	F09

18.12 Substance/Alcohol and Other Drugs:

ALCOHOL		F10
303.90	Alcohol dependence [Same in DSM4]	
305.00	Alcohol abuse [Same in DSM4]	
303.00	Alcohol intoxication [Same in DSM4]	
291.00	Alcohol withdrawal [Delirium]	
.1	Alcohol [Persisting] amnestic disorder [Alcohol psychotic disorder with delusions]	
.2	Alcohol dementia associated with alcoholism [Persisting]	
.3	Alcohol hallucinosis [Same in DSM4]	
.4	Alcohol idiosyncratic intoxication	
.5	[Alcohol psychotic disorder with delusions]	
291.80	Uncomplicated [Alcohol Withdrawal]	
291.8	[Alcohol mood/anxiety/Sexual dysfunction disorder]	
.89	[Alcohol sleep disorder]	
.9	[Alchohol use disorder]	

CANNABIS		F12
304.30	Cannabis dependence [Same in DSM4]	
305.20	Cannabis abuse [Same in DSM4], Cannabis intoxication [Same in DSM4]	
292.	Cannabis withdrawal [Same in DSM4]	
292.11	Cannabis delusional disorder [Cannabis psychosis with delusions]	
.12	[Cannabis psychosis with Hallucinations]	
.81	Cannabis delirium [Same in DSM4]	
.84	[Cannabis mood disorder]	
.89	[Cannabis anxiety disorder]	
.90	[Cannabis use disorder, NOS]	

COCAINE		F14
304.20	Cocaine dependence [Same in DSM4]	
305.60	Cocaine abuse [Same in DSM4]	
305.60	Cocaine intoxication [Same in DSM4]	
221.00	Cocaine withdrawal	
291.11	Cocaine delusional disorder/[Persisting] Amnestic disorder [Cocaine psychotic disorder with delusions]	
.12	Cocaine hallucinosis	
291.84	[Cocaine mood disorder]	
.89	[Cocaine /anxiety/sexual dysfunction/sleep disorder]	
.90	[Cocaine use disorder, NOS]	
292.81	Cocaine delirium [Same in DSM4]	

OPIOIDS   F11
304.00   Opioid dependence [Same in DSM4]
305.50   Opioid abuse [Same in DSM4], Opioid intoxication [Same in DSM4]
291.11   [Opioid psychotic disorder with delusions]
   .12   [Opioid psychotic disorder with hallucinations]
   .84   [Opioid mood disorder]
   .89   [Opioid sleep/Sexual disorder]
292.81   [Opioid delirium]
   .90   [Opioid use disorder]

304.80   Polysubstance dependence [Same in DSM4]
304.90   Psychoactive substance dependence, NOS
304.90   Psychoactive substance abuse, NOS

292.90   Organic mental disorder, NOS [Substance Use Disorder, NOS]

18.13 Psychoses:

298.80   Brief reactive psychosis/Acute psychotic disorder [Same in DSM4]   F23.
298.90   Psychotic disorder, NOS (Atypical psychosis) [Psychotic Disorder, NOS]   F29.
295.40   Schizophreniform with/without good prognostic features [Same in DSM4]

295.   Schizophrenia   ICD-10 for Unspecified is F20.9
   .1x   Schizophrenia, disorganized [Same in DSM4]   ICD-10 for Hebephrenic is F20.1
   .2x   Schizophrenia, catatonic [Same in DSM4]   F20.2
   .3x   Schizophrenia , paranoid [Same in DSM4] (specify stable or not) /Positive type schizophrenia   F20.0
   .9x   Schizophrenia , undifferentiated [Same in DSM4]   F20.3
   .6x   Schizophrenia , residual (specify if late onset)   [Same in DSM4]   F20.5
For the above use x = 1 = subchronic, 2 = chronic, 3 = subchronic with exacerbation, 4 = chronic with exacerbation,
   5 = in remission, 6 = unspecified.

295.70   Schizo-affective (bipolar or depressive type) [Same in DSM4]   F25.
297.10   Delusional (paranoid) disorders: specify delusions as erotomanic, grandiose, jealous, persecutory,
              somatic or unspecified. [Same in DSM4]   F22.
   .30   Shared paranoid disorder [Shared Psychotic Disorder]

293.81   [Psychotic disorder due to a general medical condition, with delusions]
293.82   [Psychotic disorder due to a general medical condition, with hallucinations]

18.14 Sleep disorders:

307.40   Dysosmia, NOS [Same in DSM4] or Parasomnia, NOS   F51.9
   .42   Insomnia, primary [Same in DSM4] or related to another mental condition [Same in DSM4]   F51.0
   .44   Hypersomnia related to another mental condition [Same in DSM4]   F51.1
   .54   Primary hyposomnia [Same in DSM4]
   .45   Sleep-wake schedule disorder [Same in DSM4] (specify advanced or delayed phase type, disorganized type
              or frequently changing type)   F51.2
   .46   Sleep terror [Same in DSM4] (ICD-10 is F51.4) or sleepwalking [Same in DSM4] (ICD-10 is F51.3)
   .47   Dream anxiety/Nightmare disorder   [Same in DSM4]   F51.5

780.50   Insomnia or Hypersomnia related to a known organic condition
   .52   [Sleep disorder due to a general medical condition, hypersomnia Type]
   .54   [Sleep disorder due to a general medical condition, insomnia Type]
   .59   [Sleep disorder due to a general medical condition, parasomnia Type]
   .59   [Breathing related sleep disorder] [Mixed type]

18.15 Somatoform disorders:

? 307.70	Body dysmorphic Disorder .[71 in DSM4]	
.70	Undifferentiated or NOS Somatoform disorder [300.82 in DSM4]	F45.9
.80	[Pain disorder, associated with psychological factors]	ICD-10 for Persistent Pain is F45.4
.89	[Pain disorder, associated with both psychological factors and a general medical condition]	
.81	Somatization disorder [Same in DSM4]	F45.
.82	[Somatoform disorder, NOS]	
300.11	Conversion disorder, (or Hysterical neurosis, conversion type (specify single episode or recurrent) [Same in DSM4]	ICD-10 for NOS is F44.9
.70	Hypochondriasis [Same in DSM4]	F45.2
.70	Somatoform disorder, NOS [.89 in DSM4]	F45.9
.70	Undifferentiated somatoform disorder	F45.1
	[Autonomic arousal disorder]	F45.3 and specify system
	[Neurasthenia]	F48.

316. 00 Psychological factors affecting physical [Medical] condition [Same in DSM4] (specify physical condition on axis III).
[DSM4 asks you to choose among these factors and substitute for 'Psych. Factors': Mental disorder, Psychological symptoms, Personality traits or coping Style, Maladaptive health behaviors, and Unspecified psychological conditions

18.16 Dissociative disorders:

? 300.06	[Depersonalization disorder] [Same in DSM4]	F48.1
.14	Multiple personality [Dissociative identity disorder] [Same in DSM4]	F44.81
.13	[Dissociative] Fugue [Same in DSM4]	F44.1
.12	Psychogenic amnesia/Dissociative amnesia [Same in DSM4]	F44.
.15	Dissociative disorder, NOS [Same in DSM4]	F44.9

18.17 Sexual dysfunctions:

Specify psychogenic only or psychogenic and biogenic, if biogenic-only code on axis III. Specify lifelong or acquired. Specify generalized or situational.

302.70	Sexual dysfunction, NOS [Same in DSM4]	F52.9
.71	Hypoactive desire [Same in DSM4]	F52.0
.72	Female arousal/Male erectile disorder [Same in DSM4]	F52.2
.73	Inhibited female orgasm [Female ogasmic disorder] [Same in DSM4]	F52.3
.74	Inhibited male orgasm [Male ogasmic disorder] [Same in DSM4]	F52.3
.75	Premature Ejaculation ("Fast Ejaculation") Male ogasmic disorder] [Same in DSM4]	F52.4
.76	Dyspareunia [Same in DSM4]	F52.6
.90	Sexual disorder, NOS	F52.9
.79	Sexual aversion [Same in DSM4] ICD-10 for lack of enjoyment is F52.11	F52.1
		ICD-10 for Excessive sexual drive is F52.7
306.51	Vaginismus [Same in DSM4]	F52.5
607.84	[Male erectile disorder due to a general medical condition]	
608.89	[Male dyspareunia due to a general medical condition]	
.89	[Male hypoactive sexual desire due to a general medical condition]	
.89	[Other male sexual dysfunction due to a general medical condition]	
625.0	[Feamle dyspareunia due to a general medical condition]	
.8	[Female hypoactive sexual desire due to a general medical condition]	
.8	[Other female Sexual dysfunction due to a general medical condition]	

PARAPHILIAS

302.20	Pedophilia [Same in DSM4] (Specify same or "opposite" or same and "opposite" sex. Specify if limited to incest, specify exclusive or nonexclusive type)	F65.4
.30	Transvestic fetishism [Same in DSM4] [also pseudotransvestism, true transvestism]	F65.1

.40	Exhibitionism[Same in DSM4]	F65.2
.81	Fetishism [Same in DSM4] (Subtypes not in DSM include media or form fetishism, partialism, apotemnophilia/amputism)	F65.0
.82	Voyeurism [Same in DSM4]	F65.3
.83	Sexual masochism [Same in DSM4]	ICD-10 for Sadomasochism is F65.5
.84	Sexual sadism [Same in DSM4]	ICD-10 for Sadomasochism is F65.5
.89	Frotteurism/frottage [May be .85 in DSM4]	
.90	Paraphilia, NOS [Same in DSM4]	F65.9

[Other subtypes not separated in DSM include bestiality, zoophilia, hebephilia, mysophilia, klismaphilia/urophilia/urolagnia, coprophilia, incest, coprolalia, telephone scatologia, rape]

SEXUAL IDENTITY

302.6	[Gender identity disorder, NOS]	F64.9
302.6	[Gender identity diosorder in children]	F64.2
302.85	[Gender identity diosorder in adolescents and adults]	

18.18 Factitious disorders:

300.16	Factitious disorder with [predominantly] psychological [signs and] symptoms [Same in DSM4]	
.17	Factitious disorder [with predominantly physical signs and symptoms]	
.18	Factitious disorder with combined psychological and physical signs and symptoms]	
.19	Factitious disorder, NOS [Same in DSM4]	F68.1
.51	Factitious disorder with physical symptoms	
	[Factitious disorder by proxy]	

18.19 Medication-induced movement disorders

332.1	[Neuroleptic-induced Parkinsonism]	
333.1	[Medication-induced postural tremor]	
.7	[Neuroleptic-induced acute dystonia]	
.82	[Neuroleptic-induced tardive diskinesia]	
.92	[Neuroleptic malignant syndrome]	
.90	[Medication-induced movement disorder, NOS]	
.99	[Neuroleptic-induced acute akathisia]	
995.2	[Adverse effects of medication, NOS]	

18.20 V codes, etc.: See also Chapter 27 Relationships

V15.81	Noncompliance with medical treatment [Same in DSM4]	
V51.11	[Sexual abuse of an adult]	
V61.9	[Relational problem related to a mental disorder or general medical condition]	
.10	Marital problem [physical abuse of an adult]	
.12	[Partner relational problem]	
V61.20	Parent-child problem [Same in DSM4]	
.21	[Physical abuse of child] [Neglect of child]	
.22	[Sexual abuse of child]	
V61.80	Other specified family circumstances [Sibling relational problem]	
V62.20	Occupational problem [Same in DSM4]	
.40	[Acculturation problem] (See Section 30.12 The Refugee Process.)	
.61	[Religious or spiritual problem]	
.81	Other interpersonal problem [Relational rroblem, NOS]	
.89	Phase of life problem [Same in DSM4] or other life circumstance problem	
.82	Uncomplicated bereavement [Bereavement]	
V65.20	Malingering. [Same in DSM4] (See section 16.21 Malingering)	F68.
V71.09	No diagnosis or condition on Axis I or Axis II	
780.9	[Age-associated memory decline]	
799.9	[Diagnosis deferred on Axis I or II]	

19. Summary

In my professional opinion, and with reasonable medical certainty ...
In summary/in short /to summarize...

For a Child:

His/her behavior is more like a __ year old than his/her age of __ years

19.1 Major descriptive elements:

This (age), (sex) (any other crucial factors) ....

HISTORY: See Chapter 9. Background

19.2 Findings:

Select the most relevant three or four or tailor them to the report's audience.

19.3 Diagnosis: See also Chapter 18. Diagnosis

Generally offer only the most important one or two unless diagnosis was the reason for the referral
or you are in training, or your setting's culture requires a fuller listing.

19.4 Consultations:

Reasons/need, consultant, evaluation and recommendations

19.5 Summary of Treatment Services:

Number of sessions, first and last dates,

Services rendered: Consultation, assessment, pre-marital, marital, family, divorce, single parent, individual

Reason for termination: Refuses services, no-shows, successful completion, little/no progress, planned pause in treatment, other (specify), contract completed, referred elsewhere, planned

Treatment has been a complete/partial/minimal success

S/he has followed a productive hospital course
Is in good chemical remission/due to medications
Has received maximum benefit of treatment/hospitalization/services

Treatment received has had no success/been ineffective in removing/reducing symptoms
Treatment has had a negative outcome for this patient

Decision to terminate: by client/therapist/mutual/agency/other, discharge

Outcome: goals achieved, failed, some, majority, nearly all, exceeded
Negative patient outcome
Adverse reactions
Worsening
Stayed the same, unimproved
Improvement

Prognosis: See section 21. Prognosis

Recommendations: See section 20. Recommendations

19.6 Disposition: Inactive, closed, transfer, aftercare, referral

20. Recommendations

20.1 Treatment Recommendations/Disposition: See also Chapter 22 Treatment Planning

Treatability estimate: motivation, barriers, openness, workability, ego strength, probability of remaining in treatment

Further evaluations/diagnostic studies: physical/medical, intellectual, personality, neuropsychological, custody, family, audiological, speech/language, occupational/vocational, educational/academic

Need for treatment: justification, indication, medically necessary

Continue current treatment(s), additional/concurrent treatments referral, hospital/program/therapist transfer, discharge

Change diet to ...
Change exercise to ...
Change social/recreational etc. activities to ..., increase activities outside the home/family, take on volunteer activities such as ...

Medication(s): (name(s)) at a starting dosage of ... for a duration of .... with instructions regarding ... to be supervised/administered by patient/family/clinic staff/school nurse/Visiting Nurse, decrease/taper off by (date)
Counseling or psychotherapy: with whom, where, frequency, duration, mode/format, technique(s).

Goals: reduce symptoms, focus on/to build self esteem, provide a supportive context for the exploration of feelings, bolster defenses and prevent further decompensation

Behavior referral: self-control training, Anger Management, parenting skills/child management training, Parent Effectiveness Training, Assertiveness training, Anti-victimization program

OTHER THERAPIES:

Expressive therapies: art, music, dance/movement, poetry, bibliotherapy
Crisis intervention only, staff monitoring, spousal/family support, Aftercare services, Intensive Case Management
Body-mind Awareness: Primal scream, Rolfing, Bioenergetics, Autogenic Training, Gestalt, Rebirthing, Functional Integration, Biofeedback, the Alexander Method, Structural Patterning, Do'in, Shiatsu
Psychological Growth: Transactional Analysis, Psychoanalysis, Encounter/Marathon/Open Encounter groups, Morita Therapy, Reality Therapy, Psychosynthesis, Assertiveness training, sex therapy, Synanon/Daytop,
Consciousness development: Arica, Living Love, Erhard Seminar Training, Transcendental Meditation, Silva Mind Control, Zen, Yoga, Bhakti, Kundalini Yoga, Buddha's Middle Way, Gurdjieff's method,

Specialized community support groups: grief counseling, victim support services, Mothers Against Drunk Driving, Parents of Murdered Children, Candlelighters, Reach for Recovery, Parents Anonymous, Recovery groups, Take Off Pounds Sensibly

12 Step programs for many addictive behaviors: Narcotics/Alcohol/Overeaters/Gamblers Anonymous

Educational groups: Toastmasters International, Marriage Encounter, local college/general studies/evening classes, vocational/trade/beauty schools

Work Adjustment Training, Work Hardening program, (see also section 28. Basic Work Skills), work placement, internship program

Residential Services: foster care, "group home", Community Living Arrangements, community residential services, "half-way house", structured/supportive living arrangement, transitional services, protective services, etc.

Note: You may want to create/insert a reference list of additional or specific services available in your community or system.

For a Child:

Methods and services to be provided are to include:

Special Education, Language Stimulation classroom, Socially and Emotionally Disturbed, Learning Support, Hearing Impaired, in-home teacher/itinerant, etc.

Counseling, psychiatric consultation, behavior modification, parent-staff conference, medical consultation, due process procedures, social skill training - remedial/adaptive/for acceptance

21. Prognosis

21. 1 Prognosis for ....

SETTING:

Community/family/structured setting/institutional placement
Recovery: full/partial
Improvement
Employment - competitive/supportive/partial/sheltered workshop (see Chapter 28 Vocational)
Return to original job/alternative work placement at _____ level
therapy
life

IS:

excellent/good/uncertain because .../variable/poor/unknown/guarded/negative/grave/terminal

COURSE IS/IS EXPECTED TO BE: (<->)

benign, static, waxing and waning, acute, shows step-wise/steady progress, recuperating, fluctuating/
with remissions and exacerbations, chronic, has reached a steady state, no change with or without
treatment, hard to treat, refractory to treatment, rapidly progressing, virulent form of the disorder,
unrelenting course despite our best efforts, intractable, has failed all appropriate treatments,
malignant

21.2 Other Statements:

His/her eventual prognosis for success in later life will be a function of how well the situational
demands match his/her individual profile of abilities
The severity and chronicity of his/her symptoms indicate a poor prognosis
His/her history so far has been downhill and his/her prognosis therefore must be ...
This outcome/result of treatment is expected only if (specified) services are received and is expected
to be slow and difficult with many reversals
S/he can be salvaged with ....
The probable duration of treatment is __ with these goals of therapy:
Needs the structure of various social agencies with which s/he is involved

ALCOHOLISM:

Prognosis is poor because he/she
has no sobriety support system
lives in a high risk area
has low self-esteem/efficacy expectations
has a history of physical/emotional/sexual abuse

22. Treatment Planning Formats and Statements

We all know that diagnosis and intervention are not tightly related but what then should we use as the armature of interventions? We can focus in symptoms, complaints, problems, goals, functioning level, behavioral excesses and deficits, recovery by stressor reduction, alteration of family dynamics/ homeostasis, crisis management, etc. How you understand the problem, its cause, dynamics and goals all depend on your paradigm. Therefore listed below are some formats from which to choose and modify to suit your understanding of your work.
See also Chapter 27 Relationship evaluations for treatment planning and goals.

22.1 Goals and Objectives:

Offer both long-term **goals** and short-term **objectives**. The highest level might be **mission** statements.
   Some view the relationship as analogous to strategic and tactical efforts in military terms.
   To seek objectives ask "If we are to achieve this goal by (date, such as next year) what would we have to accomplish by (date, such as next month/week).
   Objectives are usually more behavioral, measurable, and concrete than goals.
   Divide the efforts this way: goal setting is the client's job; selecting and implementing the means is the contribution of the therapist/professional.
   Short term objectives: Develop, Improve, Maintain.

Berg and Miller (1992) offer these criteria for "well-formed treatment goals" which:
   1. Must be important to the client
   2. Small
   3. Concrete, behavioral, specific
   4. Focus on the presence rather than the absence of something
   5. Focus on the first small steps, on what to do first, on a beginning rather than an end
   6. Are realistic and achievable within the context of the client's life
   7. Are perceived as requiring "hard work" (Like Jay Haley's Prescribed Ordeal)

22.2 Treatment Plan Format A: The One Sentence Treatment Plan Format:

Who is going to do what, how often and for how long, to whom, for what problems, with what desired outcome by what date and when are we going to look to see how it is going?

22.3 Treatment Plan Format B: Is created around these headings:

1. The Problem(s):
    Foci of treatment: immediate and long term issues
    Problem-Oriented Record: Problem List, SOAP notes (<u>S</u>ubjective, <u>O</u>bjective, <u>A</u>ssessment, <u>P</u>lan)
2. The Outcomes sought: Objectives
3. The client's Strengths or Assets:
4. The client's Liabilities, or the Barriers to Change in the client or elsewhere:
5. The Treatment(s)/Methods used: What, When, by Whom?:
    Interventions/methods/means/modalities, resources required, staff and others involved, frequency of   contacts, expected date of achievement, dates of review
6. The Means and Dates of Evaluation: Measurable performances, Operationalizations

22.4 Treatment Plan Format C: From social work (Wilson, 1980, p. 144-146.) it describes:

1. The ideal means of meeting the needs of this patient.
2. What you can do realistically to meet these needs.
3. The client's willingness and ability to carry out these treatment plans.
4. Progress made or not made since the plan was written.
5. What you will now do differently.

22.5 Levels of Functioning:

Kennedy (1992) offers an inventive different approach to planning interventions. Using Axis V (see Section 18.22) he has built master treatment plans around levels of functioning in the areas of psychological impairment, social skills, dangerousness, ADL-occupational skills, substance abuse, etc.

22.6 Treatment Plan for Alcohol/Drug : See also 16.31 Responses to Alcoholism Treatment.

Lewis (1990) makes the very rational and yet often overlooked point that diverse people can be dependent on drugs in different ways for different needs, etc. and that effective treatment design and implementation must take into account these differences. She offers a comprehensive form for collecting all the relevant data and this form can be used for other problems as well.

GOALS FOR SUBSTANCE ABUSERS:

Abstinence, controlled drinking
Resolving or avoiding legal problems
Stabilizing one's finances, marriage, family, vocation/school
Improving social skills, assertion, emotional expression, communication
Improving coping skills, stress management skills, relaxation
Improving social support, friendships, social pursuits, recreation
Improving problem solving
Enhancing health and fitness
Enhancing self-esteem

22.7 Treatment Plan for Behavioral Approaches:

LISTING OF BEHAVIOR MODIFICATION METHODS:

Contingency management, contingency contracting, stimulus control, convert sensitization, time out, token economy, etc. Kratochwill and Bergan (1990) is an excellent guide to the implementation of behavioral programs as a consultant.

BEHAVIOR THERAPY:

Systematic desensitization, flooding, implosion, aversion therapy, stress inoculation training

Bellack and Hersen (1985) is a simple guide to about 150 methods with definitions, explanations and resources.

Many publishers offer tools. I particularly like the quality of those from Research Press, P. O. Box 9177, Champaign, IL 61826. (217) 352-3273.

22.8 Treatment Plan for Family Therapy:

1. Therapeutic goals:
   A. Family's goals
   B. Therapist's goals
       Symptom reduction
       Reframing of problems
       Family's values/belief systems
       Reorganization of relationships
       Redefining relationships with other systems
2. Rationale of treatment plan: Paradigm: structural, strategic, behavioral, Intergenerational, etc.
3. Treatment framework: modality, frequency, duration, person responsible, fee/payment, supervision
4. Treatment contract: with members, with other systems, who is to be included, etc.
5. A. Tentative plan: immediate objectives, focus and strategies for first phase of treatment
   B. Education about the problems, normalizing
   C. Referrals, auxiliary services
6. Problems for therapist:

22.9 Treatment Plan for Crisis Intervention:

INTERVENTIONS:

Acknowledge/appreciate/validate/take seriously the subject's distress. (Do not argue or get into a power struggle)
Encourage ventilation of feelings
Reassure subject/family of your continued availability
Reinforce/support all positive responses
Reinforce/support problem solving efforts
Offer alternative methods of coping
Negotiate a contract of not doing anything to worsen the situation for a period of time and what to do during this time periods when feeling bad.

22.10 Problem Conception/Formulation:

No consensus on how to understand the causation and dynamics of the "problem." Most accept a biopsychosocial paradigm. An early citation is Leigh and Reiser (1980) and this is from Sperry, *et al.* (1992) which offers a well thought-out but elaborate approach.

This focuses on "seven dimensions for articulating and explaining the nature and origins of the patient's presentation" and then their "subsequent treatment."

The Seven "P's":

1. **Presentation**: nature and severity of symptoms, history, course of illness, and diagnosis.
   a. Chief Complaint [or Concern]
   b. History of past treatment
   c. Problem list: Separate the "short term, acute, non-characterological, or fairly circumscribed or those that may be time limited" from the long term, "less focal, more characterological skills deficits, or chronic symptoms, behaviors or issues."
   d. DSM diagnosis: all Axes, traits/defenses, listing of stressors on Axis V, and "Rule outs"
   e. Prognostic index/capacity for treatment: Ratings are made in ten areas: Symptom severity and focality, defensive style, social supports, psychological mindedness, explanatory style, past treatment compliance both general and in therapy, motivation for treatment and information style, and then a prognostic statement is made.

2. **Predispositions**: "all the factors which render and individual vulnerable to a disorder." Physical predispositions (if any) "psychological predisposers which contribute to the present problem(s) social predisposers." [These are all diatheses]

3. **Precipitants**: Stressors of all biopsychosocial kinds.

4. **Pattern:** The person's "pattern and level of functioning in all three spheres (biological, psychological, social/interpersonal), if germane" in terms of "the predictable and consistent style or manner in which a person thinks, feels, acts, copes, and defends the self both in stressful and non-stressful circumstances." The individual's capacity for treatment would be included here.

5. **Perpetuants:** "processes by which an individual's pattern is reinforced and confirmed by both the individual and the individual's environment."

6. **Plan** (Treatment):
   Patient's expectations for current treatment, both outcome and method. Take note of the patient's formulation - the individual's explanation for his or her symptoms or disorder.
   Treatment outcome goals: short and long term in Biological, Psychological and Social areas
   Rationale for the treatment plan:

Setting	Format	Duration
Frequency	Treatment Strategy	Somatic Treatment

   Treatment approach: setting, mode, duration, strategies/methods, etc.

7. **Prognosis:** Forecast of the individual's capacity and response to treatment.

22.11 Multi-modal Therapy:

Arnold A. Lazarus (1976, 1981) has developed a model of assessment in which treatments of choice (those whose effectiveness for a specific problem has been supported by empirical research) are matched to each problem analyzed at each of seven levels. The acronym for the levels is BASIC ID. There are no limitations on the methods of treatment which can be used and so it can fit any paradigm. Proper diagnosis/problem specification is crucial to this model.

Assessment area/Problematic Behaviors	Interventions
Behavior: Affect: Sensation: Imagery: fantasies, expectations Cognition: beliefs Interpersonal relations: Drugs: included here are all medical conditions	

22.12 Treatments of Choice:

We really need careful research to answer the question of which treatment, administered by whom, for what diagnosis/problem, in what kind of person, has what outcome?

Diagnosis	Treatments of Choice
Fears, Phobias, Anxieties	Systematic desensitization Flooding, Reinforced practice, Implosion Modeling Medications: anti-anxiety drugs. Anti-depressants for phobias.
Compulsions	Participant modeling, with imaginal exposure, *in vivo* exposure, response prevention
Unipolar Depression	Cognitive therapy (a'la Beck) Tricyclic and MAOI antidepressant medications; ECT; Interpersonal Therapy (Klerman)
Mania, Bipolar depression	Lithium, Tegritol, etc.
Sexual Dysfunctions	Masters and Johnson's techniques and variations (H. S. Kaplan, Hartman and Fithian, G. Kelly, LoPiccolo, Lieblum, Barbach)
Addictions: Over-eating	Veteran's groups (AA/12 Step programs, Weight Watchers, TOPS) Stimulus control methods and self help groups Relapse prevention (Marlatt)
Drug abuse	Methadone Self-help residential programs (Daytop Village, etc.)
Smoking	Combinations of techniques like aversion therapy, contractual management, booster sessions, group contracts and support.
Anorexia	Behavioral rehearsal, scheduling of pleasant events, modeling of proper eating Cognitive change of body image

22. Treatment Planning

Bulimia	Cognitive and cognitive-behavioral techniques
Schizophrenia	Neuroleptics Reduction of family/precipitating stress through family therapy and educations (Fallon, Hogarty) Day hospitals, Supportive living situations Brief hospitalizations

22.13 Other aspects of Treatment:

CONSENT TO TREATMENT:

In order to gain fully informed consent, couch your statements to the patient in terms like (GAP, 1990):
"... while no completely satisfactory statistics are available, (I) believe that this combination of treatments offers the best chance of success."
"The success rate of this treatment is about 85%. That is, about 85% of all patients receiving this treatment experience complete or substantial relief of their symptoms."

Fully informed consent should be obtained around issues like the confidentiality of your report, medications, managed care's limitations and procedures, etc. Zuckerman and Guyett (1992) is helpful in this regard.

JOINT TREATMENT PLANNING:

Spending the time to jointly develop a plan requires the kind of thoughtful, comprehensive, insightful efforts which will ensure successful therapy, so it is not a waste of therapy time but rather a productive focusing of it. A preliminary step could be to list, with the client, the major problems and related effects of these problems on his or her life. Review all areas of functioning. Then inquire about expectations of treatment and of change for this Problem List.

CPT CODES:

The CPT is the Current Procedural Terminology codes for actions taken in medical settings to treat, evaluate and manage patients and is the basis on which insurers pay for services. You'll need the current version. CPT 1992 (order # OP054192AA) cost $34 for non-members of the American Medical Association and a Minibook for covering psychiatry can be included for the same price (order # OP054292AA). Order Dept., American Medical Association, P.O. Box 109050, Chicago, IL 60610-9050. (800) 621-8335.

23. Confidentiality Notices

In order to insure **confidentiality** it is *not* sufficient to stamp the pages "Confidential" or "For professional use only." You could provide an notice on each page (by placing it in a footer on your word processor) using one or more of these paragraphs, or your reworded versions to every report you send out.

These records are to be:
1. used for a stated/specific purpose, and
2. used only by the authorized recipient, and
3. not disclosed to any other party including the patient/client, and
4. destroyed after the specified use/stated need has been met.

This information has been disclosed to you from records protected by Federal confidentiality rules (42 CFR Part 2, P.L. 93-282) and state law (for example, Pennsylvania Law 7100-111-4). These regulations prohibit you from making any further disclosure of this information unless further disclosure is expressly permitted by the written consent of the person to whom it pertains or as otherwise permitted by 42 CFR Part 2. A general authorization for the release of information is NOT sufficient for this purpose. The Federal rules restrict any use of the information to criminally investigate or prosecute any alcohol or drug abuse patient.

Privileged and confidential patient information. Any unauthorized disclosure is a federal offense. Not to be duplicated. The information contained in this report is private, privileged and confidential. It cannot be released outside the school system except by the examining psychologist/evaluator/creator of this report upon receipt of written consent of the parent. Not to be duplicated or transmitted.

Persons or entities granted access to this record may discuss this information with the patient only insofar as necessary to represent the patient in legal proceedings or other matters for which this record has been legally released.

I have in my possession a signed and valid authorization to supply these records to you and you alone.

Not to be used against the interests of the subject of this report.

This is strictly CONFIDENTIAL material and is for the information of only the person to whom it is addressed. No responsibility can be accepted if it is made available to any other person including the Subject of this Report. Any duplication, transmittal, re-disclosure or re-transfer of these records is expressly prohibited. Such re-disclosure may subject you to civil or criminal liability.[1]

NOTE: It is inappropriate to release the information contained herein directly to the client or other parties in a legal action. If this information is released to interested individuals before they are afforded an opportunity to discuss its meaning with a trained Mental Health Professional it is likely that the content of the report may be misunderstood leading to emotional distress on the part of the uninformed reader.

This report is to be utilized only by professional personnel. Any information released to others will require interpretation.

For a Child:

The contents of this report have/have not been shared with the child's parent/s/guardian. She/he/they may review this report with the evaluator or his or her specific designee. Copies of this report may be released only by the evaluator, his/her departmental administrator, or in accord with the school district's policy.

---

[1] This is from Zuckerman and Guyette (1992) *The Paper Office 1*. See the last pages of this book for more information about this book on ethics, malpractice risk reduction and clinical practice.

24. Closing the Report

VALUE OF THE INFORMATION:
I hope this information will be useful to you as you consider this case/person/client's needs/aid you in your tasks.
I hope this information will be sufficient for you to judge this patient's situation.
In the hope that these data will prove of assistance, and with thanks for the very kind referral, I remain ... Very truly yours

CONTINUED AVAILABILITY:
I trust that this is the information you desire/require but if it is not ....
Please feel free to contact me if I can supplement the information in this report/if other questions or issues arise.
If there are further questions I may address as a result of/on the basis of my examination of this individual please contact my at your convenience.
I am/will make myself available for further information/consultation regarding this client's needs.
If I can be of further benefit to you in this case do not hesitate to contact me.
If I can be of any further assistance with reference to this patient's treatment or problem or any patient's treatment it certainly will be my pleasure.
If clarification is needed I can best be reached on (days) _____ from ____ to ___ (time) at (phone number)
I will see this client again in _____ . I am certainly available sooner should problems arise.

Should additional examination/evaluation/testing/clarification/information be needed I am/not willing to provide it.
I am/not willing to perform additional examinations/evaluations on this person.

S/he requires no further/active/follow up from our standpoint but s/he is aware that s/he can contact us should further problems arise.
I am returning him/her to your care regarding ....

As always, I shall keep you informed of my further contacts/interactions/treatment of your patient via/by means of copies of my progress notes with the patient's full consent

THANK YOU:
Thank you for/I appreciate the opportunity/privilege of being able to evaluate your patient/this most interesting/challenging/pleasant patient/person/gentleman/woman.
Thank you for allowing me/us to participate/assist in his/her care/sending (patient's name) to us/asking me/us to see this patient.
Thanks again for the opportunity to participate in ____'s care.
I consider it a privilege to have been able to care for this patient.

It goes without saying that I appreciate your trust in allowing me to assist in the care of this patient.
I, and my colleagues, appreciate ....
As always, thank you very much for your referrals.

SIGNATURE:
Personal signature, degree, title.
Yours truly/Sincerely/Respectfully
I authorize that my name may be mechanically affixed to this report.
Dictated but not read to facilitate mailing to you.
Typed and mailed in the doctor's absence.

25. Activities of Daily Living (ADL's)

Note: If there are deficits or there has been a change generally indicate the reasons for this situation.

25.1 Living Situation/Level of Support Needed: (<->)

Lives independently in own home/apartment, uses community support services (e.g. soup kitchen, Food Bank/Community Pantry, "Meals-On-Wheels,"/homemaker services), with spouse/children/lover/ paramour/parental family/ relatives/ friends/roommate, single/sleeping room with/without cooking facilities, in monitored Independent Apartment, with relatives and attends Partial/Day hospital/Sheltered Workshop/Day Activities Center, in residential drug/alcohol treatment program, in rehabilitation facility, in Community Living Arrangement/Community Rehabilitative Residence/group home/supervised apartment, boarding home, custodial/domiciliary care facility, personal care home, nursing home, Skilled Care Facility, Acute Care Facility, private/community/state/city/Veteran's hospital, Intensive Care Unit

Note: As applicable, describe behaviors or deficits which limit independent living.

25.2 Quality of Performance: (<->)
Each area of ADL performance can be evaluated as to its *independence, appropriateness* and *effectiveness*.

Has a history of accidents/is accident-prone.
Performance of ADLs is unsafe/self/and other-endangering (E.g. gets lost, burns food).

Makes it worse, disorganized, ineffective, needs to be redone, unacceptable, sloppy, casual, neat, fussy, orderly, fastidious, meticulous, obsessive

25.3 Assistance Level: (<->)

Incapable/unable, dependent, limited only by physical/medical conditions, not psych ones, only simple tasks, directed, helps spouse/family with chores, participates, needs to be reminded/prompted/ monitored/supervised, does with help, finishes, unassisted, initiates, independent, autonomous

ADL's done by spouse by tradition/agreement/default/because of physical limitations, ADLs performed by children/relatives/landlady/live-in friend/paid helpers/publicly provided aides

25.4 Self-care Skills:

Cannot feed self, assists with own feeding, feeds self, appetite appropriate, preferences, good balance/nourishment, in/adequate nutrition/malnourishment, restrictions, allergies
Problems with elimination, toileting, urination, incontinent, uses drugs for
Bathes regularly, makeup/shaves, deodorant, grooming/haircuts, nails, hygiene,
Dresses self, appropriate for weather and occasion, does laundry, buys clothing,
Exercises:
Sleep problems: See section 16.32 Sleep disorders
Takes own medications as prescribed
Safety: Is aware of hazards such as in street crossing, dangers of gas odor, leaking water, loose wires

25.5 House Care/Chores/Domestic Skills:

Takes out trash
Food cleanup: sets the table, clears table, washes, does pots, drys, puts away, silverware, cleans up kitchen
Dusts and neatens up: runs sweeper/vacuum, straightens up bedroom, mops, cleans bathroom, shovels snow, mows grass
Laundry (recognizes dirty, collects, separates, washes/runs washer, drys, folds, puts away), sewing/repairs, ironing, washes windows/walls
House is immaculate/neat/clean/functional/cluttered/disorganized/chaotic/in disrepair/dangerous,
Maintenance: changes light bulbs, recognizes malfunctioning appliances, recognizes emergencies, calls for help/repair persons, repairs, changes faucets/switches
Decorates: (<->) bed covers, chooses and hangs curtains, slipcovers, paints, wallpapers, remodels
Pet care (<->): plants, fish, cat, dog

Hoards items which are, in the evaluator's opinion, worthless and meaningless

25.6 Cooking: (<->)

Eats irregularly, eats all meals out, eats only snacks/fast-food/prepared foods/take-out/carry-out, prepares boxed-canned foods, canned soup and sandwiches, simple, top of stove, light cooking (fries, boils), full menu, nutritionally balanced, uses all kitchen appliances, coordinates foods' types and preparation times, bakes, entertains

25.7 Child Care: (<->)

Abuses, neglects, feeds regularly/appropriately/healthily, bathes regularly/safely, changes diapers and clothes, dresses child appropriately, is affectionate with, actively interacts with, does not leave alone, baby-sits, defends, amuses/entertains, teaches, disciplines effectively, advocates for

25.8 Financial: See also section 28.4 Mathematical ability (<->)

(<->) Financial responsibility: squanders resources, impulsive/inappropriate/useless/wasteful purchases, easily duped into situations leading to mental/physical/financial risks/difficulty, not able to manage own finances, mathematically/intellectually/ emotionally incompetent, not financially competent, able to handle small sums/make own purchases/but not larger sums/checking account/bill paying/saving/investing

(<->) Counts, makes change, has receptive and expressive recognition of denominations of coins/metal money/currency, handles all finances on a cash basis, can perform simple arithmetic calculations sufficient to allow over-the-counter purchase

(<->) Buys money orders, writes checks, deposits checks, able to do routine banking, saves money for large purchases, manages financial resources

25.9 Shops: (<->)

FOR:
    Snacks, can run errands for self/others, toiletries, own clothes, simple foods, prepared foods, full menu foods, for presents, as entertainment,, waits for and recognizes bargains/sales, makes major purchases

Is able to estimate the costs of common foods/items, knows which store sells which kinds of merchandise

Can separate needs from wants and can control impulses so s/he is a wise consumer.

25.10 Transportation: (<->)

Uses special bus, para-transit, mass transit/regular buses, driven, drives with companion, drives alone, vacations
Gets about by walking/bicycling/hitchhiking, depends on family/friends/spouse, etc.

25.11 Life-style:

LOCATION:

Rural, farm/ranch, suburban, urban, small/medium/large city, inner-city, commuter

QUALITIES: (<->)

Nomadic	Unstable	low variety	solitary	low activity	comfortable
vagrant	limited by	low stress	vegetative	no productive	independent
wanders	poverty	low intensity	occupying	activities	autonomous
migratory	survival	low demand	home-bound	low ambition	satisfied
predatory	marginal	minimal	reclusive	unproductive	ambitious
symbiotic	chaotic	mundane			adaptive
parasitic		circumscribed			
roams		constricted			
street person		limited			
panhandles		regressed			
		centers around TV			
		routine			
		simple			
		recumbent			
		monotonous regularity			
		home-based			

25.12 Summary Statements:

Level of personal independence is adequate given socioeconomic status and life-style.
Adapted well to circumstances

S/he is intellectually and psychologically capable of performing ADLs but does not due to physical limitations/limited primarily by physical/medical circumstances

He/she is not able to care for his/her own needs and so requires _____ support services. See section 20. Recommendations

For a child:

Goes to bed by self, does not need a night light, does not go into parent's bed during night, can sleep at friend's house
Washes his body
Performs chores

26. Social Functioning

This Chapter covers social and community activities. Interpersonal behavior in the interview can be found in Chapter 12. and the evaluation of couples and family relationships is in Chapter 27. For sexual relating see section 7.22, for questions, 9.4, for Sexual Adjustment, 14.9, Sexual affects.

Note: If social relating has been reduced in any area try to indicate why this has happened.

26.1 Involvement in Social/Community Activities: (<->)

Hermit, recluse, isolated, withdrawn, aloof, avoidant, no interest in social relationships, disinterested in people and relating, no social activities, keeps to self

Doctor's etc. appointments only, no outside interests or functioning in any organizations, talks on phone, visited but does not visit, gardening and solitary pursuits, hunts/fishes

Window shops, visits/goes out with/drinks with friends, drops in on nearby friends, writes to or calls friends, hangs out with/ loafs with/visits family/neighbors, eats out, routine "coffee klatch"/breakfast/"night out," interested/participates in groups, small outings (church, bingo, bowling, senior center, movies), church attendance only on major holidays, friends help if s/he is sick, gets along selectively/appropriately with friends/family/authorities/public, shops in a variety of stores for all needs

Gregarious, church/religious/social/card club weekly or more often, sporting events as spectator, has out of town guests, goes to movies, visits museums, musical and cultural activities, votes in elections

Attends adult school or classes, active in the community, plans life goals/self-improvement, plays team sports, visits out of town alone, does volunteer work, fully participates in the society

Note: If client reports "attends church" or "plays cards" inquire what s/he does there or which games in order to assess interests, demands (active or passive, skill or chance) and the quality and intensity of her/his social performance.

26.2 Conflictual Community Relating:

AT WORK: See also section 28. Vocational evaluations and 27. Relationships

Reprimands, suspensions, firings, fighting with peers, given "cold shoulder," teases/provokes, threatening/disruptive behaviors

LEGAL ASPECTS:

Police contacts, warnings, tickets, history of fighting/drunkenness, charges filed, Protection From Abuse orders, arrests (indicate for what, when, with whom and consequences), misdemeanor, felony, trial, convictions, probation, jail/prison time, parole
Evictions, bankruptcies
Conflicts with neighbors, agency personnel, landlords, store clerks
Child/spouse/relative/animal abuse

FAMILY:

Ignored by family, distanced, never/rarely visit, only fight with, only phone contacts, estranged, struggling to individuate

26.3 Social Maturity: See also sections 15.13 Social Maturity and 15.14 Social Judgement

27. Evaluations of Families/Relationships

See also Chapter 22. Treatment Planning.
DSM diagnoses are almost exclusively about individuals, not relationships, situations, or interactions yet current understandings of disorders emphasizes interactions: stressors and diatheses, family therapy, systems thinking, etc. Therefore this chapter lists several ways to evaluate relationships and interactional processes and the author would be grateful for your suggestions of more and better ways.

27.1 Dating Relationships: (<->)

INTENSITY:

Never, seldom/rarely, only periodic/special events/holidays, group/car date/dyadic, "gets together with," interested in more dates but ..., frequently, has many/only brief relationships, "dating" same person for many years, many dating partners, exclusive relationship/"going steady" or "seeing others also," progressive relationships, has long-term relationships

QUALITY:

Abusive/abused, exploitative/exploited, dates compulsively, promiscuous
Satisfactory, rewarding

27.2 Intake Assessment of Families:

CASE FORMULATION:

1. Presenting Problem, Chief Complaint/Concern
    Abuse/Violence (spousal, child), (sexual, physical)
    Adolescent adjustment problem
    Chemical abuse (parent, child)
    Child behavior problem/parenting
    Child custody
    Enrichment (marital, family, personal, relationship)
    Heath/medical/nutritional/physical conditions of relevance
    Legal difficulties (child, parent, other) (civil, criminal, misdemeanor, felony)
    Marital conflict
    Parenting (skill enhancement)
    "Poor Communication"

School (behavior, academic, peer)
Separation, divorce, spouse absence, divorce mediation
Sexual dysfunction/patterns
Truancy/runaway
Other: cultural problems, religion, job/financial problems, education, peer problems, relatives

2. Who sought treatment?
3. Referrer's perception of problem:
4. Precipitants/why now?: changes, births, illnesses, deaths, marriages, divorces, remarriages, moves, job changes, leavings
5. Who is involved?: Current household
6. Each member's perception of the problem, major tasks/Changes desired/facing the family now, time frame for improvement, Identified Patient
7. Previous solutions: efforts/attempts/therapy, outcome, Ineffective attempts to maintain homeostasis
   Previous treatment of whom, for what, when, intervention, outcome
8. Developmental issues: for children, parents, family life cycle
   HISTORY OF RELATIONSHIP:
   How met, courtship, each family's attitude,
   Relationship to grandparents, other relatives,
   Beginning expectations, satisfaction/fulfillment levels
   Children, Blended
   FAMILY STAGE/LIFE CYCLE: Courtship, early marriage, child bearing, child rearing, parents of teenagers, launching, middle years, retirement, transitions
9. Therapist's formulation:
   COMMUNICATION STYLE
   Norms, intimacy, secrets, ghosts
   Inadequate/irrational communication: confusion, lack of a frame of reference
   Direct, clear, indirect, confused, vague, double-binded
   INTERACTION STYLE:
   AFFECT: Atmosphere, Positive, negative, aggressive, Family tone/mood/affect, Reinforcing/punishing/ratio?
   ROLES; Differentiation, roles played, intrusions
   CONFLICT AREAS: Issues, Fight management, Resources, Problem solving, Sexual compatibility, Attitudes, values
   COHESIVENESS:
   OVERALL CONCERNS:
   Risk/danger/seriousness
   Priority: emergency/critical need/special need/ordinary need
   Presenting problem: in crisis/past crisis/recurrent crisis/chronic
   EXTENDED FAMILY/FAMILY OF ORIGIN:
   Constellation: members, relatives, others,
   Relationships of Sibs: competitive, intimate, distant, hostile, emotional, legal/social problems
   Positive or negative influences
   Problems with/obligations owed to
   Intergenerational dynamics and conflicts
   OTHER INFLUENCES ON FAMILY: stress or support?
10. Other Relevant history:

Family Configuration: You can record much useful information on a genogram: See section 9.7 Genogram.

27.3 Other Aspects of Families:

LEGAL AND SOCIAL STATUS:

Never married, (single), living together, People Of Opposite Sex Sharing Living Quarters, paramour, live-in, roommate, boyfriend/girlfriend, common-law marriage, married, separated/living apart, estranged, commuter marriage, divorced, re-married, marriage of convenience, outward appearance of a marriage

Previous Relationships/marriages, living togethers, duration, satisfactions, why ended?, age/date/termination reason, number/age/sex of children, relationship with ex-spouse spouse/children, adultery/extra-marital relations/exclusivity/monogamy

Partner is in the process of divorcing/ex-spouse-to-be/"pre-ex"

QUALITY OF RELATIONSHIP: (<->)

Physical/verbal/emotional abuse, abusing spouse, abused spouse, neglecting, punishing, parasitic, avoidant, 'leaky', dead, distant, stale, stalemate, "truce", unhappy, mismatched, ill-considered, hasty, unhealthy, unsupportive, limiting, unsatisfying, symbiotic, repeatedly unfaithful, stable, functional, adequate, satisfying, intimate, enhancing, loving, fulfilling

PERCEPTIONS BY PARENTS:

Feels gets much/some/no support from spouse in parenting/child management/raising/child care, doing chores, finances, dealing with relatives, home maintenance

Child rearing is viewed as unsuccessful/overwhelming/stressful/difficult at times

27.4 A Competency-based model:

Marsh (1992a, 1992b) offers an excellent characterization of a competency-based model for viewing families which emphasizes health, competencies, coping strategies, strengths, skills, resources, problem-solving, empowerment, ecology, and professionals not as therapists but as active enablers, collaborators, advocates, and strengtheners of the family system and network using reframing, positives, and skill development.

27.5 Systemic Family Evaluations:

THEORETICAL CONSTRUCTS:

Structure/Coupling: involvement, enmeshed, disengaged, isolation, individuation, power structure,
Boundaries: rigidity/flexibility, closed/open, generational boundaries
Coalitions: schism, skew, (Lidz), enmeshment (Minuchin) disengagement, pivotal members, dyads, triangles, labels, identifications, mappings, alliances, interfaces, relationship of spouses, alliances of members
Family life-styles, themes, Family myths: security, success, taboos, secrets
Rigidity: chaotic, flexibility, rigidity, ability to change

Style: Closed (traditional/authoritarian)   Random (individualistic/permissive
         Open (collaborative/democratic)   Synchronous (perfectionistic/consentient)
         Family image on these style criteria
Pseudomutuality (Wynne)
Scapegoating (Ackerman): scapegoat, persecutor, family healer
Paradoxes, Double-binds (Bateson)
Discordant, Disturbed, Disrupted
Centripetal and Centrifugal family interaction patterns: (Robert Beavers)

Dynamics: how problem works, who is involved, who is served by the problem,
Motivators/demotivators
Strengths:
Disablement: who is blocked from which targets, collective failings,

Subsystems:
    Couple system   Sibling system
    Intergenerational system: boundaries, patterns, alliances, ethnic influences, should, conflict and
        cooperation, cutoffs,
    Other subsystems: friends, work, school, church, professionals, agencies
    Support systems: relatives, friends etc.

INTERVENTION METHODS:

Reframing   Validation
Problem-solving approaches: brainstorming   Fair Fighting Training (George Bach)
Structural and Systematic interventions   Paradoxical directives

SUMMARY:

Hypotheses re maintenance of symptoms, functional analysis, payoffs, trade-offs, homeostasis

27.6 Aspects of Child Rearing/Raising:

PARENTAL RESTRICTIVENESS:

Strictness re: feeding, mobility, interruption by children, table manners, neatness, cleanliness, bedtime,
    noise, radio and TV, chores, obedience/compliance, leniency, aggression
Restrictiveness regarding sexuality: nudity, modesty, masturbation, sex play
Inhibition of aggression: encouraged to fight back, defend self, toward parents/sibs/ peers
Ratio of maternal to paternal discipline, mother's view of father's strictness, conflicts over discipline
Faulty discipline: lack of discipline, harsh/overly serve discipline, fear/hatred of parent, decreased
    initiative/spontaneity, inconsistent discipline, unstable values

PARENTAL REJECTION:
    Warmth: response to crying, demonstrations of affection, fun in child care, warmth of bond, play time
        initiated by mother/father
    Use of praise: for table manners, for obedience, for nice play, amount of play
    Rejection, over-protection/excessive restriction, overpermissiveness/indulgence, unrealistic demands
    Other: coldness, positive/negative feelings when pregnancy discovered

PARENT-CHILD MISFIT/bad fit due to primary reactions tendencies/Temperament variables of child or expectations of mother/caregiver

> Difficult babies: irregular sleeping/eating/elimination, mainly negative moods, much crying, irritable and poor adjustment to change leads to "dissonant stress" (Thomas, Chess and Birch, 1977, 1968)
> Ways of responding to change/stress: illness, disturbed sleep, eating problems

Abusing Families, Characteristics of : See section 16.1 Abuse

Abuse, Spouse: See section 16.7 Battered Woman Syndrome

27.7 Measures Assessing Family Functioning:

Many scales of marital relationships an old and well researched one has been updated by Swenson, *et al*, (1992) which lists 43 areas of possible conflict, each rated on 5 levels of frequency clustered into six factor analysed subscales:
> 1. Problems-solving, decision-making, and the goals of marriage.
> 2. Child-rearing and home labor
> 3. Relatives and in-laws
> 4. Personal care and appearance
> 5. Money management
> 6. Outside friendships and the dissatisfactions with the expression of affection in the marriage.

ASSESSMENT OF LOVE AND AFFECTION:

Swenson, *et al.* (1992b) offers a current revision of a scale which has been well researched and which seems to address all the measurable meanings of love and affection in marriage. There are six factor analysed subscales:
1. Verbal expressions of affection to and from the loved one
2. Self-disclosure of intimate personal facts to and by the loved one
3. Toleration of loved one's bothersome aspects
4. Moral support, encouragement and interest expressed in other's activities shown and received
5. Feelings felt but not expressed overtly
6. Material evidence of affection as seen in gifts, chores performed, financial support, favors done by and for the loved one.

OTHER ASSESSMENT METHODS:

> Life chronology, time line (Satir, Toman)
> Structured Family Interview (Watzlawick)
> Genogram: See section 9.7 Genogram
> Evaluation of Marriage:
> Life cycles of Marriages
> There are many scales for marriages. I happen to like Richard Stuart and Barbara Jacobson's *Couple's Pre-counseling Inventory*. See section 37 Citations.
> Many useful questionnaires and problem lists can be found in Lasswell and Brock (1989).

CLINICIAN'S JUDGEMENTS OF FAMILY FUNCTIONING:

Kinston's (1988) Family Health Scales are a very interesting "attempt to capture formally the intuitive assessment made by clinicians." The goal is formalizing the clinician's judgements not mathematical measurement. Evaluations are made at the family-level, the network-of-relations level, and the level of individual functioning. An outline of the sections and subscales will suggest its richness:

Family character:
   Affective life: Family atmosphere, Nature of relationships, Emotional expression, Emotional responsiveness
   Communication: Overall patterns, Continuity, Expression of messages, Reception of messages
   Boundaries: Family cohesion, Family roles, Intergenerational boundary, Sexual identity, Individual autonomy
   Alliances: Family structures, Marital relations, Parental coalition, Parent/Child relationships, Sibling relationships

Family Competence:
   Conflict resolution
   Problem solving
   Family life-cycle tasks: e. g. child management

Family relationship with the environment:
   Family stability
   Community
   Extended family
   Relationship with the Interviewer/Treater

Family process:
   Family interaction
   Interaction between family and environment

28. Vocational/Academic Skills and Disability Evaluations

28.1 Basic Work Skills:

ASPECTS: (<->)

Energy level is sickly, low, adequate/normal, healthy, vital, vigorous, impressive, excessive, driven

Motor skills: poor coordination/good/adequate/normal dexterity/dextrous, eye-hand coordination

Shows minimal/unacceptable regard for personal attire or cleanliness/disheveled and sloppy/wears dirty clothes, needs a bath or shave, adheres to standards of non-offensive personal cleanliness, is cleanly but inappropriately dressed, appears typical of his/her community's workers in grooming/ cleanliness/attire choice

Deficiencies of attention, *concentration*, persistence or pace, low frustration tolerance, easily dismayed, can focus and maintain attention, conceptualizes the problem, corrects situation/alters own behavior

Motivation to work is eager/positive/minimal/compliant without complaint, willing to work at tasks seen as monotonous or unpleasant, refuses

Remembers locations/work procedures/instructions/rules

Makes no/few/occasional/an unacceptable number of errors which must be corrected by client/ coworkers/supervisors, notices exceptions/failures, monitors own quality, has low/poor/ adequate/high inspection skills, quality/accuracy/waste/scrap decreases with repetition/supervision

Productivity is minimal/below expected/equal to __ % of average competitive worker's rate, quantity of work, he/she increased production/productivity by __ % over original measured rate, quantity/productivity increases with practice/repetition/supervision, and shows acceptance of competitive work norms,

Attendance is unreliable/inadequate/minimal/spotty/deficient/adequate/as expected/excellent, has no/few/normal large number of unexcused absences per month, calls off, punctual for arrival/ breaks/lunch hours, performs without excessive tardiness/rest periods/time off/absences/ interruptions from psychological symptoms, dependable, responsible

28. 29 Voc/Rec

He/she seldom <u>communicates</u> beyond basic ideas and often misunderstands directions/is misunderstood by peers/supervisors, can comprehend some non-concrete aspects of work situation, communication is usually understood by others, communications are clear and work relevant, has the ability to ask questions or seek assistance as needed

Uses telephone properly

Response to <u>supervision</u>: rebels against supervision, resists supervision and is inappropriate interpersonally, does not seek supervision when needed, personalizes supervisor/worker relationship, requests excessive supervision, is oppositional to requests of supervisor, often withdraws/refuses offers of interaction, is difficult to get along/work with, requires firm supervision, asks for unnecessary help, interacts with the general public/co-worker/supervisors without behavioral extremes/appropriately, reports appropriately to supervisor, improves work methods/organization under supervision, works in small/large groups, is helpful to supervisor and peers

<u>Emotional responsiveness</u> on the job: he/she tends to become emotional/angry/hurt/anxious when corrected or criticized/cannot have own way and is unable to continue work, argues, responds angrily or inappropriately to comments, but with counseling or encouragement can remain at work site, verbally denies problems but ..., maintains composure and attention to task, takes corrective action, responds appropriately by adjusting behavior or work habits, reacts appropriately to conflict/authorities/peers/coworkers, maintains even temperament, accepts instructions/criticism/authority/supervision/feedback/rules

Is un/able to retain individual <u>instructions</u> for simplest of tasks, requires constant/one-on-one supervision/continual reminders/coaching/only normal instruction to perform routine tasks, requires reinforcement to retain information from day to day, requires little or no direction after initial instruction or orientation, able to learn job duties/procedures from oral instructions/demonstrations/written directions, carries out short/simple/detailed/multi-step instructions

<u>Adaptation</u>: "Set in his/her ways," exhibits serious adjustment problems when work environment changes, is unable to cope with job's pressures/displays inappropriate or disruptive behaviors, displays inappropriate or disruptive behavior only briefly after work, changes but is able to return to task with supervisory encouragement, generally adapts to/copes with/tolerates work changes/schedules/deadlines/interruptions/pressures, learns from mistakes/instruction/supervision, relies on self, able to compete

Oblivious to/aware of <u>hazards</u> and able to take precautions, seems to be "accident prone" beyond usual frequency of accidents, has an "accident" whenever eligible for promotion or transfer

Cannot make simple <u>decisions</u> to carry out a job, indecisive, confused by choices and criteria, becomes paralyzed by decisions, makes correct routine decisions, makes up own mind, effectively sequences steps in a procedure

Cannot conform to a <u>schedule</u> or tolerate a full workday, performs within a schedule, sustains a routine, organizes him/herself, prioritizes work, arranges materials, shows an even/steady work pace throughout workday, paces work, shows necessary/expected/normal/required stamina, maintains motivation, completes assignments, finishes what s/he starts, continues despite obstacles/opposition/frustrations, able to work in a time-conscious manner, conscientious worker

<u>Maintains</u>/cares for tools/supplies/equipment, repairs, adjusts, replaces, services, does not waste materials or damage equipment

<u>Travels</u> independently by public transportation or makes own arrangements to job site

Relationship to peers/coworkers is avoidant, distant, shy, self-conscious, nervous, conflictual, domineering, submissive, competitive, suspicious, attention-seeking, clowning, immature, provocative, dependent, trouble-maker, teasing, ridiculing, normal, friendly

Maladaptive or odd behaviors: too introverted/withdrawn, loud/domineering, manipulative/takes advantage of peers, limits conversation to yes or no answers, will not look at person he is addressing, gossips, will not start a conversation, seeks unwanted/ill timed/inappropriate physical contacts, has attention-getting odd behaviors, offensive personal hygiene, confuses actual and imagined abilities, excessive or unrealistic complaints

Financial competence: see section 25.8

28.2 Vocational Competence/Recommendations:

OVERALL COMPETENCE:

Normal:
S/he is capable of performing substantial gainful employment at all levels.
There are no psychological barriers to employment.
Able to relate to coworkers and supervisors, handle the stresses and demands of gainful employment within his/her intellectual/physical limitations

Somewhat limited
S/he is functional in her/his current simplified life-style/supportive situation but in a more independent setting, i.e. living independently/alone s/he appears to lack adequate self-direction and other resources for maintenance/continued functioning
S/he is intellectually limited but not to the extent which would prevent appropriate employment.
This person could understand, retain and follow instructions within the implied limitations of his/her Borderline intellectual functioning/mild/moderate mental retardation.
Able to understand, retain, and follow only simple, basic instructions.
Would/not be able to meet the quality standards and production norms in work commensurate with his/her intellectual level
Can perform activities commensurate with his/her residual physical/functional capabilities

Significantly limited:
Can function only in a stable setting/sheltered program, in a very adapted and supportive setting, can perform in a competitive work setting, in the open labor market
Requires appropriate pre-vocational experiences, Work Adjustment Training, work hardening program, diagnostic work study, evaluation of vocational potential
Can/can't tolerate pressures of workplace, unused to the regularities and demands of the world of work
No Residual Functional Capacity for Substantial Gainful Activity
The cumulative impact of the diagnoses present very significant deterrents/obstacles to employment/ productivity/substantial gainful activity

SETTING NEEDED:

Non-stressful, low/non-pressured, non-competitive setting
When performing simple, basic, repetitive, routine, non-speeded, slow-paced/unpaced/non-speeded, non-complex tasks, which do not require facility in academics
Solitary, non-social tasks, working alone, no contact with the public

Closely supervised
Sheltered/highly supportive, stable
Part-time, flexible hours, full-time, overtime

EMPLOYMENT LEVEL: (<->)

Unskilled/helper/laborer, semi-skilled, skilled, professional, managerial, self-employed

SUPERVISION: (<->)

Requires continual re-direction, repetition of instructions, working under close and supportive supervision, instruction only, monitoring only, occasional overview, can work independently

AMBITION: (<->)

None, lethargic, indolent, listless, lackadaisical, self-satisfied, content, eager, persistent, hopeful, enterprising, greedy, opportunistic, pretentious, unrealistic, grandiose

SELF-CONFIDENCE:

Impractical and unrealistic

JOB SEEKING/HUNTING: (<->)

Has no actual or realistic history of seeking, efforts have been episodic/half-hearted, efforts have been determined but initiative is now exhausted, Poor/low/adequate/high knowledge of vocational and educational resources
Employment is seen as too/highly/moderately/mildly/tolerably/not stressful
Has a feasible vocational goal/time frame for actions
Has/lacks job finding skills, interviewing skills, ability to identify obstacles to successful completion of training/skill development/employment

SUMMARY OF OBSTACLES TO SUCCESS:

Academically so deficient that s/he cannot find or hold a job

Takes unscheduled breaks/absences, engages in excessive off-task behaviors
Invents excuses for lateness/absences/mistakes/inattention, irresponsible,
Avoids some tasks
Inappropriate or disruptive behaviors
Agitates intentionally
Asks for unnecessary supervision/help/attention

Does not work effectively when under any/normal/expected pressure
Responds to criticism with anger/anxiety/hurt/withdrawal

Uses/overuses offensive language
Puts worst foot forward

While not disabled s/he is not employable because ...

28.3 Written Language Skills/Ability: See also section 29.4 Reading Materials

(Test with a paragraph from a magazine on a current topic and ask about its meanings)

READING COMPREHENSION:

Alexic, illiterate, functionally illiterate, lacks basic/survival reading skills
Names letters, says simple words, reads out-loud/silently, only small sight reading vocabulary, reads signs/directions/instructions/recipes, low/normal comprehension, deciphered word meanings, slow reader
Worked hard, asked for assistance, recognized errors, used word attack skills to successfully identify/decipher several words on a reading test.

His/her spelling/reading is limited to a small group of memorized words.

He/she has rudimentary phonetic abilities but cannot identify unfamiliar or phonetically irregular words.
Reading skills are adequate for basic literacy and utilization of written texts for getting directions.
His/her poor reading skills prohibit responding to/guidance by written instructions.
Basic functional literacy/no reading for pleasure/usual skills/literate/avid/scholarly

SPELLING:

Agraphic
Letter-sound relationships are absent/poor/good/need strengthening
Her/his spelling skills are poor/good/excellent and s/he shows/demonstrates a solid grasp of underlying phonetic principles.
Writing from dictation: reversals, inversions, omissions, substitutions, additions, confused attack at letters, labored writing, reckless
Handwriting: quality, upper and lower case letters, named the letters, inversions, reversals, confused one letter with another, degree of effort required, awkward handgrip position/use of the page, size of letters
Relationship of disorder to expected school achievement is ...
Areas of educational strength/weakness/ handicap, diagnosis, diagnosis of learning disabilities, need for interventions

28.4 Math Ability: See also section 25.8 Financial ADLs

Anumerate, can say the digits, knows the sequence, holds up the correct number of fingers when asked for a number, counts items, does/doesn't know which number is larger

Understands all prices, counts change, makes change.
Possesses basic survival math (measurements, portions, percentages, fractions, weights, etc.), basic business math
Can do simple tasks of counting and measurement but not computation beyond addition and subtraction
Could do simple addition and subtraction of only single digit numbers/double digit numbers but only when borrowing was not involved
His/her ability was limited to simple computation in orally presented arithmetic problems, could answer statement/verbally presented problems requiring addition/subtraction/multiplication/ division
Could do problems when regrouping was/wasn't required.
Could solve/not do correctly problems involving multiplication or division, decimals, fractions or measurements

28.5 Academic/Vocational History:

No problems with firings, absenteeism, conflict with customers, peers/coworkers, supervisors

Never worked/had a wage-earning job outside the home, number/duration/kind of jobs, currently employed, unemployed, laid off, underemployed, labor pool, marginal, temporary, seasonal, part-time, full time, several jobs, retired.

(<->) Regular/irregular/interrupted/sporadic employment history, number and reasons for firings

Because of genetic/home/school situations/other background s/he didn't benefit from formal education.
History of low productivity, success, and achievement throughout life

28.6 Rehabilitation Assessment:

Broadwin *et al.* (1992a and b) are useful starting places as they offer sample reports (initial evaluation, medical, background, progress) and job analysis (job description, duties, physical demands, etc.) in terms of the job's stressors.

28.7 Other:

S/he has an attorney and is not working

In disability evaluations do not indicate that the client is **disabled**. This is usually an administrative decision and made on criteria beyond just your findings.

29. Recreational Behaviors

29.1 Entertainment: TV/Radio/Tapes/Records/Music: (<->)

Avoids, dislikes, confused/over-stimulated by, just as background, passive listener, aware of news/weather, selective/chooses/plans for particular programs, "Must see my stories/soaps", recalls, actively tapes/records/purchases recordings, attends musical events regularly, plays musical instrument

29.2 Hobbies:

No hobbies, does puzzles/letter games/board games, crafts, needle-crafts, tinkers, paints by the numbers/ water/oil/acrylics, builds models, hunts/fishes, gardens, table games (cards, checkers, Monopoly), reads, collects, repairs, plans, travels, builds

Cares for pets: feeds, exercises, cleans up after, grooms, cleans, teaches, consults veterinarian, etc.

29.3 Sports: (Specify which)

Watches on TV, attends/spectates, reads about, discusses, participates, Special Olympics, bowling league, plays on sports team, has individual sport(s), regularly participates in sport, competitive player

Exercises: regularly, walks, jogs, aerobics, health club, golfs, swims, lifts weights

29.4 Reading Materials: See section 28.3 Language ability

NEWSPAPER:

Headlines only, comics, horoscopes, simple stories, advertisements/prices, classifieds, news, columnists, editorials, news analyses, arts sections, reviews

MAGAZINES:

Word-finding magazines, children's books/magazines, comic books, adventure, gossip, supermarket, women's, men's, news-weeklies/current events, crosswords, science fiction, special interest, e.g. war/detective/biker/guns/wrestling/hobby/trade/technical/professional/literary/arts

BOOKS:

Romances, short stories, mysteries, novels, westerns, horror, adventure, science fiction, contemporary literature, poetry, biographies, self-help, non-fiction, texts, classics

29.5. Summary Statements:

QUALITY OF PERFORMANCE (<->)

No recreational activities, nothing for relaxation, for fun, no pleasurable activities, no interest in recreation

Compulsively completes, finishes, usually does, finishes only the simplest, quickest, forgets activities started, is very slow, takes much longer than usual, previously, completes only at a very low quality, neglects, half finishes projects, discontinues

Active and satisfying recreational life, recreation integrated into work and social lives

For a Child:

Has imaginary playmates
Plays with toys, dolls, miniatures
Quality of play: autistic movements/manipulation, watches only, stereotyped actions built into toys, creative, makes own toys, involves others
Actively/passively participates in neighborhood/informal sporting activities
Has/maintains collections
Builds models (airplanes, cars, ships, railroading, etc.)

30. Other Areas of Evaluation

30.1 Psychological Autopsy: Adapted from Shneidman (1976) and Ebert (1987)[1]

1. Demographic data:
2. Details of death: cause or method, laboratory studies, coroner's report, police report, etc.
3. Brief Social History: the usual as well as medical illnesses, educational, employment, military history, psychotherapy, previous suicide attempts, suicide notes and other writings
4. "Death history" of victims family: suicides, fatal illnesses, age at death
5. Personality and Life-style of victim:
6. Typical reactions to stress: emotional upsets, periods of disequilibrium, mood, mental status
7. Stresses, upsets, pressures, tensions or anticipations of trouble in last year
8. Role of drugs and alcohol in life-style and in victim's death
9. Nature of interpersonal relationships: include relation with physician
10. Fantasies, dreams, thoughts, premonitions, or fears of death, accident, or suicide
11. Recent changes in the victim's habits, hobbies, eating, sexual patterns, or other life routines
12. Information about the victim's "Life side": successes, plans, upswings
13. Assessment of the role of the victim in his/her demise, presuicidal behavior
14. Rating of lethality of method(s) used
15. Reactions of informants to the victim's death
16. Comments, special feature

30.2 Beliefs, Irrational (Albert Ellis)

A LIST OF CLASSIC IBS:
1. I must be loved and approved of by every significant person in my life, and if I'm not, it's awful.
2. When others behave badly or unfairly, they should be blamed, reprimanded and punished. They are bad or rotten people.
3. It is simply awful when things are not the way I want them to be.
4. I should be very anxious about events that are uncertain or potentially dangerous.
5. I am not worthwhile unless I am thoroughly competent, adequate, and achieving at all times or at

---

[1] Ebert reiews the history and multiple uses of this evaluation and adds many factors; highly recommended.

least most of the time in one major area.

6. The world should be fair and just.
7. There's got to be a perfect solution to this problem; I must find it. I must have certainty and perfect control over things.
8. I should be comfortable and without pain at all times. It's easier to avoid than to face life's difficulties.
9. If I feel emotional distress I am going crazy and that is unbearable.
10. I need someone stronger than myself on whom to depend.
11. Misery comes from circumstances. I have little ability to control of change my feelings.
12. My past is the cause of my problems

Best current general books on RET are Dryden and DiGuiseppe (1990) and Whalen (1992).
A very long list of iBs can be found in Ellis, A. (1976). More can be found in Ellis, A (1987).

Albert Ellis' RET Institute's Catalog offers books by many authors, neat posters, and training programs. Write to the Institute for Rational-Emotive Therapy, 45 East 65th Street, NY NY 10021-6593.

30.3 Cognitive styles: See also Shapiro (1965)

Field dependent vs. Field Independent or psychological differentiation (Herman Witkin)
Global vs. Analytical or Focussing vs. Scanning or Impulsive vs. Reflective (Jerome Kagan)
Sharpeners/Levelers or Impulsive vs. Reflective
Cognitive complexity, more or fewer dimensions used (George Kelly)
Internal vs. External Locus of Control (Julian Rotter)

30.4 Competence to Manage Funds/Financial Competence: See also section 25.8 Financial ADLs. "Incapacitated" is currently preferred to "incompetent," as it focuses on receiving and evaluating information

Standards/Criteria:

Ability to manage his or her property
Likelihood to dissipate own property
Likelihood of becoming the victim of designing persons
Ability to make or communicate decisions about the use and management of his or her entitlements

Assessment of Financial competence *is based on*:

Psychological/mental status evaluation/data base of orientation, memory, judgement, reading ability, emotional disturbance, intelligence testing

Is oriented to time, place, person, common items
Has adequate memory functions, social judgement, test judgement, control of emotions
Overall/general intelligence
Make simple mathematical calculations

Psychological/psychiatric evaluation of quality of reality contact because of delusions, hallucinations, thought disorder, disordered thought processes, etc.

His/her FACTUAL KNOWLEDGE of the source and extent of his/her assets, understanding of financial terms and concepts, recognition of currency, values/costs of several common items, simple/basic arithmetic, change making ability, perception of situations of potential exploitation

His/her FUNCTIONAL ABILITY/BEHAVIOR such as observed/historical ability to conduct transactions, conserve assets, competent performance of financial management/responsibilities

AND S/HE IS THEREFORE CONSIDERED:

Incompetent in all financial areas
Competent to manage only small amounts of money
Able/not able to manage his/her property, likely/unlikely to dissipate/squander his/her property.
Able avoid exploitation, manage welfare/etc. benefits, and make long range financial decisions autonomously, responsibly and effectively
Likely/unlikely to fall victim to/become the victim of designing persons, be duped/gulled
Lacks/possesses the capacity to make or communicate responsible decisions about the use and management of his/her entitlements and assets
Unlikely to hoard funds rather than make necessary purchases

If benefits are awarded s/he would use the money for drugs/alcohol/gambling/disorganized/impulsive purchases and therefore s/he may/will/should not be the best recipient of funds for their management.

30.5 Competence to Make a Will/Testamentary Competence:
The individual must understand 1) the nature and extent of his or her property, 2) the identity and relationships of the usual beneficiaries, 3) the nature and, 4) effects of making a will.

30.6 Competence to Stand Trial:
The defendant must be able to participate in his or her own defense by understanding the nature of the 1) proceedings and the 2) charges and be able to 3) communicate and cooperate with the defense attorney. These abilities depend on the client's 4) mental status.

Melton *et al.* (1987) is the most thorough resource on this and other thorny and complex forensic issues. A useful resource is Nicholson, *et al.* (1988) for the evaluation of scales.

30.7 Coping Ability/Stress Tolerance: See also section 9.4 Adjustment History,

DIMENSIONS:

Instrumental, affective and escape coping
Low/moderate/high, frustration tolerance, ability to delay gratifications, tolerance for ambiguity/ uncertainty/conflict/low information/structure, hardiness

COPING SKILLS: (<->)

Inept, incompetent, "can't cope", unadaptable, rigid, inflexible, stubborn
Has developed self-soothing techniques
Has developed specific skills: anger management, assertiveness, rational self-talk

Uses social support system/friendships/"bitching group"
Resourceful, skilled, "survivor", courageous, realistic, adaptable, flexible, adjusts, conforms, bends
Valiant, proud, resourceful, "down on his/her luck"

ASSETS AND LIABILITIES/STRENGTHS TO BUILD UPON:

Assets, resources, qualifications, reserves, possessions, skills, abilities, aptitudes, capabilities, knowledges, dexterity, talents, prowesses, proficiencies, competencies, experience, expertise
Vigor, drive, spirit, courage, determination, valor
Strengths and weaknesses

30.8 Stages of Homosexual Identity Formation: Modified from Cass (1979)

CONFUSION: Conscious awareness that homosexuality has relevance to oneself.
"My behavior may be called homosexual. Does this mean that I am a homosexual?" -> turmoil, alienation, searching -> denial or personal relevance, anti-homosexual stance, or inhibition of homosexual behaviors -> foreclosure
COMPARISON: "I may be homosexual" -> "I'm different, I don't belong to society at large," "I do not want to be different"
TOLERANCE: "I am probably a homosexual"
ACCEPTANCE: "I am a homosexual"
PRIDE: "Gay is good", "Gay and Proud"
ACTIVISM:"How dare you presume I'm heterosexual?", Confrontation activities, disclosure as a strategy.
Also 'Them and us' - 'Homosexual is good, heterosexual is bad.'
SYNTHESIS:"... there are some heterosexual others who accept (my) homosexual identity as I do."
At this stage homosexual identity is no longer "seen as *the* identity, it is now given the status of being merely one aspect of self."

Gay men[1] may go through different stages according to Troiden (1979, 1988):
SENSITIZATION: Awareness in general.
DISSOCIATION AND SIGNIFICATION: Personal awareness and struggling with personal meaning.
COMING OUT OR IDENTITY ASSUMPTION: Exploring and integrating awareness with behavior.
COMMITMENT: With reconciliation of identity and integration of personality.

Gay relationships have been classified by Bell and Weinberg (1978) as: Close-coupled; Open-coupled; Functionals; Dysfunctionals; and Asexuals.

30.9 Effect of Impairment on Person:

(<->) Has become psychotic, suicidal, regressed, decompensated, devastated, catastrophic reaction, denial of event or its consequences, overwhelmed, maladaptive, deteriorating, depressed, adjustment disorder, prolonged/delayed mourning, saddened, marginal functioning, adjusting to disability/losses, adequate/fair functioning, functional, adapting, assimilating, accepting, accommodating, using psychological coping mechanisms, compensating, has devised compensatory/prosthetic/mnemonic devices, successful, over-compensating, mature, is challenged

The cumulative impact/effect of his/her emotional and physical impairments results in no/insignificant/mild/ significant/moderate/severe/crippling limitations

---

[1] "Gay men" is preferred to "male homosexuals" as it is not pathological or clinical sounding and highlighting (see synthesis" just above).

30.10 Classifications of Intelligence:

Consider levels of <u>A</u>daptive <u>B</u>ehavior, <u>A</u>ctivities of <u>D</u>aily <u>L</u>iving, and needs for assistance, as well as the results of intelligence testing.

Consider the potential effects of depression, dementia, distracting anxiety, relationship with the examiner, intercurrent medical illnesses, etc. on intellectual functioning.

DSM III-R CATEGORIES FOR MENTAL RETARDATION:

	IQ levels as guide
Borderline intellectual functioning (not MR, use V code 40.00)	71- 84
Mild retardation	50 to approximately 70
Moderate retardation	35-49
Severe retardation	20-34
Profound retardation	less than 20
Unspecified mental retardation	not testable

THE DSM II CATEGORIES FOR MENTAL RETARDATION:

	IQ levels as guide
Dull normal	
Borderline intellectual functioning	68-83
Mild retardation (old usage is Moron)	52-67
Moderate retardation	36-51
Severe retardation	20-35
Profound retardation	less than 20

CATEGORIES OF MENTAL DEFECTIVENESS IN THE UNITED KINGDOM:

Feeblemindedness	50-90
Moron	50-75
Imbecile	25-50
Idiot	less than 25

Each of these is qualified by *high, medium* or *low.*

WECHSLER DERIVATIONAL INTELLIGENCE QUOTIENTS FOR THE WAIS-R (1981):

Category	IQ scores as a guide	% of population included in each
Very Superior	130 and above	2.2
Superior	120-129	6.7
Bright Average	110-119	16.1
Average	90-109	50.0
Low average	80-89	16.1
Borderline intellectual functioning	70-79	6.7
Mild Retardation	60-69	
Severe retardation	20-34	
Moderate retardation	50-59	< 2
Severe retardation	20-34	
Profound retardation	less than 20	

VALIDITY OF SCORES:

The obtained test scores are believed to be valid indicators/significantly underestimate current intellectual functioning/are consistent with developmental history and degree of functional loss but not potential because ....

NOTES:
> After three years from the date of the evaluation test data and findings should be treated with caution and trusted even less when the subject is/was a child.
> Generally IQ scores below 40 are not meaningful.
> Consider the possibility that current functioning represents a decline due to Organic Brain Syndrome, etc. and, if so, give an estimate of premorbid intelligence based on current subtest results, earlier testing, changed levels of adaptive behavior, etc.

30.11 Moral Reasoning's Stages of Development: From Kohlberg (1984):

Preconventional Level	1	Avoids punishment
	2	Gains reward
Conventional Level	3	Gains approval and avoids disapproval of others
	4	Defined by rigid codes of "Law and Order"
Postconventional Level	5	Defined by a "Social Contract" agreed upon for the public good.
	6	Personal moral code based on abstract ethical principles

Carol Gilligan - Men's morality is based on *Justice* and women's on *Caring*.

30.12 Adaptation in the Refugee Process: Based on Gonsalves (1992)

PHASES:

Pre-flight: mounting anxiety, abandonment, "victims of fate", "no one cares"
Flight: traumatizing experiences, varying in intensity, duration and number, returning as intrusive memories often on anniversary dates
Resettlement: complex, a lifetime process of coping with different language, traditions, etc.

STAGES
Early arrival: from 1 week to 6 months in which they learn the surroundings/"lay of the land", remain involved with their homeland, and experience disorientation, low energy, sadness/loss, anger and guilt, relief and excitement.
Destabilization: from 6 months to 3 years in which they acquire survival tools, develop a support group, learn the language, social customs and culture due to economic pressures, experience great stress and pain, hostile withdrawal from new culture, resistance to the new culture, or compliance with the new culture uncritically, view the old county as better, feel lonely, and denial.
Exploration and restabilization: from 3 to 5 years in which they develop more flexible cultural learning methods, continued marital conflict and adjustment, resist further adaptation, and remain linked to other refugees and experience anger at lowered status, fear of failure, isolation, premature culture or identity closure.
Return to normal life: from 5-7 years in which they maintain flexible cultural accommodation while retaining some old values, develop realistic expectations of new generations, develop a positive identity, expect lasting personality changes, show delayed grief reactions, and experience rigidity and intergenerational conflict.
Decompensation: for some refugees, at any time in 1 week to 7 years, in which they struggle to meet survival needs, modify identity, enter the new culture, continue commitments, connect the past, present and future and experience psychosis, identity disorders, depression, continuity of family, and existential crises.

30.13 Evaluation of Intellect and Cognitive Functions: See also Chapter 6 Mental Status Questions

There are thousands published and hundreds with good reliable and valid instruments for evaluation of almost any aspect of mental functioning. These are the most popular.

There are more kinds of 'intelligence' than are assessed by widely available tests. Howard Gardner (1983) suggested seven.

If you suspect the presence of a learning disability, mental retardation or any physical condition which would affect school performance consultation with and referral to a school psychologist or educational specialist who can utilize the many specialized instruments for evaluation and remediation is usually appropriate. Commonly used and well standardized instruments include:

CHILD DEVELOPMENT/ADAPTIVE BEHAVIORS:

AAMD Adaptive Behavior Scale
Adaptive Performance Instrument
Bayley Scales of Infant Development
Brigance Diagnostic Inventory of Early Development
Callier-Azusa Scales
Child Behavior Checklist (Achenbach)
Connors Parent Rating Scale (CPRS)
Denver Developmental Screening Inventory
Developmental Activities Screening Inventory-II
Developmental Assessment for Severely Handicapped
Developmental Indicators for Assessment of Learning-Revised (DIAL-R)
Vineland Social Maturity Scale

Adaptive Behavior Inventory for Children
Battelle Developmental Inventory
Birth to Three Developmental Scale
Burk's Behavior Rating Scales
Camelot Behavior Checklist
Child Behavior Rating Scale
Connors Teacher Rating Scale (CTRS)
Normative Adaptive Behavior Checklist

Developmental Profile II (DP-II)

Vineland Adaptive Behavior Scale

FOR SCREENING OF INTELLIGENCE

McCarthy Scales of Children's Abilities
Peabody Picture Vocabulary Test-Revised (PPVT-R)
Expressive One Word Picture Vocabulary Test-Revised

Columbia Mental Maturity Scale (CMMS)
The Quick Test
Slosson Intelligence Test-Revised

FOR PRECISE EVALUATION AN INDIVIDUAL'S GENERAL INTELLIGENCE:

The Wechsler Preschool and Primary Scale of Intelligence (WPPSI)
The Wechsler Intelligence Scale for Uhildren - Uevised (WISC-R)
The Wechsler Adult Intelligence Scale - Revised (WAIS-R)
    All Wechsler tests offer a Verbal Intelligence Quotient, a Performance IQ, and a Full Scale IQ
The Stanford-Binet Intelligence Test - Form L-M, Revised
Cattell Infant Intelligence Scale
Leiter International Performance Scale

Kaufman Assessment Battery for Children
Raven's Progressive Matrices

SPEECH AND LANGUAGE TESTS

Bankson Language Test Second Edition
Early Language Milestone Scale
Sequenced Inventory of Communication Development-Revised
Test of Early Language Development-2

Del Rio Language Screening Test

Test of Language Development -Primary-2

EDUCATIONAL READINESS, ABILITY AND ACHIEVEMENT:

California Achievement Tests -Forms C/D
Detroit Tests of Learning Aptitude-2
Illinois Test of Psycholinguistic Ability

Detroit Tests of Learning Aptitude-Primary
Differential Ability Scales
Iowa Test of Basic Skills-Forms G and H

Kaufman Test of Educational Achievement-Comprehensive
Peabody Individual Achievement Test-Revised   Wechsler Individual Achievement Test
Jastak Wide Range Achievement Test - Revised (WRAT-2R for adults, WRAT-R for children)
Woodcock Johnson Psycho-Educational Battery-Revised (the Woodcock Johnson)

LEARNING DISABILITIES:

The Beery Developmental Test of Motor Integration   Visual Auditory Digit Span (VADS)

VOCATIONAL GUIDANCE

Differential Aptitude Tests   Strong Vocational Interest Inventory
Self-Directed Search   Geist Picture Interest Inventory

NEUROPSYCHOLOGICAL FUNCTIONING:

Halstead-Reitan Neuropsychological Test Battery   Luria-Nebraska Neuropsychological Battery
The Bender Visual Motor Gestalt Test (with the Canter Interference procedure)

MEMORY:

The Wechsler Memory Scale - Revised, and the Russell modification.
Wide Range Assessment of Memory and Learning   Benton Revised Visual Retention Test

MOTOR DEVELOPMENT:

Brazelton Neonatal Behavioral Assessment Scale   Bruininks-Oseretsky Test of Motor Proficiency
Peabody Developmental Motor Scales   Sensory Integration and Praxis Tests

30.14 Personality Assessment Tests:

Theodore Millon's (1985) perspectives and diagnostic schema are becoming more popular.

Repeated factor analyses have consistently found five factors to underlie all the variations of personality:
1. Surgency or Extraversion   2. Agreeableness   3. Conscientiousness or Dependability
4. Emotional stability (vs. Neuroticism)   5. Openness to Experience: Culture or Open-mindedness
The NEO Personality Inventory is based on this model.

OBJECTIVE:
For diagnosing clinical populations:
Minnesota Multiphasic Personality Inventory and MMPI-2   Personality Assessment Inventory
Millon Clinical Multiaxial Inventory-II   Psychological Screening Inventory

For non-clinical populations:
California Personality Inventory-Revised   Children's Personality Questionnaire
NEO Personality Inventory (NEO PI-R)   Omnibus Personality Inventory
Personality Inventory for Children   Sixteen Personality Factor test (16PF)

PROJECTIVE:

Children's Apperception Test (CAT)   Draw-A-Person test (DAP), Draw-A-Family
House-Tree-Person (drawings) test (HTP)   Koppitz Human Figure Drawing Test
Rorschach or Holtzman Inkblots   Rotter Incomplete Sentences Blank
Thematic Apperception Test (the TAT)   Three Wishes

31. Formats for Reports

This Chapter offers templates, formats or outlines for many kinds of reports. They offer other ways to structure a report for specific audiences, purposes, or paradigms. The report is usually based on an evaluation and so these Chapters are of relevance: 30 Other evaluations, 27 Family evaluations, and 25, ADLs, 26. Social Functioning, 28. Vocational , and 29. Recreational and perhaps 22. Treatment Plans.

31.1 Format for Psychoanalytic/Psychodynamic Evaluations: Adapted mainly from Kellerman and Burry (1991) which is a book on testing from a analytic perspective.

CENTRAL TOPICS TO BE ADDRESSED:

Psychosexual developmental levels   Areas of conflict   Mechanisms of defense/adaptation
Character/personality structure   Ego strength   Potential for acting out
Identity   Object relationships
Estimate of treatability, transference issues
Primary and Secondary Autonomous Ego Functioning   Integrative/Synthetic/Adaptive Ego Functions

ANXIETY: Signal anxiety/inner tension evoked by internal threat (fantasies, impulses) or external threat (other people or demands of life); How is it manifested? How is anxiety experienced: Consciously? acted out? or somatized?

IMPULSE VS. CONTROL:

Impulses, energized emotions: anger, aggression, sexuality, hostility
    Anger: hostility, fantasy, rumination, aggression, sarcasm, quarrelsomeness, passive-aggressive behaviors
    Sexuality: libidinous impulses and wishes for gratification
    Pleasure fantasies, power themes, sexual fantasies, sexual variations
    Acting out as: compulsive masturbation, perversions, promiscuity
    Impulse-dominated personality

Control Mechanisms:
    Cognitive/intellectual (concentration, attention, achievement, integration)
    Ego and superego (goal pursuit, frustration tolerance, taking actions)
    Individual defense mechanisms (anxiety management, emotion associated with the anxiety)
    Character traits (patterns for binding anxiety; sublimating, impulse, pleasure-dominated, anger-
       dominated, fear-dominated, dependency-dominated)
    Fantasy   Fears/phobic reactions   Control-dominated personality

DEFENSE MECHANISMS:

Acting out, Acting In	Compartmentalization	Compensation, Overcompensation
Denial: seven kinds, See section 16.10	Displacement	Fantasizing
Fixation	Identification	Insulation, emotional
Intellectualization	Internalization	Introjection
Isolation	Projection	Rationalization
Reaction formation	Regression	Repression, Dissociation
Resistance	Restitution	Splitting
Sublimation	Substitution	Suppression
Symbolization	Turning Against the Self	Undoing

DIAGNOSIS-DEFENSE CORRESPONDENCE:

Diagnosis	*Preferred Defenses*
Hysteric	Denial, Repression
Obsessive-Compulsive	Intellectualization, Isolation, Undoing, Rationalization, Sublimation
Passive-Aggressive	Displacement
Depression	Compensation, Turning Against the Self
Narcissistic disturbance	Compensation
Paranoid	Denial, Reaction Formation, Projection
Borderline	Splitting
Psychopathic Personality	Regression
Mania	Reaction formation, Compensation, Sublimation

31.2 Behavioral Diagnosis: Summarized from Kanfer and Saslow (1965) present an alternative to the usual dynamic and personological evaluation for clinical evaluations and interventions.

THE PROBLEM

  I. Count the excesses, deficits, and qualities of the maladaptive behavior(s)
  II. Circumstantial/functional analysis
     A. Original initiating circumstances
     B. Antecedent maintaining and inhibiting circumstances
        1. environment : location, time,
        2. physical: illness, injury, sleep, diet, exercise, chemical intake

        3. social: others present, and their actions
        4. affect, mood
        5. cognitive: thoughts, meanings, ideas about self, situation, others
        6. other factors: values, attitudes, opinions
     C. Sequence: what happened, happens, and what can upset the sequence
     D. Payoffs, reinforcements: immediate and long-term
     E. Competing or enhancing higher level cognitive functions: ideals, values, self-talk

THE PERSON

III. Skills
A. Self-control: sex, aggression, self-injurious habits, persistence, delay of gratification, relaxation
B. Expressive: sex, aggression, any strong emotion, artistic activities: art, music, dance, religion, humor
C. Cognitive: self-awareness, psychological-mindedness, academic intelligence, job skills, verbal and analytical facility
D. Physical: strength, coordination, attractiveness
E. Social:
F. Payoffs in past for exercising skills

IV. Reaction to incentives and aversions: Techniques for changing behavior used in the past
A. Reinforcements: What has worked or would work to change behavior: self-image, goal achievement, approval, money, access to activity, free time, power, competition, status, etc.
B. Withdrawal of reinforcements or punishment: time out, being ignored, withdrawal of privileges, reactions toward punisher and punishment
C. Schedule of reinforcement: subgoals, step size

THE ENVIRONMENT

V. Psychosocial-cultural context
A. Social class: expectations of authority, therapy, opportunities, previous treatment
B. Effects of changes on family, friends, coworkers, bosses, etc.
C. Health behaviors

THE FUTURE
VI. Predicted response to various kinds of interventions
A. Environmental manipulation
B. Therapy
VII. Prognosis:
A. Changeability of maintaining circumstances and skills
B. Habit strength
C. Cost of interventions

31.3 Nursing Diagnoses and Treatment Planning: I am most grateful to Patricia Hurzeler, MS, RN, CS of Bloomfield, CT for these materials.

Nursing thinks clearly and comprehensively (biopsychosocial diagnoses) and productively (Nursing Care Plans). Townsend (1988) is a good resource.

COMPONENTS OF A NURSING DIAGNOSIS: PES
1. Health Problems: Human response to actual or potential health problems as assessed by the nurse.
   1A. "Related to":
2. Etiology: Past experiences of individual, genetic influences, current environmental factors, or pathophysiological changes.   2A. "Evidenced by":
3. Clustered Signs or symptoms/defining characteristics: What the client says and what the nurse observes about the existence of a problem.

NURSING CARE PLAN:
1. Selected and Prioritized Nursing Diagnoses
2. Goal/Objectives: in behavioral/objective terminology, measurable, for evaluating effectiveness of interventions Long term usually means "by discharge."

3. Interventions with their Rationales: 4. Desired Patient Outcomes/Discharge Criteria:
5. Date of Evaluation: 6. Medication Information   7. Revisions of Plan on Evaluation Dates

31.4 Adlerian Evaluations: These are from of Henry T. Stein, Ph. D. of San Francisco, CA

LIFE STYLE ANALYSIS:

Activity Level and Radius: Friendships, social life, occupation, recreation, love and sex.
Degree of Cooperation and Social Interest: Thinking about needs and feelings of others, actions to help others:
Courage and Conquests:
Discouragements and Stopping Points:
Excesses and Omissions:
Level and Type of Intelligence:
Emotions and Feelings: Conjunctive and disjunctive, Depth and Range
Scheme of Apperception: Antiethical Scheme of Apperception, Perceived Minus and Plus Situations
Use of Capabilities: Intelligence (Social Purpose), Abilities and Talents (Socially Useful and Useless), Feelings and Emotions (Move Ahead or Stop), Memory and Imagination, (Encouragement/Discouragement)
Pattern of Dealing with Tasks and Difficulties: Childhood Prototype, Adolescent Experimentation, Repetitive Adult Style
Inferiority Feelings, Compensatory Goal, and Style of Life: Inferiority Feelings (What to Avoid, Painful Insecurity), Fictional Goal of Superiority (Imagined Compensation, Security and Success)
Style of Life (How to Get to Goal and Deal with Life's Major Tasks: Social Relationships, Occupation, Love and Sex), Connection of Presenting Problem with Life Style and Goal Use of Symptoms to Excuse Avoidance of Normal Tasks

31.5 The Sequential Report Model: Huber (1984) offers an outline which combines the chronological (to understand causation) with the topical (to understand the presentation).

1. Intellectual functioning
    Level of present functioning, comparison with his group
    Level of capacity
    Reasons for failure to function up to capacity
    Areas of strength and weakness
2. Dynamics
    What is he attempting to accomplish with his present mode of behavior?
    What thoughts and feelings is he having?
    What events or people produce conflict? Anxiety?
    Major and minor conflicts
    People with whom the conflicts are manifested:
    Times and places where the conflicts arise
    How did his present situation arise?, What pressures and supports were given by significant figures?, What was the sequence of learning the defenses symptoms, adaptations, etc.?
3. Methods of handling conflicts
    Manifestations of anxiety, symptoms, defense mechanisms
    Overt behavior
4. Strengths and weaknesses in relation to goals
    Needs and wishes, manifest and latent
    Strengths for pursuing them: What are the pressures, supports, and strengths (environmental and intrapsychic) which can changes his life?

Weaknesses: What can produce dangerous and/or crippling behaviors (suicide, psychotic reactions, psychosomatic difficulties, antisocial acts)?
What does he need to function more effectively?
How much impairment is there? What is the nature of the impairment?
5. Recommendations
Therapy/no therapy, environmental change
Form(s) of therapy
Predictions about therapy.

31.6 A Case Summary Report: This very elaborate outline is modified from Wolberg (1954). It is commonly used in hospital/clinic settings which have departments and is perhaps best suited to research or teaching settings. It is also called a Source Oriented Record, or the Treatment Team or Orthopsychiatric format.

1. Chief complaint
2. History and development of complaint (date of onset, circumstances under which complaint developed, progression from the onset to the time of the initial interview)
3. Other complaints and symptoms (physical, emotional, psychic and behavior symptoms other than those of the complaint factor).
4. Medical, surgical, and in women, gynecologic history.
5. Environmental disturbance at onset of therapy (economic, work, housing, neighborhood and family difficulties).
6. Relationship difficulties at onset of therapy (disturbances in relationships with people, attitudes toward the world, authority, and self).
7. Heredity, constitutional and early developmental influences (significant physical and psychiatric disorders in patient's family, socioeconomic status of family, important early traumatic experiences and relationships, neurotic traits in childhood and adolescence).
8. Family data (mother, father, siblings, spouse, children - ages, state of health, personality adjustment, and patient's attitude toward each). Summary of social service contacts
9. Previous attacks of emotional illness (as a child and later). When did patient feel him/herself to be completely free from emotional illness?
10. Initial interview (brief description of condition of patient at first contact, including clinical findings).
11. Initial assessment of mental status: Level of insight and motivation at onset of therapy (How long did the patient feel that he or she needed treatment? For what? Awareness of emotional nature of problem. Willingness to accept psychotherapy.)
12. Previous treatments (When did the patient first seek treatment? What treatment did he/she get? Any hospitalizations?).
13. Clinical examination (significant findings in physical, neurological, laboratory, psychiatric and psychological examinations).
14. Differential diagnosis (at time of initial interview).
15. Estimate of prognosis (at time of initial interview).
16. Psychodynamics/Dynamic formulation and psychopathology
17. Course of treatment: Treatment plan and goals, recommendations, disposition
    a. Type of therapy employed, frequency, total number of sessions, response to treatment.
    b. Significant events during therapy, dynamics that were revealed, verbatim report of important dreams, nature of transference and resistance.
    c. Progress in therapy, insight acquired, translation of insight into action, change in symptoms, mental status, attitudes and relationships with people.
18. Condition on discharge (areas of improvement, remaining problems).
19. Recommendations to patient.
20. Statistical classification.

31.7 Format for Therapy notes: See also Zuckerman and Guyett (1992)
First decide these questions 1. To whom am I writing?, 2. for what purpose am I making these notes? and, 3. What is my system for recording data?
Include the content (facts, actions, words) and some interpretations and keep these distinguished.

INDIVIDUAL PSYCHODYNAMIC THERAPY NOTE:: Modified from Wolberg (1954)
  a. Present state of symptoms/complaint (absent, improved, the same, worse).
  b. How the patient feels (mood and emotion)
  c. Important life situations and developments since the last visit and how they were handled.
  d. Content of the session.
  e. Insight, Translation of insight into action
  e. Significant transference and resistance reactions: Appointments (timely, tardy, attitude), Communicativeness, Relationship with therapist
  f. Dreams (in the patient's words).
Huber (1984) adds:
  g. Countertransference reactions.
  h. Goals of therapy (as seen by the therapist)

A Simple Format: Modified from Huber (1984): (Notes in brackets are my, ELZ, way of marking these)
  1. Content (or Behavior): What each did and said. (I record these with no modifiers)
  2. What the therapist thought and felt about the content and may have said to the patient. (I put these in parentheses.)
  3. How the therapist felt about the patient, the interview, the content. [and probably did not tell the patient. I put these comments in square brackets]
  4. Outside: Anything bearing on the therapy which happened outside the interview.
      For Between-Therapy Sessions: Menninger (1952) adds to this:
        Compliance with the therapeutic program
        Steps taken to overcome the patient's resistance and who took them
        Telephone calls   Consultations with colleagues and the results
  5. Plans for the next interview (promises made, what to pursue, questions). I use the headings "HW" for work to be done by either of us and "RX" for topics to be followed up.

31.8 Child Assessment Outline: Modified from Jenkins, *et al.* (1990)

I. Overview
  A. Establish rapport: Find out why the child thinks he or she is being seen; Discuss the nature and procedures of the interview; Explain confidentiality's limits
  B. Gather general information: Chief complaint from child and from adult; Age, school grade, physical condition, intelligence; Character, temperament, judgement, attitudes; History of present illness

II. Development history
  A. Family: Individual interviews with the parents; Child's attitude toward each parent; Child's relationship with sibling's; Family psychiatric history; Level of education and current occupation
  B. History of parent's childhoods: Relationships with their parents and siblings; Discipline methods used; evidence of abuse or dysfunction
  C. Developmental milestones
      1. Physical: Pregnancy, circumstances of patient's birth/adoption, feeding, and weaning; neonatal illnesses; Early or significant medical illnesses or injury; Neuromuscular development of speech, motor milestones (sit, stand, walk, first words, play)
      2. Behavioral: Toilet training and other training (response to discipline, methods used); Reactions to beginning day care and school; Sleep patterns/disturbances; Phobias; Habit disorders (e.g. bed-wetting and thumb-sucking)

D. Significant events: moves, parent's illnesses, death, divorce

E. Current level of functioning: School performance; Hobbies and extracurricular activities; Peer relationships; Relationships with adults other than parents; Unusual habits and habit disorders; Aims and ambitions; Current health and medications

III. Interview with the child; Possible topics of discussion

A. Child's ideas about the problem: Expectations for outcome; What the child would like to change in self or others; "What problems have we not talked about yet?"

B. Symptom review: Vegetative symptoms; Anxiety symptoms; Psychotic symptoms; Suicidal ideation, other self-destructive acts; Ruminations or acts of violence; Substance abuse; Victimization experiences

C. Mental Status Examination. See 31.9 below

D. Drawings - House/Tree/person, self-portrait, Kinetic Family Drawing

IV. Consider other information to be sought: Psychological testing; Medical consultations - pediatric, neurological; School records, interview with teachers; Interviews with other significant adults (noncustodial parents, grandparents, social worker); Records of previous treatment or evaluations

31.9 Child's Mental Status Report: Simmons (1987) offers this format:

1. Appearance
2. Mood or affect
3. Orientation and perception
4. Coping mechanisms   a. Major defenses
           b. Expression and control of affectional and aggressive impulses
5. Neuromuscular integration
6. Thought processes and verbalizations: speech quality; vocabulary
7. Fantasy   a. Dreams   b. Drawings   c. Wishes   d. Play
8. Superego   a. Ego ideals and values
           b. Integration into personality
9. Concepts of self   a. Object relations
           b. Identification
10. Awareness of problems
11. Estimate of intelligence
12. Summary of Mental Status Examination

31.10 Vocational and Non-clinical Personality Evaluations: Huber (1984) quotes these skeletal Industrial/Organizational report outlines:

From Roher, Hibler and Replogle:

1. Intelligence   2. Emotional control   3. Skill in human relations
4. Insight and self-criticism   5. Organization and planning ability, direction of others
6. Recommendations and prognosis (for candidates) or Conclusions and prognosis (for non-candidates)

Huber also suggests asking the reader or recipient of the report these questions:

Describe the characteristics of the most satisfactory/ideal candidate in this job?

What characteristics of this person stand in the way of your hiring him or her without any hesitation?

What specific questions keep coming into your mind about this candidate?

What do you not want to see in a candidate for this job?

31.11 Neuropsychological Evaluations: This section detail the topics not covered in this book so far.

GENERALIZED NEUROPSYCHOLOGICAL REPORT FORMAT:

Background:
   Educational performance: levels, grades, most difficult and areas of best performance, future plans
   Occupational functioning: nature of work, demands, future plans

Pertinent:
   Histories: medical, developmental, psychiatric, substance abuse, education, occupational demands,
   History of Accident/Illness
      Trauma: Closed Head Injury, Traumatic Brain Injury,
      Neurological finding on arrival at hospital
         Loss/compromise of consciousness, unresponsiveness, Glasgow Coma Scale, Ranchos Los
            Amigos Scale. See section 6.2.
   Amnesia: Anteriograde, retrograde
   Medical tests: EEG, Q-EEG, Scannings: CT, CAT, MRI, NMR, SPECT
   Medications and responses
   Progress, changes, complications

Symptoms/Complaints/Problems: See Chapter 10 Referral Reasons

Tests administered/Test Procedures:

Sensory/Perceptual Functioning: See below

Motor functions
   Grip strength, speed, eye-hand coordination, motor speech, gross motor

Memory functions: See section 15.7 Memory

Cognitive-Communicative Functions: See sections 11.5 Speech and 15.9 Stream of Thought

Functional assessment: See also Chapter 25. ADLs

Executive functions:
   Goal-directed activities: initiation, follow through
   Concept formation: abstraction/concreteness,
   Frustration tolerance
   Judgement, organization, planning, impulsivity, problem solving
   Simple/basic calculations
   Speed of information processing

Intelligence/General intellectual functioning: See below

Academics/Achievement: See Chapter 28.3, 28.4, and 28.5

Mental status examination: See Chapter 6. for questions and Chapter 15. for descriptors

Personality: Testing results. See Chapter 17. Personality

Conclusions and recommendations:

FOCUS ON INTEGRATION OF SENSORY-PERCEPTUAL-MOTOR COMPONENTS:

Visuo-perceptual processing with and without a motor component
Reorganizing visual stimuli into a cohesive whole
Organization and planning
Featural vs. configural approach
Visuo-constructive processing
Visuo-motor speed
Visual scanning
Coordination - bilateral
Attentional capacity

FOCUS ON MEMORY FUNCTIONS: See also section 15.7 Memory
Immediate, delayed,
Acquisition, recognition, recall, decay
Ability to hold visual information in working memory
Verbal
    With and without category cues   Semantic "intrusions", "false positives"
    Encoding strategies   Response/word discrimination
    Retrieval   Memory for thematic material
Non-verbal
    Recognition for designs which she had just seen   Immediate recall
    Identify designs which repeated in a longer sequence   Configural information/designs
    Reproduce geometric designs   Memory for a more complex designs

FOCUS ON INTELLECTUAL-ACADEMIC-CONCEPTUAL RESOURCES:
IQ scores: verbal knowledge and reasoning, attentional processes, visuo-constructive ability and
    visuo-motor speed,
Academics:
    Reading comprehension, speed, word/color interference
    Spelling: errors
    Arithmetic: single step,
    Writing sample: organization, spelling, speed, errors, handwriting legibility, motorically intact,
    Oral expression: fluency, prosody, volume,
    Oral reading: speed, substitutions

Problem solving: flexibility, shift problem solving set, perseveration of strategies, effect of verbal
    prompts,
    Visual scanning and motor speed
    Information processing speed
    Shifting cognitive set
    Verbal concept formation , abstract reasoning,
Summary

RESOURCES:
A good introduction to neuropsychology for the clinician is Berg, Franzen, and Wedding (1987).

31.12 Some Advice on Report Writing: See also Chapter 22. Treatment Planning

In reporting responses to objective questions it is clearer to the reader if you underline the erroneous responses, as for example on serial sevens: 93, <u>84</u>, 77, 70, <u>62</u>.

To prevent confusion do not indicate ages with 13.5 but use 13/5mo., or 13'5" or 13 5/12

Avoid the use of **acronyms**, abbreviations and names for local service providers and programs if the report is addressed to or might be useful to those unfamiliar with such references. Instead use the local language and then describe the program in general terms. For example, "TSI, a transitional community residential services provider" or "7 West, the alcohol detoxification ward."

Where you are concerned about confidentiality and yet know you will be releasing the report to readers with whom you wish to maintain the subject's anonymity you might use this method: list the subject's name at the top of only page one and use the subject's first (for children) or last (for adults) initial in all subsequent references to the subject. This way you will have only one occurrence of the name to remove. Also see Chapter 24. Confidentiality notices

For the prevention of tampering with and loss of the pages of a report they can be numbered as "Page 1 of 6", "Page 2 of 6", etc.

Because of concerns with test security and copyrights do not repeat the questions from standardized tests or the mental status questions in your reports but only the responses you received.

Sattler (1982) offers advice worth repeating. In writing reports:
1. Prefer the specific to the general, the definite to the vague, the concrete to the abstract.
2. Do not take shortcuts at the cost of clarity.
3. Avoid fancy words.
4. Omit needless words. Make every word tell.
5. Express coordinate ideas in similar form. The content not the style, should protect the report from monotony. Use a clear order of presentation so the ideas can be followed.)
6. Do not overstate. (Avoid overgeneralizations, over-interpretations, "Barnum Statements")
7. Avoid the use of qualifiers. Rather, very, little, pretty ... these are the leeches that infest the pond of prose, sucking the blood of words.
8. Put statements in positive form. Make definite assertions, Avoid tame, colorless, hesitating noncommittal language.

Thomas Esser (1974) points out these common problems with reports:
1. Failure to answer referral questions or provide desired information.
2. Too long or too short. The report should be the shortest way to convey the essential information. Balance brevity and thoroughness.
3. Telling the referrer what he or she already knows.
4. Failure to use referrer-provided information.
5. The presence of contradictions in the report.
6. Reluctance to provide realistic or negative findings.
7. Failure to backup recommendations and plans with facts and reasons.
8. Pure data. Findings without interpretations, judgements, impressions.
9. Making unrealistic plans for the client.
10. Failure to consider alternatives in recommendations, courses of action, objectives.
11. A summary which isn't. It fails to bring together the information, fails to create a composite picture.

32. Listing of Psychoactive Medications

This listing is not to be used for prescription guidance or medical evaluation but simply for reference by the active clinician to the sometimes confusing mass of names.
Some medications appear in more than one category as they have multiple uses. Many have multiple formulations but, for simplicity, are listed under only one name.
They are **listed in alphabetic order within each grouping.**

32.1 Listing of Medications by Trade Name:
FORMAT:
PURPOSE/DESIRED EFFECT
    DRUG CLASS OR TYPE
        TRADE NAME   GENERIC NAME

Trade Name	Generic Name	Trade Name	Generic Name
ANTI-ANXIETY AGENTS:			
Benzodiazepines:[1]			
Ativan	lorazepam	Paxipam	halazepam
Centrax	prazepam	Restoril	temazepam
Dalmane	flurazepam	Serax	oxazepam
Doral	quezepam	Tranxene[1]	chlorazepate
Halcion	triazolam	Valium	diazepam
Klonopin	clonazepam	Valrelease	diazepam
Librium	chlordiazepoxide	Versed	midrazolam
Libritabs	chlordiazepoxide	Xanax	alprazolam
Non-benzodiazepines:			
Atarax	hydroxyzine	Inderal	propranolol
BuSpar	buspirone	Lopressor	metoprolol
Catapres	clonidine	Miltown	meprobamate
Corgard	nadolol	Tenormin	atenolol
Deprol	meprobamate + benactyzine	Transcopal	chlormezanone
Equanil	meprobamate	Vistaril	hydroxyzine
ANTI-CONVULSANTS:			
Barbituates: (see also Sedatives, below)			
Amytal	amobarbitol	Mebaral	mephobarbital
Anxanil	amobarbitol	Nebutal	pentobarbital
Gemonil	methobarbital	Seconal	secobarbital
			phenobarbital
Hydantoins:			
Dilantin	phenytoin	Mesantoin	mephenytoin
Peganone	ethosuximide		

[1] Benzodiazapines have addicting properties.
* There are laboratory tests for these drugs' therapeutic levels.

Succinimides:

Celontin	methsuximide	Milontin	phensuximide
Zarontin	ethosuximide		

Others:

Depakene	valproic acid	Phenurone	phenacemide
Depakote	divalproex	Tegretol	carbamazepine
Diamox	acetazolamide	Tridione	trimethadione
Klonopin	clonazepam	Tranxene[1]	chlorazepate
Myidol	primidone	Valium	diazepam
Mysoline	primidone		

ANTI-DEPRESSANTS:

Tricyclics:

Adapin	doxepin	Norpramine	desipramine
Anafranil	clomipramine	Pamelor	nortriptyine
Asendin	amoxapine	Pertofrane	desipramine
Aventyl	nortriptyine	Sinequan	doxepin
Elavil	amitriptyline	Surmontil	trimipramine
Endep	amitriptyline	Tofranil	imipramine
Etrafon	perphenazine & amitriptyline	Triavil	perphenazine & amitriptyline
Janimine	imipramine	Vivactil	protriptyline
Limitrol	chlordiazepoxide & amitriptyline		

Tetracyclics:

Ludiomil	maprotiline

MAO inhibitors:[2]

Marplan	isocarboxazid	Nardil	phenelzine
Parnate	tranylcypromine		

Triazolopyridine:

Desyrel	trazadone

Bicyclic:

Prozac	fluoxetine

Monocyclic:

Wellbutrin	buproprion

Other:

Zoloft	sertraline

Antidepressants not currently available in the US:

alaproclate, citalopram, clovoxamine, femoxetine, fluvoxamine, indalapine, paroxetine, sertraline, nisoxetine, oxaprotiline, tandamine, diclofensine, mianserin, viloxazine

Antidepressants withdrawn from the US market:

ANTI-MANIC AGENTS:

Lithium:

Cibalith	lithium citrate	Lithionate/	lithium carbonate
Eskalith/Lithane/	lithium carbonate	Lithobid/Lithotab	lithium carbonate

---

* There are laboratory tests for these drugs' therapeutic levels.
[2] Note restrictions on food containing tyramine for MAO users.

Other:

Haldol/Haldol	haloperidol decanoate	Klonopin	clonazepam

Calcium channel blockers:

Adalat	nifedipine	Isoptin	verapamil
Calan	verapamil	Procardia	nifedipine
Diltiazem	cardizem		

ANTI-OBSESSIVE:

Anafranil	clomipramine

ANTI-PARKINSON:

Akineton	biperiden	Inderal	propranolol
Aldomet	methyldopa	Kimadrin	procyclidine
Artane	trihexyphenidyl	Larodopa	L-dopa
Benadryl	diphenydramine	Norflex	orphenadrine
Cogentin	benztropine	Pagitane	cycrimine
Dantrium	dantrolene	Parlodel	bromocriptine
Disipal	orphenadrine	Parsidol	ethopropazine
Dopar	levodopa	Sinemet	carbidopa & levodopa
Eldepryl	selegiline	Symmetrel	amantadine

ANTI-ALZHEIMERS:

Cogex	tacrine

ANTI-PSYCHOTICS:[1]

Butyrophenones:

Haldol/Haldol	haloperidol**[2] decanoate	Inapsine	droperidol

Dibenzoxapines:

Clozaril	clozapine	Daxoline	loxapine
Loxitane	loxapine		

Dihyroindolones:

Moban	molindone

Diphenybutylpeperadines:

Orap	pimozide

Phenothiazines:

Compazine	prochlorperazine	Sparine	promazine
Etrafon	perphenazine + amitriptyline	Stelazine	trifluroperazine
Mellaril	thioridazine**	Thorazine	chlorpromazine
Orazine	chlorpromazine	Tindal	acetophenazine
Permitil	fluphenazine**	Triavil	perphenazine + amitriptyline
Prolixin	fluphenazine**	Trilafon	perphenazine
Permitil	fluphenazine**	Vesprin	triflupromazine
Serentil	mesoridazine		

Rauwolfias:

Serpasil	reserpine

---

[1] There are tables to compare these drugs' potency by comparing them to a dose of 100 mgs of chlorpromazine.
** Denotes higher risk of Neuroleptic Malignant Syndrome

32 Medications Listing

Thioxanthenes:
Navane	thiothixene**	Taractan	chlorprothixene

Antipsychotics not currently available in the US: sulpiride, fluperlapine, remoxipride, raclopride

PSYCHOSTIMULANTS:
Amphedroxyn	methamphetamine	Deaner	deanol
Benzedrine	amphetamine	Desoxyn	methamphetamine
Biphetamine	amphetamine + dextroamphetamine	Dexedrine	dextroamphetamine
Cylert	pemoline	Ritalin	methylphenidate

SEDATIVES/HYPNOTICS:

Barbituates:[1] (see also Barbituates, above)
Alurate	aprobarbital	Seconal	secobarbital
Amytal	amobarbital	Solfoton	phenobarbital
Mebaral	mephobarbital	Tuinal	secobarbital + amobarbital
Nembutal	pentobarbital		
	phenobarbital		

Non-barbituates:
Dalmane	flurazepam	Paral	paraldehyde
Doral	quazepam	Placidyl	ethchlorvynol
Doriden	gluthimide	ProSom	estazolam
Halcion	triazolam	Quaalude	methaqualone
Noctec	chloralhydrate	Restoril	temazepam
Noludar	methyprylon		

ANTIHYPERTENSIVES:
Aldomet	methyldopa	Inderal	propranolol
Apresoline	hydrazine	Ismelin	guanethidine
Catapress	clonidine	Serpasil	reserpine

CORTICOSTEROIDS AND OTHER HORMONES:
Cortone	cortisone	Lipo-Lutin,	
Evex, Menrium,		Progestasert,	
Femest,	estrogen	Proluton	progesterone

OTHERS MEDICATIONS:
Anectine	succinylcholine	Lioresal	baclofen
Antabuse	disulfram	Limbitrol	chlordiazepoxide + amitriptyline
Compazine	prochloroperazine	Mepergan	promethazine
Deprol	meprobamate + benactyzine	Narcan	naloxone
Dolophine	methadone	Neo-Synephrine	phenylephrine
Dopram	doxapram	Noctec	chloral hydrate
Feldene	piroxicam	Norpace	disopyramide
Gerimal	ergoloid	Phenergan	promethazine
Hydergine	ergoloid	Questran	cholestyramine
Indocin	indomethacin	Synthroid	levothyroxine
Lasix	furosemide	Tegretol	carbamazepine
Levithroid	levothyroxine	Trexan	naltrexone

---

[1] Barbituates have addicting properties.

32.2 Your list of drugs applicable to your practice setting:

32.3 List of street drugs: As these change so often you may want to make your own.

Lewis (1990) contains a good listing of street drugs.

32.4 Results of Medication Treatment:

Tolerated without difficulty
Rapid and dramatic improvement, abatement of symptoms, symptomatology improved
Highly sensitive to all medications
Multiple/distressing side effects
It was quite difficult to find a medication regimen which was tolerated.
Polypharmacy
Distressing and extreme reactions to all medications tried despite changes in dosage and schedule.
Adverse drug reactions
Contraindicated

32.5 Resources for the Clinician:

For technical information about medicating a good reference is Jenkins, *et al.* (1990).

Appleton (1991) contains pearls of wisdom about psychopharmacology and comparison of different choices. E. g. for Bipolar II use MAO inhibitors; for rapid cyclers use carbamazepine.

Bassuk, Schoonover and Gelenberg's (1983) *The Practitioner's Guide to Psychoactive Drugs* is an extraordinarily book on psychopharmacology: complete and yet highly readable, factual and yet full of clinical wisdom, thorough and detailed yet it is easy to find what you need to know. Its section on abuse is very complete, and sections on geriatrics and pregnancy are appreciated.

Information on uses, side effects and interactions can be found in these books:
PDR: Physician's desk reference.
PDR guide to drug interactions side effects and indications.
Many pharmaceutical companies supply pocket guides to drugs.

33. Psychiatric/Psychological Masquerade

33.1 Introduction:

DEFINITION:

Psychiatric masquerade is the commonly accepted term for the situation in which a patient presents to the clinician with psychological or psychiatric symptoms which come from a medical condition or illness which is not immediately (and sadly, sometimes never) recognized.[1] It is the masquerade (or concealment) of a medical condition, presenting with the mask of a psych. condition. Adams notes that calling it "psychiatric masquerade" focuses on the presentation and if we were to focus on the causation it would be called "medical masquerade."

There are numerous excellent articles and books which describe the psych. effects of medical conditions or of medications but these are useless to the professional who sees only the patient who presents with psych. symptoms and not with a medical diagnosis. However, all we clinicians have the ethical obligation to be sensitive to the possibility of masquerade and to investigate appropriately any possibilities.

REFERENCES:

The interactions of medication is a complex subject. There are many articles, a number of books and several computer databases for reference. Ask your local medical librarian for the most current and usable materials.

Good general references in this area are Pincus and Tucker (1975) and Taylor (1982) which is highly recommended for its educational approach and reasonableness and well as the contents which focus on the most common problem presentations.

A good overview from the medical-disease-causes-the-psychiatic-disorder perspective is Hall and Beresford (1986).

Lishman (1978) is an encyclopedic resource.

The *Merck Manual of Diagnosis and Therapy* (latest edition) is an excellent and standard resource and commonly available.

The listings below are not meant to be complete or in any way replace a thorough medical work up. They are merely meant to raise the practitioner's awareness of the physical illness basis of some psych. symptoms he or she is likely to see in clinical practice.

---

[1] The overlap of medical and psych. conditons is common. There is substantial research evidence and commonly accepted wisdom: that as many as half of medically hospitalized patients have undiagnosed (and, of course untreated) psych. conditons and vice versa, that a single visit with a mental health professional drastically reduces the over-use of medical facilities by patients presenting with "medical" complaints who have diagnosable and treatable MH conditions, etc.

33.2 Anxiety:

MEDICATIONS WHICH MAY INDUCE ANXIETY:

Anticholinergics and Antihistamines
Antidepressants: fluoxetine, monoamine oxidase inhibitors, tricyclic antidepressants (especially early in therapy)
Benzodiazepines: (paradoxical reactions, withdrawal states)
Euphoriants and Hallucinogens: cocaine, cannabis, LSD, mescaline, psilocybin, phencyclidine (PCP)
Hormones: androgens, estrogens, progesterones, corticosteroids, thyroid supplements
Neuroleptics:
Stimulants and sympathomimetics: amphetamines; methylphenidate, pemoline; ephedrine, pseudoephedrine, phenylpropanolamine; xanthenes: caffeine, theobromine, theophylline
Withdrawal states: especially from alcohol, sedatives, narcotics
Asthma medications
Caffeine
Others: cycloserine, metrizamide, quinacrine, nasal decongestant sprays

MEDICAL CONDITIONS WHICH ARE ASSOCIATED WITH ANXIETY:

Mitral valve prolapse, adrenal tumor, alcoholism, carcinoid syndrome, CNS degenerative diseases, Cushing's disease, coronary insufficiency, delirium, hypoglycemia, hyperthyroidism, Meniere's disease (early stages), post-concussion syndrome

33.3 Sexual dysfunction:
About a hundred medications may cause sexual dysfunction. A good listing can be found in Drugs that induce sexual dysfunction (1987). *Medical Letter on Drugs and Therapeutics. 29,* 65-70. Crenshaw and Goldberg (1993) is current and complete. Highly recommended.

33.4 Depression: See Section 14.5 Depression

MEDICATIONS WHICH MAY INDUCE DEPRESSION:

Antiarrhythematics: digitalis, disopyramide, nifedipine
Anticonvulsants:
Antihypertensives: clonidine, guanethidine, hydralazine, methyldopa, prazosin, propranolol, b-blockers, reserpine, trichloromethiazide
Antimicrobials: cycloserine, isoniazid, metronidazole, nalidixic acid
Antiparkinson agents: levodopa, amantadine, carbidopa
Chemotherapeutic agents: asparaginase, vinblastine, vincristine
Hormone preparations: corticosteroids, oral contraceptives, thyroid supplements
Non-Steroidal Anti-Inflammatory Drugs:
Sedatives: alcohol, barbiturates, benzodiazepines, hypnotics, marijuana, hallucinogens
Withdrawal states: especially from cocaine and other stimulants, amphetamines
Other: cimetidine, ranitidine, disulfiram, levodopa, a-methyldopa, carbidopa, metoclopramide, metrizamide, cholinesterase inhibitor insecticides

DISEASES THAT MAY PRODUCE DEPRESSION:

Influenza, TB, general paresis,, hypothyroidism, Cushing's, Addison's, Parkinson's, Systemic Lupus Erythematosus, Rheumatoid Arthritis, stroke, multiple sclerosis, cerebral tumors, sleep apnea, early stages of dementing diseases

33.5 Mania: See section 14.7 Mania

MEDICATIONS WHICH MAY INDUCE MANIA:

Amphetamines, bromides, cocaine, isoniazid, procarbazine, corticosteroids, levodopa, MAO Inhibitors, tricyclic antidepressants, methylphenidate, over-the-counter stimulants/appetite suppressants, vitamin deficiencies and excess of fat-soluble vitamins

DISEASES WHICH MAY INDUCE MANIA:

Influenza, general paresis, St. Louis encephalitis, Q Fever, thyrotoxicosis, rheumatic chorea, stroke, multiple sclerosis, cerebellar, diencephalic and third ventricle tumors, hyperthyroidism, Cushing's, hyperparathyroidism

33.6 Organic Brain Syndrome/dementia: See section 15.6 Dementia

NEUROLOGICAL CONDITIONS WHICH COMMONLY EXHIBIT PSYCHOLOGICAL SYMPTOMS: Bondi (1992) offers this basic orienting information to this issue:

1. Neurological conditions have a base rate of 2.5% of general population.
2. General symptoms: paranoia, attentional deficits, mood swings, euphoria, sleep disturbance, personality changes, depression, impaired memory, anxiety, apathy, violence.
3. Temporal lobe epilepsy/complex partial seizure disorder -> global diminution in sexual behavior, impulsive-irritable behaviors, especially in a context of hyperethical and hyperreligious behaviors, hypergraphia, and overconcern and overemphasis on the trivial.
4. Frontal lobe damage -> apathy (empty indifference as contrasted with the depressive's preoccupation with worry), total loss of initiative, euphoria, lack of adult restraint/tact, incontinence.
5. Traumatic head injury -> like 4 as well as depression (psychomotor retardation, apathy, lack of initiative, blunted or flat affect), and memory dysfunction.
6. Huntington's disease -> intermittent affective disorder with onset before the chorea and dementia. Besides the affective components there may be paranoia, delusions, hallucinations, and mood swings. Always seek a family history.
7. Hypothyroidism -> progressive cognitive deterioration, insidious onset, sluggishness, lethargy, poor attention and concentration, memory disturbances.
8. Multiple sclerosis -> muscle weakness, fatigue, double vision, numbness, paraesthesia, pain, bowel and bladder dysfunction, sexual disturbance. Euphoria and/or depression, "conversion" symptoms.
9. Headache:
   -If it is the worst ever experience by the patient, a new type of headache, or accompanied by neurological signs, is much more likely to be organic than one which is dull, generalized, constant for days, or present for a year.
   -Tumor caused headaches have no one quality. They may occur on awakening and recede during the day, often bifrontal or bioccipital, lateralized or localized, ameliorated or exacerbated by changes in body position.

SOME CLUES SUGGESTIVE OF ORGANIC MENTAL DISORDER: Adapted from Hoffmam and Koran (1984).

1. Psychiatric symptom onset after age 40
2. Psychiatric symptoms begin ...
    a. during a major illness
    b. while taking drugs known to cause mental symptoms (see below)
    c. suddenly, in a patient without prior psychiatric history or know stressors
3. With a history of ...
    a. alcohol or drug abuse
    b. a physical illness impairing a major organ's function
    c. taking multiple medications (prescribed or over-the-counter)
    d. a history of poor response to apparently adequate psychiatric treatment
4. With a family history of ...
    a. degenerative or inheritable brain disease
    b. metabolic disease (diabetes, pernicious anemia, etc.)
5. Whose mental signs include ...
    a. altered level of consciousness
    b. fluctuating mental status
    c. cognitive impairment
    d. episodic, recurrent, or cyclic course
    e. visual, tactile, or olfactory hallucinations
6. Physical signs include ...
    a. signs of organ malfunction that can affect the brain
    b. focal neurological deficits
    c. difuse subcortical dysfunction (slowed speech/mentation/movement, ataxia, incoordination, tremor, chorea, asterixis, dysarthria, etc.)
    d. cortical dysfunction (dysphasia, apraxias, agnosia, visuospatial deficits, or defective cortical sensation, etc.)

DRUGS THAT MAY INDUCE DELIRIUM, HALLUCINATIONS, OR PARANOIA:

Antiarrhythmics: digitalis, lidocaine, procainamide, quinacrine
Anticholinergics:
Anticonvulsants:
Antidepressants: tricyclics
Antimicrobials, antiparasitics, antivirals: amantadine, amphotericin B, metronidazole, thiabendazole, cycloserine, isoniazid, chloroquine, hydroxychloroquine, dapsone, procaine   penicillin
Antihistamines: H2 blockers: cimetidine, rantidine
β-adrenergic blockers
Chemotherapeutic agents (especially intrathecal administration): asparaginase, cisplatin, vincristine
Euphoriants and Hallucinogens: cannabis, LSD, mescaline, psilocybin, phencyclidine (PCP)
Hormone preparations: corticosteroids,
Non-Steroidal Anti-Inflammatory Drugs:
Sedatives: alcohol, barbiturates, benzodiazepines, hypnotics
Stimulants and sympathomimetics: amphetamines; cocaine, methylphenidate, pemoline;
Withdrawal states: especially from alcohol, sedatives, delirium tremens
Other: albuterol, bromides, bromocriptine, disulfiram, levodopa, carbidopa, methyldopa, methysergide, metrizamide.

TREATABLE/MORE EASILY REVERSIBLE CAUSES OF OBS: From Slaby (1980)

Some angiomas of the cerebral vessels, intracranial aneurysms, normal pressure hydrocephalus, cerebral anoxia secondary to cardiac (arrhythmias, infarct, congestive heart failure) or respiratory disease (chronic obstructive pulmonary disease, emboli), cerebral abscess, some cerebral neoplasms, chronic subdural hematoma(s), electrolyte imbalance (hyponatremia, hypernatremia, hypercalcemia), endogenous toxins (as with hepatic or renal failure), exogenous toxins (such as carbon monoxide, heavy metals, insecticides, pesticides), drug effects (alcohol, medications), endocrine disorders (hypothyroidism, hypoglycemia, adrenals, parathyroid, Addison's, Cushing's), cerebral infections (neurosyphilis, herpes, parasites, tuberculosis), depression/pseudodementia, , vitamin deficiencies (thiamine leads to Werneke's and Korsakoff's; niacin leads to pellagra), pernicious anemia, hyponatremia, diabetic ketosis and non-ketotic hyperosmolarity, delirium tremens, anticholinergic intoxication, subarachnoid hemorrhage, subdural hematoma, myocardial infarct, pneumonia, post-ictal states, Dilantin toxicity, renal failure

33.7 Psychosis:

DRUGS WHICH CAN CAUSE PSYCHOSIS:

Sympathomimetics (e.g. cocaine, "crack", many over-the-counter cold medications)
Antinflamatory drugs: steroids
Anticholinergics: antiparkinsonian agents
Hallucinogens
L-dopa (in schizophrenic patients)

MEDICAL CONDITIONS PRESENTING AS PSYCHOSIS:

Addison's, CNS infections, CNS neoplasms, CNS trauma, Cushing's, Folic acid deficiency, Huntington's, multiple sclerosis, myxedema, pancreatitis, pellagra, pernicious anemia, porphyria, systematic lupus erythematosus, temperal lobe epilepsy, thyrotoxicosis,

33.8 Medication-Induced Psych. Conditions:
The following quick reference table is modified from Estroff and Gold (1986).

Key: P=Psychoses   M=Mania   A=Anxiety   D=Depression O=Organic   H=Hallucinations and Other Effects

Psychiatric Medications

	P	M	A	D	O	H / Other Effects
Tricyclic Anti-depressants	P	M			O	H-Visual
MAOI Anti-depressants	P	M	A			Agitation, insomnia
Antipsychotics	P			D	O	Oversedation,Neurological Malignant syndrome
Lithium						
Sedative/Hypnotics						Oversedation, disinhibition
Benzodiazepines	P			D		
Disulfiram	P	M	A	D	O	

Key: P=Psychoses M=Mania A=Anxiety D=Depression O=Organic H=Hallucinations and
  Other Effects

Antihypertensives

	P	M	A	D	O	H	Other Effects
Reserpine	P			D	O		
α methyl dopa	P			D	O		Nightmares, disordered sleep
Clonidine	P	M	A	D			Sedation, fatigue
Propranolol						Hypnopompic Hypnogogic	Nightmares, fatigue

Cardiovascular medications:

	P	M	A	D	O	H	Other Effects
Lidocaine	P						
Procainamide	P	M					
Disopyramide	P					Auditory, Visual	
Digitalis	P					Auditory, Visual	Mutism, lability Mood swings

Neurological medications:

	P	M	A	D	O	H	Other Effects
Phenytoin	P				O		Visual and Somatic delusions, tactile
Barbiturates				D	O		Tearfulness, hyperactive, aggression in children
Primidone	P	M			O		Mood swings, personality changes, paranoia
Ethosuzimide	P	M	A	D		H-Yes	Aggression, night terrors, lethargy
Carbamazepine	P		A				Restlessness, drowsiness
Baclofen	P	M		D		Auditory, visual	
L-Dopa	P	M		D	O	Auditory	Vivid dreams and visual illusions
Bromocriptine	P	M			O		Vivid dreams
Anticolinergics	P		AA	D	O		Prominent anxiety

Gastrointestinal medications

	P	M	A	D	O	H	Other Effects
Cimetidine	P			D	O	Auditory, visual	

Over the counter medications

	P	M	A	D	O	H	Other Effects
Phenylpropanolamine	P			D			
Ephedrine	P			D			
Pseudoephedrine	P			D			
Aminophyline	P			D			

Non-steroidal Antiinflamatory agents

	P	M	A	D	O	H	Other Effects
Indomethacin	P		A	D			Agitation, hostile, depersonalization
Sulindac	P			D			Angry, combative, homicidal, obsessive talking

Key: P=Psychoses M=Mania A=Anxiety D=Depression O=Organic H=Hallucinations and Other Effects

Anticancer medications

	P	M	A	D	O	H	Other Effects
Steroids	P	M		D			
Decarbazine				D	O		
Hexamethylamine				D	O	H	
Methotrexate					O		
5 FU					O		Labile mood
Vincristine				D	O	H	
Vinblastine			A	D			
Mithramycin			A				Agitation, irritability
Asparaginase				D	O		Personality changes
Procarbazine		M					Drowsiness

Anesthetic medications

	P	M	A	D	O	Hallucinations	Other Effects
Nalophine						Auditory, visual	Panic, suffocation, fear of impending death
Levorphan							Fear, "queer behavior"
Atropine							Postanesthetic excitement
Scopalamine							Postanesthetic excitement
Cyclopropane							Postanesthetic excitement
Halothane				D	O		Anger, tension fatigue
Isoflurane				D	O		Anger, tension, fatigue
Pentazocine							Overactive, rambling, crazy thoughts, fear of dying

Antibiotic medications

	P	M	A	D	O	Hallucinations	Other Effects
Iproniazid	P	M			O	H	
Isoniazid	P			D	O	Auditory, visual	Catatonia
Cycloserine	P	M	A	D	O		Nervousness, irritability
Procaine/Penicillin G	P	M			O	H	Extreme agitation, fear of impending death
Amphotercin B					O		
Chloroquine	P	M				H	
Quinacrine	P	M				H	

Heavy metals and Toxins

	P	M	A	D	O	Hallucinations	Other Effects
Lead							Lowered IQs and hyperactivity in children
Mercury	P		AA	D	O		Extreme anxiety, strange form of xenophobia
Arsenic	P	M		D	O	Visual	
Manganese	P	M		D			Destruction of nigro striatum
Bismuth	P		A	D	O	Visual	
Thallium	P			D	O		
Aluminum				D	O	H	
Tin (organic)				D			Unprovoked rage attacks
Magnesium	P			D	O		
Copper	P	M		D	O	H	
Vanadium	?			D			
Cadmium							Associated with learning disabilities in children
Bromine	P	M		D	O	Auditory, visual	
Carbon monoxide	P			D	O		Catatonia, panic attack
Carbon dioxide							Precipitates panic attack
Volatile hydrocarbons		M	A	D	O	Auditory, visual	Conduct disorder, panic, personality change

34. Abbreviations

The following are some commonly used and the author's own list of abbreviations found useful:

CLINICIANS/MENTAL HEALTH PROFESSIONALS:

Psychologist	ψ or ψo	Psychiatrist	ψi or ψMD
Amer. Psychological Assn.	APoA	American Psychiatric Assn.	APiA

MSW	Master's degree in Social Work	BSW	Bachelor's in Social Work
ACSW	Academy of Certified Social Workers	CSW	Clinical or Certified Social Worker

Ph. D.	Doctor of Philosophy degree	M. A. Master's in Arts
Psy. D	Doctor of Psychology	M. S. Master's in Science
NBCC	National Board Certified Counselor	National Register of Health Service Providers
NCSP	National Certified School Psychologist	in Psychology
ABMP	American Board of Medical Psychotherapists	

CCC	Certified Communication Counselor		
CAC	Certified Alcoholism Counselor		
SLP	Speech and Language Pathologist		
APRN	Advanced Practice Registed Nurses	CS	Certified Specialist in psychiatric nursing.

TREATMENT:

Interview	IV	Psychotherapy	P/T	Psychoanalysis	P/A
Summary	S	Treatment	Rx/Tx	Therapist	th
History	Hx	Prognosis	Px	History of	h/o
Homework	HW	Symptom	Sx		
Handwriting	h/w	Diagnosis	Dx		
Not Otherwise Specified	NOS	Intelligence	I		
Discontinue/ed	d/c	Prior to admission	PTA		
Discharge/ed	d/ch	Within Normal Limits	WNL		

DIAGNOSES AND CONDITIONS:

Heart Attack	H/A	Headache	h/a	Diabetes Melitus	DM
Closed Head Injury	CHI	Low Back Pain	LBP	Seizures	sz
Mitral Valve Prolapse	MVP				
Cerebral Vascular Accident	CVA	Hypertension	HBP		

Anxiety	$\underline{A}$	Paranoia	Pa	Panic	$\underline{P}$
Alcohol and Other Drugs	$\overline{A}$OD (Preferred to "Substance Abuse")			Drug and Alcohol	$\underline{D+A}$
Generalized Anxiety Disorder		GAD		Depression	$\underline{D}$
Chronic Undifferentiated Schizophrenia		CUS or CUSc			
Delusions and Hallucinations		D+H			
Bipolar Affective Disorder		Bip			
Chronic Obstructive Pulmonary Dis.		COPD		Low Back Pain	LBP

Motor Vehicle Accident	MVA	Motorcycle Accident	MCA	Gun Shot Wound	GSW

RELATIONS (each person can be circled):

Husband	Ⓗ	Wife	Ⓦ	Brother-in-law	bil
Brother	B	Sister	S	Sister-in-law	sil
Grandparent	GP	Daughter	d	Son	s
Mother	Mo	Father	Fa		
Boyfriend	bf	Girlfriend	gf		
Maternal/Paternal Grandparents		MGM(other) or MGF(ather)			
Household	HH				

AIDS TO RECORDING:

About	c or ~				
At	@	Therefore	∴	Change	Δ
With	c̄	Without	s or w/o	Within	w/i or c/in
After, by history, post	p or s/p	Before	ā		
Date of Birth	DoB	Died	D	Date of Death	DoD
Divorced	d or d/				
Intercourse	I/C				

Anyone	AO	No one	NO	Everyone	EO
Question	?, Q	Times (3)	X3	Occasional	occl
Increasing	↑	More, greater, larger	>	Present, positive for	⊕
Decreasing	↓	Less, lesser, smaller	<	Not present, absent	Θ, Ø
Frequency	f	Number	#	Change	Δ

Interview	IV	Psychotherapy	P/T	Disorder	D/O
Intake	ntk	Summary	S	Biofeedback	Bf
Signs and symptoms	s/s				

Discontinued or Discharged	d/c	Withdrawal/withdrew	w/d		
Did-not-show	DNS	Return to Work	RTW	Return To Clinic	RTC
Failed to keep appointment	FTKA	Did not keep appointment	DNKA		

LEGAL

Involuntary Deviate Sexual Intercourse	IDSI	Corrupting the Morals of a Minor	CMM
Indecent Assault	IA		

ABBREVIATIONS IN EDUCATIONAL SETTINGS:

MDT	Multidisciplinary Team	MDE	Multidisciplinary Evaluation
IEP	Indicidual Educational Plan		
EMR	Educable Mentally Retarded/Learning Support	TMR	Trainable Mentally Retarded
SEM or SED	Socially and Emotionally Maladjusted or Disturbed		
S/PMR	Severely/Profoundly Mentally Retarded	LD	Learning Disabled
VI	Visually Impaired	HI	Hearing Impaired

Also: Itinerant teacher, Resource Room, Regular classes, Special Classes in regular school, Special Classes in Special Facility, Gifted and Talented

35. Conversions of Scores Based on the Normal Curve of Distibution

	−4	−3	−2	−1	0	+1	+2	+3	+4
Percentage of cases under portions of the normal curve	0.13	2.14	13.59	34.13		34.13	13.59	2.14	0.13
Standard Deviations −SD or σ +4	−4	−3	−2	−1	0	+1	+2	+3	
Cumulative percentages		0.1	2.3	15.9	50.0	84.1	97.7	99.9	

Percentile equivalents

1   5   10   20   30 40 50 60   70   80   90   95   99

| **Stanines** (Mean = 5, SD = 2) | | 1 | 2 | 3 | 4 | 5 | 6 | 7 | 8 | 9 |
| **Percent in each Stanine** | | 4 | 7 | 12 | 17 | 20 | 17 | 12 | 7 | 2 |

	−4	−3	−2	−1	0	+1	+2	+3	+4
Z - Scores (Mean = 0, SD = 1)	−4.0	−3.0	−2.0	−1.0	0.0	+1.0	+2.0	+3.0	+4.0
T - Scores (Mean = 50, SD = 10)		20	30	40	50	60	70	80	
Deviation IQs (Mean = 100, SD = 15)	40	55	70	85	100	115	130	145	
Wechsler Subtest Scaled Scores (Mean = 10, SD = 3)		1	4	7	10	13	16	19	
Binet IQs (Mean = 100, SD = 16)		50	66	84	100	116	132	148	

36. Feedback and Order Form   TCT3rd Edition/2

Dear Fellow Clinician,

I created this book to meet my needs as a clinician writing reports and gave it my best shot. I really would appreciate your best shot too so it may develop to aid all of us. New versions will come out at intervals (the next is planned for 1996) and could be designed to better meet our needs if we work together. If you will send your suggestions, modifications and ideas (perhaps by photocopying the relevant pages) I will give you credit in the revised editions, send you a FREE copy of the next edition. Also if you want another or later copy of *The Clinician's Thesaurus 3,* there is an offer below, which you can take advantage of if you will just give me some feedback. Thanks.

Ed Zuckerman

Would you answer a few questions for me so I can better understand you professional life, please?

Your Professional Title: _____ Years in practice when you bought this book ___.

How often do you refer to this book? ❑ Whenever I evaluate people. ❑ Every time I write a report. ❑ Fairly often, when I need some specific ideas and wording choices. ❑ Never now; but it was useful when I was learning to write reports. Other times: _____

How do you use it? ❑ I use it for questions in evaluating people. ❑ I use it to structure my report writing. ❑ I refer to it for specific information and wording choices. ❑ I use it to teach evaluation or report writing. Some other use(s)?: _____

What is your overall evaluation of *The Clinician's Thesaurus 3* in just a few words? _____
_____

I would suggest the following changes.

Increase the _____

Add the following sections _____

Decrease or eliminate _____

As a clinician I really wish there were a "tool" to: _____

We at The Clinician's ToolBox are always interested in other "Tools" for clinicians.
If you are developing something please call and let's talk.

Ordering Information

❑ The Current (3rd) Edition - $29.95 plus shipping and handling of $3.55 = $23.50 ($35.30 to addresses in PA) for new purchasers or

❑ The Current Edition if you bought any earlier edition - $14.97 plus Shipping of $3.55 = $18.52 and the front cover (no alternatives) from your copy (There is, of course, a limit of one copy).

❑ For bookstores, inservice training, or graduate programs with eleven copies sent to one address there is a discount of 25% from the list price. Just add UPS shipping costs.

Please make your check to The Clinician's ToolBox, and send it or all your VISA or MC numbers and Exp. Date with this page with the questions answered and your name and full mailing address to
P. O. Box 81033, Dept. TCT3R, Pittsburgh, PA 15217. (412) 521-1057

IF YOU ARE IN PRIVATE PRACTICE YOU REALLY SHOULD CONSIDER *THE PAPER OFFICE 1*
PLEASE SEE THE NEXT PAGE.

Do you write your reports on a word processor?
TCTEE - The Clinician's Thesaurus 3: Electronic Edition

Wouldn't it be convenient to have this whole book available to you instantly when you write a report? Would you like to add all your standard text, sentences, recommendations, prescriptions, referral statements, in fact, any text on your computer to *The Clinician's Thesaurus*, and have it available with a click or two, to paste into your current report? The Electronic Edition fits IBM and Macintosh computers and will make report-writing easier. For more information see the last pages of this book or write for a FREE DEMO DISK (Please indicate Macintosh or IBM, Windows or DOS).

Protect yourself and your practice with
The Paper Office 1

Now you can easily update your office's practices to current legal/ethical standards for less than a single paid hour of your time!
- *The* only 4 routes to obtaining fully Informed Consent: a) an elegant Structured Interview method; b) create a exhaustive Rules-of-My-Practice brochure in 3 hours; c) 7 Therapy Contracts for adults, groups, children; d) 5 Client's Rights Lists
- 5 detailed Releases of Information and a complete Cover Letter which meet all standards.
- Informative and protective Patient Education handouts on Sexual Intimacies, the Limits of Confidentiality, avoiding Dual Relationships/Double Agentry, Malpractice in Testing, etc.
- Simple yet complete forms for Intake, History, Development, Financial Data, Agreement to Pay, Termination Letters, etc.
- All 37 forms, handouts, and checklists on a 5.25" or 3.5" disk for IBM and compatibles or for Macintosh so you can tailor them to your practice and revise them as your practice evolves.

302 pages of checklists, guidelines, resources, and advice. Just $49.95 US plus shipping of $3.55 (total of $53.50, $56.50 to PA addresses) and the kind of Computer Disk your computer uses.

Thinking of Computerizing your office?
UpDate: Office Computerization

Helps you to evaluate the competing systems
- The Computerized Clinician: What can computers can do for clinicians?
- An Exhaustive Listing of the Developers of Computer Billing Programs (addresses, phone numbers, costs, and which computers they run on) so you can find all the programs you want to evaluate. More than 65 Office Management Programs and several dozen other programs of interest to clinicians.
- A Very Complete 6 page Checklist of the Features and Functions of these programs for you to use when comparing office computerization programs. It is written in ordinary language and organized the way therapists think about their practices.
- A Form Letter to Simplify Sending for More Info and/or Demonstration Disks
- Resources, Readings and References for further study.

26+ pages of Information, Continuously Revised so it is Absolutely Current - $12.00 US inclusive

The Handouts Book™

What do you give your patients to read to explain or teach or guide them?
Would you share these with our fellow therapists? Send me copies and when the book is published you'll get full credit, a free copy, and a really usable resource.

Send your check or VISA/MasterCard numbers to The Clinician's ToolBox, Dept. TCT3R, P. O. Box 81033, Pittsburgh PA 15217. Immediate Shipment and Immediate Refund if Dissatisfied. *Thanks*

38. References

I have endeavored to remove from *The Clinician's Thesaurus 3* all copyrighted material (such as questions and formats of descriptions) out of respect for the efforts of the authors and out of awareness that borrowed materials would not necessarily be valid in another context. If any copyrighted materials remain I apologize and explain that they entered *The Clinician's Thesaurus 3* by oversight and from the reports written by the consulting examiners whose reports I have read to compile this manual.

Indicatied here are many variations and specializations of the Mental Status Exam which have had the benefit of empirical evaluation.

---*DSM III-R Diagnostic and Statistical Manual,* Version three, Revised. (1987). Washington: American Psychiatric Association Press. Information at 800/368-5777

--- *Physician's desk reference.* 47rd Edition, (1993). Medical Economics Company Inc., Oradell, NJ 07649. $57.95. Also available on CD-ROM for $595.

--- *PDR guide to drug interactions side effects and indications.* 47nd Edition, (1993). Medical Economics Data, Montvale, NJ 07649. $45.95. This is also avaliable on IBM Diskettes for $225.

Ables, B., Brandsma, J., and Henry, G. M. (1983). An empirical approach to the mental status examination. *Journal of Psychiatric Education, 7* (3), 232-239.
The Empirical Mental Status Examination

Achenbach, T. M. and Edelbrock, C. (1983) *Manual for the child behavior checklist and revised child behavior profile.* Burlington, VT: University of Vermont.

Ackerman, R. J. (1987). *Children of alcoholics: A bibliography and resource guide.* Pompano Beach, FL: Health Communications.

Adams, David (1991). Factitious disorders and malingering: Choosing the appropriate role for the psychologist. *American Psychological Association Division 29 Newsletter,* Pp10-13.

Akiskal, H. S., Khani, M. K., and Scott-Strauss, A. (1979). Cyclothymic temperamental disorders. *Psychiatric Clinics of North America, 2,* 527-554.

Alber, M.S., Butters, N., and Levin, J. (1979). Temporal gradients in retrograde amnesia of patients with alcoholic Korsakoff's disease. *Archives of Neurology, 36,* 211-216.
The Test of Remote Memory

Alden, Lynn, E. (1992). Cognitive-interpersonal treatment of avoidant personality disorder. In Leon Vandecreek, S. Knapp and T. L . Jackson (Eds.) *Innovations in clinical practice: A source book, 11,* Sarasota, FL: Professional Resource Press.

Alcoholics Anonymous (1976). *The big book.* Third edition. NY: AA World Service

Appleton, William S. (1991). *Psychoactive drug usage guide.* Fifth edition. Memphis, TN: Physicians Postgraduate Press.

Archibald, H. C. and Tuddenham, R. D. (1965). Persistent stress reaction after combat. *Archives of General Psychiatry, 12,* 475-481.

Attwell, Arthur A. (1972). *The school psychologist's handbook.* Los Angeles, CA: Western Psychological Services.

Baird, J. *et al.* (1982). *Psychological Assessment Manual.* Bridgeville PA: Mayview State Hospital.

Barth, R. J. and Kinder, B. N. (1987). The mislabeling of sexual impulsivity. *Journal of Sex and Marital Therapy, 13,* 15-23.

Bassuk, Ellen L., Schoonover, Stephen C., and Gelenberg, Alan J. (1983). *The practitioner's guide to psychoactive drugs.* Second Edition. NY: Plenum.

Beck, A. T. (1987). *Beck Hopelessness Scale.* San Antonio, TX: The Psychological Corporation.

Beck, A. T., *et al.* (1961). An inventory for measuring depression. *Archives of General Psychiatry, 4,* 561-171.

Beck, A. T., Kovacs, M., and Weisman, A. (1979). Assessment of suicidal ideation: The Scale for Suicide Ideators. *Journal of Consulting and Clinical Psychology, 47,* 343-352.

Beck, A. T., Schyler, D. and Herman, I. (1974). Development of suicide intent scales. In A. T. Beck, H. L. P. Resnick, and D. J. Lettieri (Eds.) *The prediction of suicide.* Bowie, MD: Charles Press. Pp 45-56.

Beck, James C. (1990). The potentially violent patient: Clinical, legal and ethical implications. In Eric Margenau (Ed.) *The encyclopedic handbook of private practice.* NY: Gardner Press.

Bell, A. P. and Weinberg, M. S. (1978). Homosexualities: A study of diversity among men and women. NY: Simon and Schuster.

Bellack, Alan S. and Hersen, Michel (1985). *Dictionary of behavior therapy techniques.* NY: Pergamon.

Benjamin, Lirna S. (1982). The use of structural analysis of social behavior (SASB) to guide intervention in psychotherapy. In J. C. Anchin and D. L. Kiesler (Eds.) *Handbook of interpersonal psychotherapy.* NY: Pergamon.

Berg, Insoo K. and Miller, Scott D. (1992). *Working with the problem drinker.* NY: W. W. Norton.

Berg, Richard, Franzen, Michael, and Wedding, Danny (1987). *Screening for brain impairment: A manual for mental health practice.* NY: Springer.

Bernard, Sam D. (1991). A substance use checklist. In Peter Keller and Steven R. Heyman (Eds.) *Innovations in Clinical Practice: A source book, 10,* Sarasota, FL: Professional Resource Exchange. Pp 381-386.

Berne, Eric (1964). *Games people play.* NY: Grove Press.

Bernstein, E. M. and Putnam, F. W. (1986). Development, reliability, and validity of a dissociation scale. *The Journal of Nervous and Mental Disease, 174,* 727-735.

Bernstein, J. G. (1989). Prescribing antipsychotics. *Drug Therapy, 9,* 79.

Biele, A. M. (1974). The mental status examination. Unpublished manuscript. Quoted in Dubin and Stolberg (1981). *Emergency psychiatry for the house officer.* NY: SP Medical and Scientific Books.

Blakiston (1972). *Gould Medical Dictionary.* Third Edition. NY: McGraw-Hill.

Bondi, Mark (1992). Distinguishing psychological disorders from neurological disorders: Taking Axis III seriously. *Professional Psychology: Research and Practice, 23,* 4, 306-309.

Braun, P. R. and Reynolds, D. J. (1969). A factor analysis of a 100-item fear survey inventory. *Behavior Research and Therapy, 7,* 399-402.

Breznitz, S. (1988). The seven kinds of denial. In Charles Speilberger, et al. (Eds.) *Stress and anxiety,* Volume 2, Washington: Hemisphere Publishing. Pp. 73-90.

Brodwin, Sandra K., Brodwin, Martin G., and Liebman, Robert. (1992a). Initial case assessment forms in rehabilitation counseling. In Leon Vandercreek, Samuel Knapp, and Thomas L. Johnson (Eds.) *Innovations in clinical practice: A source book, 11.* Sarasota, FL: Professional Resource Press. Pp 351-62.

Brodwin, Sandra K., Brodwin, Martin G., and Liebman, Robert. (1992b). Job analysis procedures in rehabilitation counseling. In Leon Vandercreek, Samuel Knapp, and Thomas L. Johnson (Eds.) *Innovations in clinical practice: A source book, 11.* Sarasota, FL: Professional Resource Press. Pp 363-86.

Burgess, T. and Holmstrom, B. (1974). Rape trauma syndrome. *American Journal of Psychiatry, 131,* (9) 981-986.

Burns, David D. (1980). *Feeling good.* NY: Morrow.

Callahan, E. J., Hamilton-Oravetz, S. and Walker, A. (1992). Psychotherapeutic intervention for unresolved grief in primary care medicine. In Leon Vandecreek, S. Knapp and T. L. Jackson (Eds.) *Innovations in clinical practice: A source book, 11,* Sarasota, FL: Professional Resource Press.

Cass, Vivienne, C. (1979). Homosexual identity formation: A theoretical model. *Journal of Homosexuality, 4,* 3, 219-235.

Cermak, Timmen L. (1991). *Evaluation and treating adult children of alcoholics II.* Minneapolis, MN: Johnson Institute.

Chess, S. and Birch, H. G. (1986). *Termperament in clinical practice.* NY: Guilford.

Cleckley, Hervey M. 1976). *The Mask of Sanity*, 5th Edition, St. Louis: C. V.. Mosby.

Cloninger, C. R. (1987). Neurogenic adaptive mechanisms in alcoholism. *Science, 236,* 410-416.

Coffman, Sandra and Fallon, Patricia (1990). Unmasking and treating victimization in women: cognitive and non-verbal approaches. In Keller, P and Heyman, S. (Eds.) *Innovations in clinical practice: A source book, 9*. Sarasota, FL: Professional Resource Exchange.

Connors, C. K. (1983). *Conners' Abbreviated Teacher Rating Scale* (ATRS). Washington, DC: Children's Hospital National Medical Center.

Coons, P. M. and Milstein, V. (1986). Psychosexual disturbances in multiple personality: Characteristics, etiology, and treatment. *Journal of Clinical Psychiatry, 47,* 107.

Crenshaw, Theresa L. and Goldberg, James P. (1993). ^ NY: Norton.

Davis, Neil M. (1990). *Medical abbreviations: 7000 conveniences at the expense of communication and safety.* Neil M. Davis, 1143 Wright Drive, Huntington Valley, PA 19006.

Davis, P., Morris, J., and Grant, E. (1990). Brief screening tests vs. clinical staging in senile dementia of the Alzheimer type. *Journal of the American Geriatric Society, 38,* (2), 129-135.

Dinwiddie, S. H. and Cloninger, C. R. (1991). Family and adoption studies in alcoholism and drug addiction. *Psychiatric Annals, 21,* 206-213.

Dryden, Windy and DiGuiseppe, Ray (1990). *A primer on rational emotive therapy.* Champaign, IL: Research Press.

Ebert, Bruce W. (1987). Guide to conducting a psychological autopsy. *Professional Psychology: Research and Practice, 18,* 1, 52-56.

Edinger, Jack D. (1985). Sleep history questionnaire for evaluating insomnia complaints. In Peter A. Keller and Lawrence G. Ritt (Eds.) *Innovations in clinical practice: A source book, 4.* Sarasota, FL: Professional Resource Exchange. Pp. 295-303.

Ellis, A. (1976). The biological basis of human irrationality. *Journal of Individual Psychology, 32,* 145-168.

Ellis, A (1987). The impossibility of achieving consistently good mental health. *American Psychologist, 42,* 4, 364-375.

Endicott, J, and Spitzer, R. L. (1978). A diagnostic interview: The Schedule for Affective Disorders and Schizophrenia. *Archives of General Psychiatry, 35,* 837-844.

Erkinjunti, T., Sulkava, R., Wilkstrom, J. and Autio, L. (1987). Short Portable Mental Status Questionnaire as a screening test for dementia and delirium among the elderly. *Journal of the American Geriatrics Society, 35,* (5), 412-416.

Esser, Thomas J. (1974). *Effective report writing in vocational evaluation and work adjustment training.* Materials Development Center, Dept. of Rehabilitation and Manpower, University of Wisconsin, Menomonie, WI 54751.

Estroff, Todd W. and Gold, Mark S. (1986). Medication-induced and toxin-induced psychiatric disorders. In Extein, Irl and Gold, Mark S. (Eds.) *Medical mimics of psychiatric disorders.* Washington, DC: American Psychiatric Press.

Favier, C. M.. (1986). The mental status examination-revised. In P.A. Keller and Ritt, L. G. (Eds.) *Innovations in clinical practice: A source book, 5.* Sarasota, FL: Professional Resource Exchange. Pp. 279-285.

Feuerstein, M. and Skjei, E. (1979). *Mastering pain.* New York: Bantam Books.

Firestone, Lisa. (1991). *Firestone Voice Scale for Self-Destructive Behavior.* The Glendon Association, 2049 Century Park East, Suite 3000, Los Angeles, CA 90067.

Folstein, M. F., Folstein, S. E., and McHugh, P. R. (1975). Mini Mental State: A practical method for grading the cognitive state of patients for the clinician. *Journal of Psychiatric Research, 12,* 189-198.

Frisch, Michael B. (1992). Clinical validation of the Quality of Life Inventory. *Psychological Assessment, 4,* (1), 92-101.

Gardner, Howard (1983). *Frames of mind: The theory of multiple intelligences.* NY: Basic Books.

Garner, D. M. and Garfinkel, P. E. (1979). The eating attitudes test: An index of the symptoms of anorexia nervosa. *Psychological Medicine, 9,* 273-279.

Gonsalves, Carlos (1992). Psychological stages of the refugee process: a model for therapeutic interventions. *Professional Psychology: Research and Practice, 23,* 5, 382-389.

Goldberg, Lewis R. (1992). The development of markers for the Big Five factor structure. *Psychological Assessment, 4,* 26-42.

Goldenberg, B. and Chiverton, P. (1984). Assessing behavior: The nurses's mental status exam. *Geriatric Nursing, 5,* (2), 94-98.

Goodman, W. K., *et al.* (1989). Yale-Brown obsessive compulsive scale. Clinical Neuroscience Research Unit, Connecticut Mental Health Center, 34 Park Street, New Haven, CT 06508.

Gordon, M. (1986). Microprocessor-based assessment of attention-deficit disorders. *Psychopharmacology Bulletin, 22,* 228-290.

Greenwood, Debra U. (1991). Neuropsychological aspects of AIDS dementia complex: What clinicians need to know. *Professional Psychology: Research and Practice, 22,* (5), 407-409.

Greist, J. H., Jefferson, J. W., Marks, I. M. (1986). *Anxiety and its treatment: Help is available.* Washington, DC: American Psychiatric Press.

Hamilton, M. (1960). A rating scale for depression. *Journal of Neurology, Neurosurgery and Psychiatry, 23,* 56-62.

Hare, R. D. (1980). A research scale for the assessment of psychopathy in criminal populations. *Personality and Individual Differences, 1,* 111-119.

Hase, Harold D. (1992). McGill pain questionnaire: revised format. In Leon Vandecreek, *et al.* (Eds.) *Innovations in clinical practice: A source book, 11,* Sarasota, FL: Professional Resource Press. Pp. 285-291.
This revision is expanded and is methodologically more sophisticated and should be more valid.

Hersen, Michel and Turner, Samuel (1985). *Diagnostic interviewing.* NY: Plenum.

Horacek, H. Joseph (1992). Neurobehavioral perspective may help in treating ADDH. *Psychiatric Times, 9,* 9, 32-35.

Hackett, T. P. (1978). The pain Patient: evaluation and treatment. In Hackett, T. P. and Cassem, N. H. (Eds.) *Massachusetts General Hospital handbook of general hospital psychiatry.* St. Louis: C. V. Mosby.

Haddad, L. and Coffman, T. L. (1987). A brief neuropsychological screening examination for psycho-geriatric patients. *Clinical Gerontologist, 6,* (3), 3-10.

Hall, Richard C. W. and Beresford, Thomas P. (1986). Psychiatric manifestations of physical illness. In Jeffrey L. Houpt and H. Keith H. Brodie (Eds.) *Consultation-Liaison psychiatry and behavioral medicine.* NY: Basic Books. Pp. 95-112.

Hays, A. (1984). The Set Test to screen mental status quickly. *Geriatric Nursing, 5,* (2) 96-97.

Hersen, M. and Turner, S. (Eds.) (1985). *Diagnostic interviewing.* New York: Plenum Publishing.

Hinsie, L. E. and Campbell, R. J. (1970). *Psychiatric dictionary.* Fourth Edition. New York: Oxford Press.

Hoffman, R. S. and Koran, L. M. (1984). Detecting physical illness in patients with mental disorders. *Psychosomatics, 25,* 654-660.

Hyler, S. E. and Spitzer, R. T. (1978). Hysteria split asunder. *American Journal of Psychiatry, 135,* 1500-1504.

Jacobs, J. W., Bernhard, M. R., Delgado, A., and Strain, J. J. (1977). Screening for organic mental syndromes in the medically ill. *Annals of Internal Medicine, 86,* 40-46.
The Cognitive Capacity Screening Examination.

Jahoda, Marie (1958). *Current concepts of positive mental health.* NY: Basic Books.

Jenkins, Susan C., Gibbs, Timothy P., and Szymanski, Sally R. (1990). *A pocket reference for psychiatrists.* Washington, DC: American Psychiatric Press.

Kanfer, Fredrick, H. and Saslow, K. (1965). Behavioral analysis: An alternative to diagnostic classification. *Archives of General Psychiatry, 12,* 529-538.

Kaufman, A. S. (1979). *Intelligent testing with the WISC.* NY: Wiley.

Kaplan, Helen S. (1983). *The evaluation of sexual disorders: Psychological and medical aspects.* NY: Brunner/Mazel.

Kellerman, Henry and Burry, Anthony (1991). *Handbook of psychodiagnostic testing: An analysis of personality in the psychological report.* Second edition. Boston: Allyn and Bacon.

Kennedy, James A (1992). *Fundamentals of psychiatric treatment planning.* Washington, DC: American Psychiatric Press.

Kertez, A. (1982). *The Western Aphasia Battery.* NY: Grune and Stratton

Kinston, W., (1988). The family health scales for global assessment of family functioning. In Peter A. Keller and Steven R. Heyman (Eds). *Innovations in clinical practice: a source book, 7.* Sarasota, FL: Professional Resource Exchange. Pp. 299-330.

Kohlberg, Lawrence (Ed.) (1984). *The psychology of moral development: The nature and validity of moral stages.* San Francisco; Harper and Row.

Kratochwill, Thomas and Bergan, John (1990) *Behavioral consulting in applied settings: An individual guide.* NY: Plenum Press.

Krupp, K. B., Mendelson, W. B., and Friedman, R. (1991). An overview of Chronic Fatigue Syndrome. *Journal of Clinical Psychiatry, 52,* (10), 403-410.

La Rue, A. (1982). Memory loss and aging: Distinguishing dementia from benign senescent forgetfulness and depressive pseudodementia. *Psychiatric Clinics of North America, 5,* 90.

Lasswell, Marcia and Brock, Gregory (Eds.) (1989). *AAMFT Forms book.* Washington, DC: American Association for Marriage and Family Therapy. 1717 K Street, NW, Washington, DC 20006. About $55.

Lazarus, Arnold A. (Ed.) (1976). *Multimodal behavior therapy.* NY: Springer.

Lazarus, Arnold A. (1981). *The practice of multimodal therapy.* NY: McGraw-Hill.

Leary, Timothy (1957). *Interpersonal diagnosis of personality: A functional theory and methodology for personality evaluation.* NY: The Ronald Press.

Lefkovitz, P. M., Morrison, D.P., and Davis, H. J. (1982). The Assessment of Current Functioning Scale (ACFS). *Journal of Psychiatric Treatment and Evaluation, 4,* (3), 297-305.

Leigh, H. and Reiser, M. F. (1980). *The patient: Biological, psychological and social dimensions of medical practice.* NY: Plenum.

Levin, H. S., O'Donnell, V. M., and Grossman, R. G. (1979). The Galveston Orientation and Amnesia Test ,(GOAT): A practical scale to assess cognition after head injury. *Journal of Nervous and Mental Disease, 167,* 675-684.

Lewis, Judith A. (1990). A psychosocial and substance use history form. In Keller, P and Heyman, S. (Eds.) *Innovations in clinical practice: A sourcebook, 9.* Sarasota, FL: Professional Resource Exchange. Pp. 289-300.

Lezak, M.D. (1983). *Neuropsychological assessment.* Second edition. NY: Oxford Press.

Lishman, William (1978). *Organic psychiatry: The psychological consequences of cerebral disorder.* Oxford: Blackwell Scientific Publications.

Logue, Mary Beth, Sher, Kenneth J. and Frensch, Peter A. (1992). Purported characteristics of adult children of alcoholics: A possible "Barnum Effect." *Professional Psychology: Research and Practice, 23,* (3), 226-232.

Lopez-Ibor, J. J. Jr. (1990). The masking and unmasking of depression. In J. P. Feighner and W. F. Boyer (Eds.) *The diagnosis of depression.* NY: John Wiley and Sons.

Lubin, B. (1965). Adjective checklists for measuring depression. *Archives of General Psychiatry, 12,* 57-62.

Lukas, C. and Seiden, H. M. (1990). *Silent grief: Living in the wake of suicide.* NY: Bantam.

Lukas, Susan (1993). *Where to start and what to ask: An assessment handbook.* NY: Norton.

Marsh, Diane T. (1992a). *Families and mental illness: New directions in professional practice.* NY: Praeger.

Marsh, Diane T. (1992b). Working with families of people with serious mental illness. In Leon Vandecreek, Samuel Knapp, and Thomas L. Jackson (Eds.) *Innovations in clinical practice: A source book. 11.* Sarasota, FL: Professional Resource Press. Pp. 389-402.

Masters, William H. and Johnson, Virginia, E. (1970). *Human Sexual Inadequacy.* Boston: Little, Brown.

McGoldrick, Monica and Gerson, Randy (1985). *Genograms in family assessment.* NY: W. W. Norton.

Mclemore, Clinton and Benjamin, Lorna S. (1979). Whatever happened to interpersonal diagnosis?: A psychological alternative to DSM-III. *American Psychologist, 34,* 17-34.

Melton, Gary B., Petrilla, John, Poythress, Norman G., and Slobogin, Christopher (1987). *Psychological evaluations for the courts: A handbook for mental health professionals and lawyers. NY:* Guilford.

Melzak, R. and Wall, P. D. (1983). *The challenge of pain.* New York: Basic Books.

Miller, P. S., Richardson, S. J., Jyu, C. A., Lemay, J. S. *et al.* (1988). Association of low serum anticholinergic levels and cognitive impairment in elderly presurgical patients. *American Journal of Psychiatry, 145,* (3), 342-345. The Saskatoon Delirium Checklist

Millon, Theodore and Everly, G. S. (1985). *Personality and its disorders.* NY: Wiley.

Millon, T. (1986). Personality prototypes and their diagnostic criteria. In Millon, T. and Klerman, G. (Eds.) *Contemporary directions in psychopathology.* New York: The Guilford Press.

Monahan, John (1981). *Predicting violent behavior: An assessment of clinical techniques.* Beverly Hills, CA: Sage Publications.

Morey, L. C. and Ochoa, E. S. (1989). An investigation of adherence to diagnostic criteria: Clinical diagnosis of the DSM-III personality disorders. *Journal of Personality Disorders, 3,* 180-192.

Mosher, D. L. (1968). Measurement of guilt in females by self-report inventories. *Journal of Consulting and Clinical Psychology, 32,* 690-695.

Mueller, J. (1984). The mental status examination. In H. H. Goldman (Ed.) *Review of General Psychiatry.* Los Altos, CA: Lange. Pp. 206-220. The Neurobehavioral Cognitive Status Examination.

Nadelson, Theodore (1986). The false patient: Chronic factitious disease, Munchausen syndrome, and malingering. In Jeffry L Houpt and H. Keith H. Brodie (Eds.) *Consultation-liaison psychiatry and behavioral medicine.* NY: Basic Books. Pp. 195-205.

NiCarthy, G. and Davidson, S. (1989). *You can be free: An easy to read handbook for abused women.* Seattle, WA: Seal Press.

Nicholson, Robert A., Briggs, Stephen R. and Robertson, Helen C. (1988). Instruments for assessing competency to stand trial: How do they work? *Professional Psychology, 19,* 383-394.

Nietzel, M. T. and Himelein, M. J. (1986). Prevention of crime and delinquency. In B. A. Edelstein and L. Michelson (Eds.) *Handbook of prevention.* NY: Plenum.

Othmer, E., Penick, E. C., and Powell, B. J. (1981). *Psychiatric Diagnostic Interview (PDI).* Los Angeles, CA: Western Psychological Services.

Overall, J. E. and Gorham, D. R. (1962). The Brief Psychiatric Rating Scale. *Psychological Reports, 10,* 799-812.

Paul, Gordon L. (1966). *Insight vs. desensitization in psychotherapy.* Stanford, CA: Stanford University Press. "The Timed Behavioral Checklist for Performance Anxiety."

Pearlman, C. A. (1986). Neuroleptic malignant syndrome: A review of the literature. *Journal of Clinical Psychopharmacology, 6,* 257-273.

Pfeiffer, E. (1975). A short, portable mental status questionnaire for the assessment of organic brain deficit in elderly patients. *Journal of the Geriatric Society, 23,* 433.

Pies, Ronald (1993). The psychopharmacology of PTSD. *Psychiatric Times*, June, 21.

Pincus, H. H. and Tucker, G. J. (1975). *Behavioral neurology.* (Third Ed.) NY: Oxford University Press.

Pomeroy, W. B., Flax, C. and Wheeler, C. C. (1982). *Taking a sex history: Interviewing and recording.* New York: The Free Press.

Potter-Effron, R. T. (1988). Shame and guilt: definitions, processes, and treatment issues with AODA clients. In R. T. Potter-Effron and P. S. Potter-Effron (Eds.) *The treatment of shame and guilt in alcoholism counseling.* NY: Haworth Press.

Putnam, Frank (991). Recent research on Multiple Personality Disorder. *Psychiatric Clinics of North America, 14, (3),* 489-502.

Reber, Arthur (1985). *The Penguin dictionary of psychology.* NY: Penguin Books.

Reynolds, W. M. (1987). *Suicide ideation questionnaires.* Odessa, FL: Psychological Assessment Resources.

Reisberg, B. (1983). Clinical presentation, diagnosis, and symptomology of age-associated cognitive decline and Alzheimer's disease. In B. Reisberg (Ed.) *Alzheimer's disease.* NY: Free Press.

Reisberg, B. (1985). Alzheimer's disease updated. *Psychiatric Annals, 15,* 319-322.

Reisberg, B., Ferris, S., deLeon, M. J. and Crook, T. (1982). The Global Deterioration Scale for assessment of primary degenerative dementia. *American Journal of Psychiatry, 139, (9),* 1136-39.

Robertson, D., Rockwood, K., and Stolee, P. (1982). A short mental status questionnaire. *Canadian Journal on Aging, 1, (1-2),* 16-20.

Rogers, Richard (1984). Toward an empirical model of malingering and deception. *Behavioral Science, 2,* 544 ff.

Rodgers, Richard (Ed.) (1988). *Clinical assessment of malingering and deception.* NY: Guilford Press.

Rodgers, Richard (1990). Development of a new classificatory model of malingering. *Bulletin of the American Academy of Psychiatry and the Law, 18,* 323-333.

Root, M. P. P. and Fallon, P. (1988). The incidence of victimization in a bulimic sample. *Journal of Interpersonal Violence, 3,* 161-173.

Rosen, W. G. Verbal fluency in aging and dementia. *Journal of Clinical Neuropsychology, 80, 2,* 135-46.

Ross, C. A. (1989). *Multiple personality disorder: Diagnosis, clinical features, and treatment.* NY: Wiley.

Ross, C., *et al.* (1989). Differences between multiple personality disorder and other diagnostic groups on structured interview. *Journal of Nervous and Mental Diseases, 177,* 487-491.

Ross, et al., (1990). Structured interview data on 102 cases of multiple personality disorder from four centers. *American Journal of Psychiatry, 147,* 596-601.

Sattler, J. M. (1988). *Assessment of children.* San Diego, CA: Jerome M. Sattler.

Schaef, Anne Wilson (1986). *Codependency: Misunderstood-mistreated.* San Francisco, CA: Harper & Row.

Schroeder, Marsha L., Wormworth, Janice A., and Livesley, W. John (1992). Dimensions of personality disorder and their relationships to the Big Five dimensions of personality. *Psychological Assessment, 4,* Pp. 47-53.

Schutz, William C. (1958). *FIRO: A three dimensional theory of interpersonal behavior.* NY: Rinehart.

Seligman, M. E. P. (1975). *Helplessness: On depression, development, and death.* San Francisco: Freeman.

Severino Sally K. and Molino, Margaret L. (1989). *Premenstrual syndrome: A clinician's guide.* NY: Guilford.

Shapiro, D. (1965). *Neurotic styles.* New York: Basic Books.

Shepard, Martin (1970). *Games analysts play.* NY: Berkeley Publishing

Sher, Kenneth J. (1991). *Children of alcoholics: A critical appraisal of theory and research.* Chicago: University of Chicago Press.

Shneidman, Edwin S. (1971). Suicide among the gifted. In E. S. Shneidman, (Ed.), *Suicidology: Contemporary developments.* NY: Grune and Stratton.

Shoben, Edward J. (1956). *The psychology of adjustment: A dynamic and experiential approach to personality and mental hygiene.* Boston: Houghton Mifflin.

Simmons, J. E. (1987). *Psychiatric examination of children.* Philadelphia, PA: Lea and Febiger.

Slaby, A. E., Liev, J. and Tancredi, L. R. (1980). *Handbook of psychiatric emergencies.* (Second edition). Flushing, NY: Medical Examination Publishing Co.

Sovner, R. and Hurley, A. D. (1983). The mental status examination I: Behavior, speech, and thought. *Psychiatric Aspects of Mental Retardation Newsletter, 2,* (2), 5-8.

Sperry, Len, Gudeman, Jon E., Blackwell, Barry, Faulkner, Larry R. (1992). *Psychiatric case formulations.* Washington, DC: American Psychiatric Press.

Spitzer, R. L., Endicott, J., Mesnikoff, A., and Cohen, G. (1967-8). *Psychiatric Evaluation Form: Diagnostic Version.* New York: Biometric Research, New York Psychiatric Institute.

Steege, J. F., Stout, A. L., and Rupp, S. L. (1988). Clinical features. In William R. Keye (Ed.) *The premenstrual syndrome.* Philadelphia, PA: W. B. Saunders Co.

Steiner, Claude (1971). *Games alcoholics play.* NY: Grove Press.

Strub, R. L. and Black, F. W. (1985). *The Mental Status Exam in Neurology.* Second edition. Philadelphia: F. A. Davis.

Stuart, Richard and Jacobson, Barbara (1991). *Couple's pre-counseling Inventory.* Research Press, P. O. Box 9177, Champaign, IL 61826. 217-352-3273.

Summers, W., *et al.* (1983). The General Adult Inpatient Psychiatric Assessment Scale (GAIPAS). *Psychiatry Research, 10,* (3) 217-236.

Sundberg, N. D. (1977). *Assessment of persons.* Englewood Cliffs, NJ:Prentice Hall.

Swenson, Clifford H., Nelson, Michele K., Warner, Jan, and Dunlap, David. (1992a). Scale of marriage problems: Revised. In Leon Vandecreek, Samuel Knapp, and Thomas L. Jackson (Eds.) *Innovations in clinical practice: A source book, 11.* Sarasota, FL: Professional Resource Press. Pp. 293-302.

Swenson, Clifford H., Nelson, Michele K., Warner, Jan, and Dunlap, David. (1992b). Scale of feelings and behavior of love: Revised. In Leon Vandecreek, Samuel Knapp, and Thomas L. Jackson (Eds.) *Innovations in clinical practice: A source book, 11.* Sarasota, FL: Professional Resource Press, Pp. 303-314.

Tallent, N. (1976). *Psychological report writing.* Englewood Cliffs, NJ: Prentice-Hall.

Taylor, Robert L. (1990). *Distinguishing psychological from organic disorders: Screening for psychological masquerade.* NY: Springer.

Teasdale, G. and Jenvet, B. (1974). Assessment of coma and impaired consciousness. *The Lancet,* July 13, 1974, 81-83. The Glasgow Coma Scale

Terman, L. M. and Merrill, M. A. (1960). *Stanford-Binet Intelligence Scale: Manual for the third revised edition.* Boston: Houghton Mifflin Company.

Thomas, A. and Chess, S. (1977). *Termperament and development.* NY: Brunner/Mazel.

Thomas, A., Chess, S. and Birch, H. G. (1968). *Temperament and behavior disorders in children.* NY: New York University Press.

Troiden, Richard R. (1979). Becoming homosexual: A model of gay identity acquisition. *Psychiatry, 42,* 362-373.

Troiden, Richard R. (1988). Homosexual identity development. *Journal of Adolescent Health Care, 9,* 105-113.

Townsend, Mary C. (1988). *Nursing diagnoses in psychiatric nursing.* Philadelphia, PA: F. A. Davis.

Turk, Dennis C. and Melzack, Ronald (1992). *Handbook of pain assessment.* NY: Guilford.

Tyrer, Peter, *et al.* (1990). A plea for the diagnosis of hyponchondrical personality disorder. *Journal of Psychosomatic Research, 34,* 6, 637-642.

Walen, Susan (1992). *A practitioner's guide to Rational Emotive Therapy.* Second Edition. NY: Oxford University Press.

Walker, Leonore (1984). *The battered woman syndrome.* NY: Springer.

Walker, Leonore (1991). PTSD in women: Diagnosis and treatment of Battered Woman Syndrome. *Psychotherapy, 28,* 21-29.

Wechsler, D. (1987). *Manual for the Wechsler Memory Scale - Revised.* New York: The Psychological Corporation.

Whelihan, W., Lesher, E. L., and Kleban, M. H. (1984). Mental status and memory assessment as predictors of dementia. *Journal of Gerontology, 39,* (5), 572-76
The Extended Mental Status Questionnaire

Limbered, T. S. (1978). Sadism and masochism: Sociological perspectives. *Bulletin of the American Academy of Psychiatry and the Law, 6,* 284-295.

Zung, W. W. (1965). A self-rating depression scale. *Archives of General Psychiatry, 12,* 63-70.

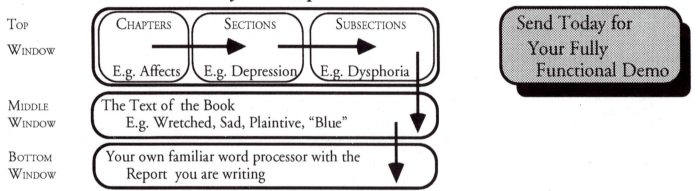